DEMOCRACY, REVOLUTION, AND MONARCHISM IN EARLY AMERICAN LITERATURE

Paul Downes combines literary criticism and political history in order to explore responses to the rejection of monarchism in the American revolutionary era. Downes' analysis considers the Declaration of Independence, Franklin's autobiography, Crèvecoeur's *Letters From An American Farmer*, and the works of America's first significant literary figures including Charles Brockden Brown, Washington Irving, and James Fenimore Cooper. He claims that the post-revolutionary American state and the new democratic citizen inherited some of the complex features of absolute monarchy, even as they were strenuously trying to assert their difference from it. In chapters that consider the revolution's mock execution of George III, the Elizabethan notion of the "king's two bodies," and the political significance of the secret ballot, Downes points to the traces of monarchical political structures within the practices and discourses of early American democracy. This is an ambitious study of an important theme in early American culture and society.

PAUL DOWNES is an Associate Professor in the Department of English at the University of Toronto. He is the author of a number of articles on eighteenth- and nineteenth-century American literature.

DEMOCRACY, REVOLUTION, AND MONARCHISM IN EARLY AMERICAN LITERATURE

PAUL DOWNES

CAMBRIDGE
UNIVERSITY PRESS

PUBLISHED BY THE PRESS SYNDICATE OF THE UNIVERSITY OF CAMBRIDGE
The Pitt Building, Trumpington Street, Cambridge, United Kingdom

CAMBRIDGE UNIVERSITY PRESS
The Edinburgh Building, Cambridge CB2 2RU, UK
40 West 20th Street, New York, NY 10011-4211, USA
477 Williamstown Road, Port Melbourne, VIC 3207, Australia
Ruiz de Alarcón 13, 28014 Madrid, Spain
Dock House, The Waterfront, Cape Town 8001, South Africa

http://www.cambridge.org

First published 2002

Printed in the United Kingdom at the University Press, Cambridge

Typeface Baskerville Monotype 11 / 12.5 pt   *System* LaTeX 2ε   [TB]

A catalogue record for this book is available from the British Library

Library of Congress Cataloguing in Publication data

Downes, Paul, 1965–
Democracy, revolution, and monarchism in early American literature / Paul Downes.
p.   cm. – (Cambridge studies in American literature and culture; 130)
Includes bibliographical references (p. 223) and index.
ISBN 0 521 81339 5
1. American literature – Revolutionary period, 1775–1783 – History and criticism.   2. United
States – History – Revolution, 1775–1783 – Literature and the revolution.   3. Politics and
literature – United States – History – 18th century.   4. Revolutionary literature,
American – History and criticism.   5. United States – Intellectual life – 18th century.
6. Revolutions in literature.   7. Democracy in literature.   8. Monarchy in literature.
I. Title.   II. Series
PS193 .D69 2002
810.9'358 – dc21   2002017399

ISBN 0 521 81339 5

For Naomi

Just here, the idea of a total separation of the colonies from the crown was born! It was a startling idea, much more so, than we, at this distance of time, regard it.

Frederick Douglass, July 5, 1852

Contents

Preface

This book attempts to deconstruct the revolutionary opposition between democracy and monarchism by considering some of the ways in which the democratic state and the democratic subject inherit the *arcana imperii* of the absolute monarch. The monarch provided Americans with a model of sovereign autonomy that might be reproduced on an individual level; but he also exemplified a self-dissolution and mystification that would be associated with everything the revolution had come to replace. This book suggests that the American Revolution initiated a democratization of the monarch's relationship to secrecy, duplicity, arbitrariness, and magisterial madness even as it redistributed the monarch's singular autonomy. The figure of the absolute monarch, I insist, is the American Revolution's constitutive other; the democracy it confronted can only be understood as a political order compelled to translate – even as it condemns – monarchism's attempts to transcend its political aporias. One of the American Revolution's most persistent claims is that it has done away with monarchism's miracles and restored an order of common sense. In the introduction to this book I will spell out at some length how we might go about undoing that claim, *not* in order to expose a lie, but to propose that the ideology of democratic monarchophobia undermined some of the revolution's most valuable political innovations. Determined to defend its purity through an absolute rejection (or exorcism) of all traces of monarchic obfuscation, democratic idealism proceeded to abandon some of the ways in which its own mysteries (mysteries which I have gathered together under the rubric of the *spell* of democracy) might contribute to expanded political participation and opportunity.

In chapter one I consider the specific role played by the figure of George III in the heat of the American Revolution and work towards a better understanding of Emerson's striking retrospective description of the monarch as the "hieroglyphic" by which men "obscurely signified their consciousness of their own right and comeliness, the right of every man" ("Self-Reliance," 38). This chapter also includes a discussion of the Elizabethan notion of the "king's two bodies," an idea central to the version of monarchic absolutism that was contested in both the English Civil War and the American Revolution. Chapter two consists of a close reading of what is perhaps the best first-hand literary account we have of what it means to be ambivalent about the transition to a post-monarchical political order in America: J. Hector St. John de Crèvecoeur's *Letters From An American Farmer* (1782). Chapter three compares the very different models of exemplary revolutionary subjectivity offered by Benjamin Franklin, on the one hand, and Stephen Burroughs on the other. These characters' various self-concealments figure the sovereign disruption of presence that is at work in every extension of democratization. The concealed citizen is also the centre of attention in chapter four's discussion of the secret ballot and of Charles Brockden Brown's fictional secret-keepers. Democracy, while it is initiated and sustained by a revolutionary critique of monarchism's impenetrable logic, nevertheless registers (often with some degree of anxiety) the post-monarchic redistribution of impenetrability in the language and structures of the citizen's right to secrecy at the moment of his political intervention. It is the inseparability of power and self-difference (the self as never fully available to – and hence always a secret to – the self) that democracy both performs and conceals in the event of the secret ballot. If Brockden Brown gives us a portrait of the democratic subject of the secret ballot, Washington Irving, in "Rip Van Winkle," gives us insight into the anxiety generated by an expanded body politic. This anxiety is recorded in specific attempts to limit the franchise in the early republic and in "Rip Van Winkle"'s aggressive embodiment of "tyrannous" authority in the figure of Dame Van Winkle and in the tongues of democratic politicians. Rather than simply remind us of the shortcomings of post-revolutionary democracy, chapter five attempts to show how the resistance to non-white and female voters participated in a revolutionary monarchophobia. The bodies of non-white, non-male (and even non-adult) Americans come to inherit (for democratic monarchophobes) the rejected corporeality of the monarch.

As an "exile in his own land," the hero of Fenimore Cooper's *The Spy* recalls the marginal figures disenfranchised in the new republic, but he is also presented, of course, as the exemplary American, the necessarily secret embodiment of the spirit of '76. In this book's afterword, I propose that Cooper's depiction of Washington and his spy (and of their secret relationship) figures a democratic translation of the absolute monarch's two bodies (a figure hinted at in the spectral associations each man gathers in the course of the novel). But, I conclude, Cooper's attempt to contain the revolution within fiction coincides with an attempt, dramatized in the novel, to put an end to a secrecy that revolutionary idealism uncomfortably associates with its monarchic other. *The Spy*, in other words, dramatizes both the appeal and the threat of democracy's relationship to monarchism: Cooper's post-revolutionary America finds itself in debt to a figure of radical independence whose sovereign obscurity can only be claimed for democracy via the perpetual reassurance of its dissolution.

Acknowledgments

I would like to take this opportunity to thank the following people for their help and encouragement at various stages of this project. Virginia Rock, Marie-Christine Leps, and Ian Balfour at York University in Toronto; Cynthia Chase, Shirley Samuels, Mark Seltzer, and Isaac Kramnick at Cornell University; Ross Pudaloff at Wayne State University; David Waldstreicher at the University of Notre Dame; Timothy Melley at Miami University; Deborah Esch at the University of Toronto; and the readers and editors for Cambridge University Press. A version of chapter 4 appeared in *Criticism*, and I appreciate their permission to reprint it. My wife, Naomi Morgenstern of the University of Toronto, has been my most constant and careful intellectual advisor.

Introduction: the spell of democracy

J'avoue que dans l'Amérique j'ai vu plus que l'Amérique.
(Alexis de Tocqueville, *De la démocratie en Amérique*, 14)

DEMOCRACY, REVOLUTION, AND MONARCHISM

"There is something exceedingly ridiculous in the composition of monarchy," wrote Thomas Paine in 1776:

it first excludes a man from the means of information, yet empowers him to act in cases where the highest judgement is required. The state of a king shuts him from the world, yet the business of a king requires him to know it thoroughly; wherefore the different parts, unnaturally opposing and destroying each other, prove the whole character to be absurd and useless. (*Common Sense*, 69)

These sentiments can be found in one of the most powerful and effective expressions of anti-monarchism in the western political tradition. As such, they also helped to achieve the creation of the west's first post-monarchical political state. The American Revolution begins with a rejection of monarchism and with it a rejection of the kind of decadent absurdity that would shut a man from the world even as he is asked to exercise his decisive political judgment. To recognize this madness and call it by its name is, according to the American Revolution, to come out from under the spell of monarchy.

In June of 1995, *The New York Times* carried a brief guest editorial on the recent elections in Haiti written by J. Brian Atwood, Administrator of the United States Agency for International Development. The piece included this account of an incident that took place while he was observing a polling station:

The problem was that symbols intended to identify candidates for illiterate voters had been left off the ballots – inadvertently, it seemed – and the polling officials

I

were attempting to help voters read the ballots. The poll watchers thought they were influencing the voters' choices. International observers like myself sought to explain to the poll watchers what the election officials were doing and calm their fears.

A few minutes later an elderly man poked his head out from behind the cardboard wall that was guarding his secret ballot. "Someone has to tell me who to vote for," he said. Whereupon the election officials and poll watchers alike almost screamed in unison, "You have to decide for yourself!" (A27)

There is nothing particularly exotic about this scene: for all the inevitable condescension that might enter into Euro-American accounts of "fledgling" democracies around the world, this is not a scene that is foreign to democracy.[1] Indeed, there is something exemplary about the drama of enforced isolation that this story records. The "elderly" man's frank imperative activates a scream that is more or less silently at work in every scene of democratic election. Watching over the man are a succession of "polling officials," "poll watchers" (watching the officials), and "international observers" (watching the watchers). The man, exercising his sovereign democratic will, would seem to be at the center of the law here: the law – via its representatives – surrounds him. And yet the officials do not want to see him; they do not want to hear from him or speak to him. They are almost hysterical about this. They are mad about his freedom. The man is all alone, in an outside–inside that defies simple description. This enigmatic and necessary space can only be located within or under what we could call the spell of democracy.

The study that follows will repeatedly suggest that the "fabulous" and "chimerical" features of monarchism, as it was condemned in America from as early as 1750 (when Jonathan Mayhew employed the words I have just quoted) to the post-revolutionary era, persist in displaced forms in the democratic state.[2] To claim as much, and to make reference to the *spell* of democracy, is, of course, to fly in the face of the revolution's explicit assertion that it had come to put an end to the magic and mystery of monarchism. "Titles," wrote Thomas Paine, referring to royal nomenclature, "are like circles drawn by the magician's wand, to contract the sphere of man's felicity" (*Rights of Man*, 227); "May [The Declaration of Independence]," wrote Thomas Jefferson, "be to the world . . . the signal of arousing men to burst the chains, under which monkish ignorance and superstition had persuaded them to bind themselves."[3] The American Revolution, so we have been told, brought things down to earth, brought things into the light of day, grounded itself in the common, the natural, and the ordinary. The thirteen governments of the newly united states, explained John Adams in 1787, were founded "on the natural authority of the people alone, without a pretense of miracle or mystery" ("Defense," *Political Writings*, 118).

By resisting the story of demystification that the American Revolution tells about itself, this book will approach monarchic and democratic political orders as two forms of political organization not just as the terms of an absolute opposition between which we have to make a political (or ethical) choice. To reject democracy's inheritance from monarchism, I argue, is to participate in the discourse of the revolution, not to analyze it, and it is to participate in what I will call, in chapter one, monarchophobia. In the pages of this introduction and in the chapters that follow, I will pursue some of the ways in which the political order and the political subject produced by the American Revolution can be thought of as being, in Jonathan Mayhew's words, "as fabulous and chimerical, as transubstantiation; or any of those most absurd reveries of ancient or modern visionaries" ("Discourse," 407).[4] I want to consider the consequences for the democratic citizen of the founding rupture between the political subjectivity that had initiated the revolution (colonial and rebellious) and that which emerged in the wake of its success (republican and constitutional); I want to draw attention to the figural excess generated by the concept of representation in the late eighteenth century; and I want to think about the strange temporality of democratic citizenship (how is it possible that one can retroactively become a subject of the revolution's liberation and empowerment?). I will repeatedly return to the relationship between political power and the rhetoric of immortality, and, finally, to the opportunity and anxiety generated by the particular forms of the citizen's realization under democracy. All these questions are raised and implicitly addressed by an ongoing reflection on an overdetermined reference to democracy's "spell." The American Revolution only brings its subjects out from under the spell of monarchy, this study suggests, insofar as it binds them to the spell of democracy.

To re-mystify the language we use to describe democracy is, for some, to participate in a discourse that has been far more at home in English departments than in history departments over the last thirty or so years. The language of structuralist, post-structuralist, and post-Marxist literary, political, and philosophical analysis threatens at times to provoke a replaying of the revolutionary moment in which an ethic of plain speech and common sense, of the ordinary and the natural, is pitted against the "monkish" gibberish of the high priests of theory. I will return to the question of how a certain post-modern discourse might be said to displace the charisma of monarchic mystique, but for now I want to admit that for many readers the study that follows will appear to be merely one more example of the kind of theoretical obfuscation that is incapable of reading the revolution's own language about itself. To that end, this book has an unapologetic founding question: "How might literary theory contribute to our understanding of the American Revolution?" This question does not ask after the representation of revolutionary events in literary texts, nor does it interrogate the political leanings of particular authors. I am not particularly interested in the aesthetic or formal elegance of the era's political writings, nor am I going to suggest that an ear for poetry makes one a better reader of the Declaration of Independence (although this may be true). Instead, this book finds in literary theory a productive series of reflections on the rhetorical dimension of all attempts – literary, historical, or political – to establish empirical distinctions and identities. Literary theory insists on a rhetorical supplement at work in any founding moment and in any founding structure. This book's literary approach, in other words, introduces into a field dominated by political science and American history an infuriating insistence on the extent to which every text, every claim, every category of revolutionary experience is at odds with itself and hence with the revolutionary project of which it is a part. To bring literary theory to bear on our understanding of the American Revolution, means, among other things, to attempt to demonstrate (and suggest the implications of) an irreducible tension between the rhetorical and the logical in every moment of what we call the founding. Those founding categories that would seem to give stability and certainty to the revolutionary effort (the monarch as absolute enemy; the "people" as sovereign source of democratic legitimacy; nature's God and God's nature; individual inalienable rights etc.) must be examined with attention to the performative disruption of their cognitive force. Literary theory refuses to take the revolution's version of its world at face value, not because it is committed to the revolution's failure or because it wants to accuse the revolution of deceit. The literary theory that I am bringing to bear on the American Revolution will be as useful for expanding the effects of the revolution as for contracting its claims to authority. Furthermore, I will suggest that the American Revolution distinguishes itself as an era in which a peculiar sensitivity to the rhetorical production of meaning emerges out of a radically politicized experience of the historical production of the social order, of justice, and of political subjecthood. Literary theory and the American Revolution share an engagement with history as the paradoxical experience of a meaningful break with precedent and convention.

The American Revolution's defining gesture, the gesture that gave it the profile of a revolution as opposed to merely an intra-state dispute, was its rejection of the English crown and with it the rejection of absolute monarchy in general. "[We must] besiege the throne of heaven," wrote Thomas Jefferson, "to extirpate from creation this class of human lions, tigers, and mammoths called kings, from whom let him perish who does not say 'good Lord deliver us.'"[5] The antagonism between monarchism and democracy was, I will contend, the most far-reaching of the revolution's political oppositions and thus it is the deconstruction of this opposition that will continually inform the readings that follow. This deconstruction follows a literary, or rhetorical, insistence on the textual instability of any set of grounding antitheses (such as that between monarchism and democracy), but it also participates in a post-modern analysis of the constitutive role played by an antagonist or enemy in the construction of any political identity. The American Revolution's crucial opposition between monarchism and democracy cannot be disentangled, I will show, from the revolution's immediate reincorporation, by way of translation and displacement, of the structures and aporias of monarchism. Understanding the post-revolutionary United States means, among other things, understanding the ways in which the discourse of democracy persistently reinscribes its defining antagonism towards monarchism *and* the ways in which it inherits, in altered form, some of the features of the monarchic political order. Thus we have to take note of a founding complication. To reassert the centrality of anti-monarchism to the revolution's political transformation is to insist on an absolute distinction: the pre- and post-revolutionary American states are divided by the wall of a political event that knows no compromise ("I do not see any tolerable middle ground," wrote Rousseau in 1767, "between the most austere democracy and the most perfect Hobbesian regime"[6]). But this wall is undermined by the suggestion that monarchism and republicanism not be seen as the poles of an opposition but as different but related attempts to manage the same political problems and as different but related attempts to assert their transcendence of politics as such. This latter claim finds in Rousseau's comment the invocation of a peculiar intimacy: there is no middle ground between monarchism and republicanism because nothing comes between them.

Thus, *Democracy, Revolution, and Monarchism* suggests that displaced or translated elements of monarchic political culture can be found at work in key revolutionary ideas and constructs. The citizen, the State, and the founding documents of American democracy emerge from this analysis

augmented by reinscribed versions of the same paradoxes, inconsistencies, and aporias that structure the monarchic political order. At the same
time, this study is not simply interested in revealing (cynically or pejora-
tively) these political inheritances. Instead, I will suggest that a recognition of the complex and irreducible relationship between democracy and
monarchism is essential for understanding how democracy works and
how it can be put to work in new and potentially more effective ways. One
of the results of this approach is to disturb simple reductions of political
affiliation in the literature of this period. Hence, a character who laments
the American break with England emerges as the author of a nuanced
allegory of revolution; a post-revolutionary outlaw's philosophy finds an
echo behind the closed doors of the constitutional convention; Benjamin
Franklin's exemplary civic personality performs one of its most crucial
interventions in the name of a secret sacrifice; and the subject of revolutionary freedom finds itself enclosed by the walls of the voting booth.
The subject of the American founding, I repeatedly show, inherits the
monarch's political authority by simultaneously inheriting the monarch's
arbitrariness, extravagance, and obscurity. This monarchic inheritance
(announced in the exemplary form of Philip Freneau's excessive denial:
"Without a king, we till the smiling plain; / Without a king, we trace the
unbounded sea, / ... Without a king, to see the end of time"[7]) enriches
the subject of American democracy and of American literary study.

Deconstructing the opposition between monarchism and democracy
also allows us to develop new insights into some of the major political
and cultural preoccupations of the early United States. In the course of
this book I will consider, among other things, political loyalism, the adoption of the secret ballot, the revolutionary appropriation of the
Native American, the debate over the franchise, and the critical debate over print-based or oratorical models of revolutionary persuasion.
The discussion will involve a series of fictional letters, two late-eighteenth
century autobiographies, and the novels and stories of Charles Brockden
Brown, Washington Irving, and James Fenimore Cooper; but as the
study of a period in which political writing and political events presented
Americans with their most compelling occasions for speculation and innovation, we will also pay close attention to the words of Thomas Paine,
Thomas Jefferson, and James Madison, as well as to the language generated in and around the Declaration of Independence, the Constitutional
Convention, and the various post-revolutionary attempts to secure or
contain the radicalism of the revolution's transformations. *Democracy,
Revolution, and Monarchism* subjects these texts and events to readings

that repeatedly ask after the traces or reconfigurations of monarchical political structures within the practices and discourses of democracy. We will persistently return to a distinction between the othering of monarchism that is necessary for the transition to democracy and the post-revolutionary recognition of democracy's political relationship to monarchism, a recognition that allows for a political philosophy that is not spell-bound by a simple revolutionary antagonism. Democracy resists its relationship to monarchism, and this resistance produces a range of fascinating figures, voices, and narratives in the polemics and plots of the new nation's novels, memoirs, and pamphlets. In the pages that follow, I want to track the fortunes of terms that link an antipathy towards monarchism to anxieties about political power *per se* and about the subject transformed by the accession to political power. Does democracy succeed by giving each and every citizen a share in the power *and* the madness of the monarch? Is sovereignty something to be desired or feared? Will the revolution have brought "ordinary people" to power, as one distinguished observer has recently put it, only to have rendered them incurably and unrecognizably extraordinary?[8] I want to begin to answer these questions by considering in more detail what it means to suggest that in bringing them out from under the spell of monarchism, democracy introduces its subjects to a new set of mysteries. What exactly falls under the spell of democracy?

REVOLUTIONARY EXORCISM

Spell *sb.1* **3. a.** A set of words, a formula or verse, supposed to possess occult or magical powers; a charm or incantation; a means of accomplishing enchantment or exorcism.[9]

Political revolution always finds itself repudiating a particular form of political organization (monarchism, for example, or totalitarian communism), but it simultaneously repudiates politics in general in the name of a revolutionary transcendence of politics. Overcoming the political failings of one regime becomes indistinguishable, in revolutionary rhetoric, from overcoming the constitutive aporias of the political (everything that, under the name of politics, resists the passage between the constative theory of the state and its performative history). This collapse of two distinct gestures would seem to be an inevitable feature of the modern revolution. In order to constitute a revolution, its discourse has to reject absolutely the principle of authority in one political regime and replace it with its own authority, the authority of the revolutionary voice. This act of usurpation can only justify itself as a legitimate, original, and self-justifying event insofar as it replaces a political force that had *itself* claimed a meta-historical transcendence of politics. The democratic revolution's new beginning, that is to say, depends upon, and repeats, monarchism's blasphemous appropriation of divine, which is to say extra-legal, authority. (This structure is wonderfully reproduced in one of the climactic scenes of Charles Brockden Brown's *Wieland* [1798] in which the "biloquist," Carwin, produces the illusion of a divine voice in order to tell the psychotic Theodore Wieland that the voice of God that he thought he had heard commanding him to murder his family was a delusion.[10]) That the American Revolution engages in this divine appropriation at the very moment of revolution is evident from a close scrutiny of the Declaration of Independence. The text in which the independent people of the United States produce themselves as such – and thereby *become* what they claim already to be – succeeds insofar as it earns itself the right to command this impossibility. The effect, in other words, is rhetorical, and it produces the revolutionary people as the god-like figures who stand outside of, and are not subject to, mortal and historical patterns of temporality and causality.[11] The Declaration of Independence cannot but perform a monarchic gesture precisely insofar as it claims an authority that is not preceded by (but is said to coincide with) the "approbation and consent" of the people in whose name it denounces and rejects monarchism.[12]

Similarly, we ought to consider the complexity of the revolutionary claim that the subject of post-monarchism is the subject of birth (the subject of what the nineteenth-century African American abolitionist James Forten called " the birth-right of the human race" [quoted in Nash, *Race and Revolution*, 78][13]). This idea, Hannah Arendt writes, was absolutely original to the American Revolution: "inalienable political rights of all men by virtue of birth would have appeared to all ages prior to our own as they appeared to Burke – a contradiction in terms" (*On Revolution*, 45).[14] This is certainly not a subject that democracy (our democracy) wants to give up ("Civil rights," wrote Malcolm X, "means you're asking Uncle Sam to treat you right. Human rights are something you were born with. Human rights are your God-given rights. Human rights are the rights that are recognized by all nations of this earth," "The Ballot," 2549). The idealism and the antagonism of this element of anti-monarchism are part of the inheritance of democracy. But *post*-revolutionary political philosophy reminds us that this very antagonism registers a contamination:

the subject of universal, inalienable rights is also always the subject of an othered – and thus displaced – monarchism; monarchic subjectivity (that of the monarch himself, but also, as we shall see in chapter one, that of the obedient people) is an integral part of the structure of democratic subjectivity. This contamination can be glimpsed in the various revolutionary condemnations of the absolute monarch's privileged relationship to the rights of birth: "The following," writes Thomas Paine, "is the system of logic upon which are founded the claims of Royalty: 'I,' says the hereditary prince, owe my authority to my birth; I owe my birth to God; therefore, I owe nothing to men'" ("An Essay," 389–90). "Just consider;" Paine continues, "a person cannot be a mere workman without some sort of ability; to be a king all that a man requires is to be born" (391). If today it is becoming possible to challenge the unexamined efficacy of an appeal to the rights of man (the rights of birth), it is because we may finally be able to resist the revolutionary injunction against thinking through the relations of inheritance and displacement that connect monarchism and democracy.[15] Democratic subjectivity, as we shall see, is in perpetual negotiation with the structures of monarchism.

Now the revolutionary subject of the rights of birth and of the Declaration's monarchic "coup of force" is also the subject of one of the most enduring legacies of revolutionary anti-monarchism: the Bill of Rights, that original supplement to the juridical founding of the federally united states. The Bill's principle gesture opposes an inalienable extra-legal freedom to the encroachments of any form of political power; it is, as Thomas Jefferson put it, "what the people are entitled to against every government on earth, general or particular, and what no just government should refuse or rest on inference."[16] "Congress shall make no law ... abridging the freedom of speech," asserts the most famous element of the Bill. Lawmaking forces, the forces of political power, must be restrained from encroaching upon an originally free speech. The subject of the Bill of Rights is the subject of Jefferson's Declaration of Independence, the subject endowed at birth with "certain inalienable rights" including the right "to alter or to abolish" any government that fails to secure these rights.

But the subject of American democracy is also, of course, the subject of the Constitution – the subject of that text which the Bill of Rights amends. Who is *that* subject if he or she is *not* the subject of an original and inalienable freedom? That subject, it seems clear, is the subject of politico-juridical structure, the subject of (constitutional) convention.[17] If the subject of the Bill of Rights finds its figural space outside, or before, the law (the people "out of doors" as Paine among others liked to say), the subject of the Constitution might be expected to show up *inside* the law, framed by its articles and sections, defined by its delineation of acceptable representatives and eligible voters. (In chapters three and four I will suggest at more length how the subject of the Constitution can be thought of not just as the subject of convention but as the subject of *the* Convention, the subject of that insistently secretive and rhetorically quite extravagant founding process that took place in Annapolis and Philadelphia in 1786 and 1787.) That this subject is as crucial to the identity of the democratic citizen as the open-air subject of the Bill of Rights is brought home to us, I will argue, by the centrality for democracy of the secret ballot. The democratic subject-citizen, in other words, is simultaneously and irreducibly the subject outside and before the law (the subject of an originary freedom) and the subject isolated and secreted within the frame of the ballot box or the voting booth.[18] One could even say that the history of political antagonism within democracy can be rewritten as an ongoing confrontation between the discourse of the subject outside and before the law, the subject of the Bill of Rights, and the subject of the law's structures and concealments (and this confrontation has recently been replayed for us in the academic study of late-eighteenth century America in the form of an "opposition" between an oratorical understanding of revolutionary rhetoric and a print-privileging analysis: the subject of print's concealments versus the subject of the spoken voice's revelations). But without dismissing the importance of this "confrontation," we should consider the possibility that it maintains a false opposition. For as the *New York Times* piece with which I began suggests, the constitutional subject of the ballot box, in his or her secrecy and isolation, is as much the subject of a disorienting "outside" as the Bill of Rights' subject "out of doors." Hidden behind a cardboard wall that "guards his ballot" (Atwood, "Fragile," A27), but which also, as with Paine's "ridiculous" monarch, leaves him "shut off from the world" (Paine, *Common Sense*, 69), the Haitian voter experiences the deconstruction of a simple opposition between the law and its outside, between democracy and monarchism as a kind of border crisis that for all its danger and for all the anxiety it generates, nevertheless belongs to democracy (the guest editorial was entitled "Fragile – But Democratic").

But something, it is important to remember, could be said to interrupt the isolation of the voting booth. The democratic voter shares his or her secret space with writing, that writing with which the voter *must* engage at the moment of decision. For the Haitian voter, this writing may well be readable only as a message that does not speak to him ("symbols intended to identify candidates for illiterate voters had been left off the ballots"). But he must read in order to vote, just as he must write – even if it is only the minimal writing of a mark added to the right set of letters – if he is to have been there at all. In a democracy, this relationship to writing guarantees the voter's free speech. The Haitian example, once again, calls to mind Paine's description of monarchism's tendency to "exclude" the king from the "means of information" needed to make the decision that he is nevertheless "required" to make. The arbitrariness of monarchic rule that Paine here despises in the name of a familiar ethic of Enlightenment relocates itself under democracy in the form of a critical engagement with writing.

What is meant by the "writing" that shares the space of the voting booth? It would be possible, after all, to imagine a voting machine that announced the candidates and recorded the spoken will of a person who was unable to read or write anything at all. It is not a simple distinction between speech and writing that the voting booth gives us to consider, then, but an understanding of writing as the name for that in language which allows it to function in the absence of any particular receiver (thus to be recordable and reproducible by a machine). The model of language that resists the humanizing emphasis on communication as an interpersonal act, that insists on the play of absence (and thus on a "death," or "non-human" element that can always be mistaken for a divine transcendence) as a constitutive feature of language, is that which democracy relies upon even as it does so in the name of the original freedom of the subject of inalienable human rights (the rights of the born, even, for some, the unborn). Democracy, founded on the fantasy of a singular will, the fantasy of a coincidence of the author and product of law, of a god-like transcendence of time (and thus of the discrepancy between general law and particular application that produces an experience of time), performs (and hides) its impossibility in the ballot box – the magician's box of democracy. As if to say, in an entirely revolutionary appropriation of monarchism's rallying cry: the democratic citizen is dead (subject to history; subject to death; subject to the letter); long live the democratic citizen.

One of the earliest and most enduring portraits of a liberated American exemplifies this complex post-mortem independence of the democratic citizen. In the chapter, "What is an American?" from Hector St. John de Crèvecoeur's *Letters from An American Farmer* (1782), the narrator, James, describes a scene in which a recently arrived emigrant from the Scottish island of Barra is told that the lease he holds on "Mr. A.V.'s" land can be passed on to his children after his death in accordance with his wishes. Andrew, the Scotsman, is "impressed with astonishment and confusion," and James can understand this: "he was an actor introduced upon a new scene; it required some time ere he could reconcile himself to the part he was to perform." "However," continues James, "he was soon enlightened and introduced into those mysteries with which we native Americans are but too well acquainted" (*Letters*, 101–2).

Referring to legal rights as "mysteries" is of course a little bit of rhetorical play on James' part; it is precisely, some might say, the non-mysterious quality of this legal system that James wants to introduce but which Andrew finds so disconcerting. And yet we cannot be sure. For what precisely is the right that so floors Andrew? It is a certain right to immortality: "You may sell the lease, or if you die, you may previously dispose of it as if the land was your own," explains Mr. A.V. This is the moment at which Andrew becomes speechless, or, we might say, dumbfounded: Andrew "starts into being" and "expressive yet inarticulate joy was mixed in his countenance, which seemed impressed with astonishment and confusion" (83, 101). And "No wonder," says James: "for how could the man who had hardly a will of his own since he was born imagine he could have one after his death? How could the person who never possessed anything conceive that he could extend his new dominion over this land, even after he should be laid in his grave?" (102). What are we to make of this language? Is it merely rhetorical play? To say that Andrew would be able to have a will "after his death" is to indulge in a trope (the legal force of his written words is anthropomorphized as a "will") that points to an aspect of the law that can hardly be stated literally. American liberty (at this point, in colonial America, it is a liberty that prefigures the revolution's achievements) coincides with a deployment of the gap that opens up between physical presence and effective will in the moment of writing. In his own small way, Andrew participates here in an aspect of monarchic power as it had been developed in England since at least Elizabethan times: Andrew has inherited the king's duplicitous ontology (his mortal and immortal bodies). I will address this concept (the king's two bodies) at more length in chapter one, but I want to note it here in order to begin to suggest that a mystificatory language of self-analysis is not foreign to the discourse of revolutionary transformation in late-eighteenth century America. "America," writes a suspiciously sanguine James, "has tended to regenerate [the poor of Europe]." "Formerly they were not numbered in any civil lists of their country, except in those of the poor; here they rank as citizens. By what invisible power hath this surprising metamorphosis been performed? By that of the laws and that of their industry" (Crèvecoeur, *Letters*, 68–9). Here again, James' reference to "invisible power" can be dismissed as an ironic registration of the insistently visible and open structures of American liberty. But the insistence with which James deploys these figures of fantastic power is in fact one early indication of what will turn out to be a very anxious account of American political transformation. For, as we shall see in chapter two, Crèvecoeur's James is not at all sure about American "innovations," and not at all sure that he will feel safer once his chosen country has abandoned the "ancient connexion" with the crown of England. James is not sure, finally, if he is ready for the "mysteries" of democracy. But then again, who is?

REVOLUTIONARY GRAMMAR

Spell *sb.1* **1. a.** Discourse, narration, speech; *Obs.*
Spell *v.2* **I.** *Trans.* **1. a.** To read (a book, etc.) letter by letter; to peruse, or make out, slowly or with difficulty.
Spell II. Intr. **6. a.** To form words by means of letters; to repeat or set down the letters of words; to read off the separate letters forming a word or words.

Who, according to the Declaration of Independence, is the subject of the revolution? First of all, it is a plural subject: It is "we" who hold certain truths to be "self evident"; it is "we" who "mutually pledge to each other our lives, our fortunes and our sacred honour." But this "we" speaks "in the name, and by the authority of" the "people" of the United States of America, and what this "we" knows and states is that "all men" are born equal. The individual rights guaranteed by mere birth that the Declaration announces and privileges are inaccessible, so this document would suggest, without recourse to the grammatical first person plural. There can be a politically empowered "I" only because of the possibility of a politically empowered "we." The independent American of the Declaration is indissociably bound to the representative "we" of the text's enunciation. The Declaration was – and is – a dramatic instance of the tension and mutual dependency that persists between the first person singular of a democratic individualism and the first person plural of a representative voice that appears to be necessary in order to claim inalienable rights. Even Jefferson, as we know, was caught up in this tension. "Neither aiming at originality of principle or sentiment, nor yet copied from any particular and previous writing," wrote Jefferson, the

Declaration was "an expression of the American mind" (in Fliegelman, *Declaring Independence*, 165). Nevertheless, in the epitaph Jefferson wrote for himself, he was to be known as, among other things, the "Author of the Declaration of American Independence," an assumption of individual agency that he never fully relinquished (*Declaring Independence*, 166). Uncertain to the end whether or not in the moment of Revolution he had found his voice or, as representative, he had been possessed by the voice of a hypostasized (thus, resolutely figural) "American mind," Jefferson played out in a particular way what we can see having general effects throughout the literary and political writing of the revolutionary and post-revolutionary period.[19] The subject of the Declaration of Independence is powerfully and effectively doubled: it is impossible to say, finally, whether he or she is the individual born with rights or the individual represented in the first person plural of the Declaration's textual voice.[20]

But the complexity does not stop there. For in addition to the play of first person singular and plural voices at work in this text there is also another "voice." The Declaration's opening sentence turns on this "voice"; one could even dare to suggest that in so far as it occupies this position, it is the most important voice in the text: "When in the course of human events it becomes necessary for one people to dissolve political bands which have connected them with another, and to assume among the powers of the earth the separate & equal station to which the laws of nature and of nature's god entitle them . . . " What "becomes necessary"? A people's dissolution of political bands? *This* people's dissolution of political bands? *This* revolution? All of the above, perhaps, and yet what we hear, of course, is the indefinite indicator, "it."[21] The famously effective passive construction here (an example of what John Adams called Jefferson's "peculiar felicity of expression" [quoted in Becker, *The Declaration of Independence*, 223]) suggests that this "it" is a strategic, if not downright deceptive, substitute for the people who do not want to be too closely identified with their revolutionary break. Jay Fliegelman has given us one of the best accounts of the extent to which the Declaration's opening lines participate in a widespread appeal to a "mechanical determinism" that served to "shield and exculpate individuals from the ultimate and uncomfortable responsibility of their newly heightened historical agency" (Fliegelman, *Declaring Independence*, 143).[22] For Fliegelman, the Declaration in general has a great deal invested in reducing intimations of calculated decision on the part of its subjects. By way of impressive contrast, the Declaration holds George III personally accountable for a multitude of attacks on colonial liberty, all carried out "without a mask."

Fliegelman explains: "Tyranny thus becomes defined not only as the abuse of power but more fundamentally as the principle of a free and independent will ... By demonizing George, the Declaration stigmatizes individual willfulness at the same time that it articulates an ideology of individual liberty. Independence is thus carefully separated from, and paradoxically made antithetical to, free will" (*Declaring Independence*, 144). Following Fliegelman, then, we could say that in these passages from the Declaration the subject of revolution is repudiated even as it is announced in a structure that can (as it is in Fliegelman's analysis) be presented as the work of a strategic duplicity. Fliegelman also suggests that what we find here is more enigmatic than even a careful attention to rhetorical strategy can explain. "Independence" is "*paradoxically* made antithetical to free will" (my emphasis). How is this possible? What does it mean to suggest that a *paradoxical* structure of independence and free will is announced in the founding document of the United States?

Let us look again at Jefferson's passive construction. If the third person singular pronoun "it" (of "it becomes necessary") is a passive substitute for the militant revolutionary people, it is nevertheless not simply a placeholder: the substitution also names an anxiety – or a constitutive indeterminability – with regard to the subject of the revolution. This indeterminability, or undecidability concerning the people's sovereign exercise of political will, is here registered with what is the grammatical equivalent of nature "herself" : this *it*, after all, is related to the *it* that rains or snows ("*it* is raining"), and it performs the same work done elsewhere in revolutionary rhetoric by nature as the supra-human site of political legitimization. The passive construction, "it becomes necessary," is the grammatical equivalent of all those substitute agents of revolutionary transformation – the "laws of nature" and of "nature's god" – that "entitle" and "impel" the people of the United States. Indeed, we might even consider the possibility that these agents (God, nature, and the laws of reason, with all their impersonal imperative force) are themselves somewhat anxious substitutes for this enigmatic "it." A whole range of rhetorical figures and narratives would proliferate in the revolutionary moment precisely as a means of defusing this revolutionary imperative ("it becomes necessary") for an ideology that is not at all at ease with the transformation it is encouraging.[23]

But grammar, as we know, cannot be relied upon. In the opening sentence of the Declaration, language plays a trick on itself (or on its subjects): the sentence that performs the work of masking agency can also be read self-reflexively to be drawing attention to its own devices:

"*it* becomes necessary." The Declaration itself, read in what some may regard as a perverse and illegitimate manner, declares that a time comes in the course of human events when the equivocal agency of the third person passive construction becomes necessary. And the time is now. It is at this moment, the moment of speaking the revolution into being, that something given to Jefferson by language, the impersonal pronoun "it" and its possibility of being used in a passive construction such as "it becomes necessary," demonstrates its value. Jefferson (and the "one people" of the United States) would be in debt to this grammar in something like the way in which the absolute monarch is in debt to his body politic (see chapter one). Without this substitution, perhaps, no revolution; without this trick of grammar, this vital undecidability, this game grammar plays with subjectivity, no revolution. The revolution that proceeds in the name of inalienable birth-rights needs something in language in order to be successful, but that something (perhaps we should not be surprised) bears all the marks of a repudiated stand-in, a body-double, or a spy. The impersonal pronoun "it" – the revolution's other body – hides; it keeps a secret, even as it stands in for the revolution itself. "It" is nowhere to be acknowledged by the revolution it serves. It is there at the beginning, and yet like the figure at the center of Cooper's *The Spy* to whom I will return at the end of this book, it must remain unseen, unrewarded. To be a subject of the American Revolution, then, is not just to be a beneficiary of the enlightening and humanizing possibilities of a world of reasonable discourse, productively printed or resolutely oral, but to be bound to negotiate a relationship to this disembodying (or body-doubling) substitution, this linguistic sleight-of-hand, this revolutionary grammar.[24]

REVOLUTIONARY TIME

Spell *sb.3* **4. a.** A period or space of time of indefinite length;
Spell *sb.3* **5. a.** A continuous period or stretch of a specified kind of weather.

When does one become a member of the American Revolution? Many accounts of the founding era have included more or less scandalous revelations of the limited beneficiaries of the revolution's achievements. Few would argue that the most important political advances in America so far have consisted in expanding the number of individuals and classes of individuals for whom the revolution can be said to have taken place. To borrow Gordon Wood's word again, more and more Americans have become the "ordinary" people for whom the revolution was enacted.

This fact alone would seem to alert us to the far-from-ordinary temporality of the revolutionary American. For whom will there have been an American Revolution? When can one become a member of the revolution? These questions, the very possibility of their being asked, suggest that one of the things the revolution achieved was the institution of a fantastic political subjectivity, a political subjectivity vulnerable to, or with the potential for generating, radical shifts in temporal identity. Women and African Americans, to take the most obvious examples, did not just become subjects of the American Revolution belatedly; in certain crucial respects they always were, from 1776 on.[25] Which is also to say that they became subjects of the revolution of 1776 at various times throughout the nineteenth and twentieth centuries. There is no way to acknowledge this structure of citizenship without engaging in what may seem like literary, or at least, unorthodox, complications of historical context. The subjects of political exclusion lived through a relationship to democratic citizenship that was at the very least doubled: they became the citizens they already were; they had always been and not been subjects of the revolution. As such, however, these subjects should also alert us to a concealed complexity at work in every example of citizenship in the revolutionary and post-revolutionary United States. What we might want to call the deferred citizenship of women and African Americans ought to tell us something about the fundamental or constitutive capacity for deferral that is part of the very structure of revolutionary American subjecthood. To invoke a constitutive deferral in the structure of revolutionary subjecthood is, then, one way of countering traces of a derogatory secondariness that may still cling to the positions of those Americans who had to fight for their full recognition as citizens of the post-revolutionary United States. Instead, these experiences could be seen to open up, for the first time, the force of the revolution's transformation of political subjectivity. The subjectivity of the white, propertied adult American male, in other words, awaited the enfranchisement of African Americans and women in order to be able to recognize the self that it had found(ed) in the revolutionary event (this would be another way to gloss Martin Luther King's suggestion, in 1963, that "[white people] have come to realize that their freedom is inextricably bound to our freedom," "I have A Dream," 1424).

Temporality is, of course, a concern of the Declaration of Independence too. In fact, the first word of the Declaration immediately alerts us to the temporal peculiarities of the revolution, "*When* in the course of human events . . ." And, as Jay Fliegelman points out, "the 'when' is not an externally and naturally determined moment but a chosen one, no less calculated a decision than the designation of the moment when suffering is no longer 'sufferable' " (*Declaring Independence*, 144).[26] The Declaration's "when" seems to speak of another order of time, a revolutionary or rhetorical temporality, and this should not be surprising. "Revolutions," wrote Hannah Arendt, "are the only political events which confront us directly and inevitably with the problem of beginning":

Antiquity was well acquainted with political change and the violence that went with change, but neither of them appeared to it to bring about something altogether new. Changes did not interrupt the course of what the modern age has called history, which, far from starting with a new beginning, was seen as falling back into a different stage of its cycle, prescribing a course which was preordained by the very nature of human affairs and which therefore itself was unchangeable. (*On Revolution*, 21)

Modern revolution requires a "new beginning," then ("America," wrote Thomas Paine in 1776, "has a blank sheet to write upon" ["Forester's Letters," 82]), and this in turn forces revolutionaries to deploy a language that might best be described as temporally charged. Revolutionary discourse often speaks as though time itself becomes palpable in the heat of revolution as the revolutionary *new* becomes indissociable from the revolutionary *now*. The revolution presents its participants with a sense of what Walter Benjamin called "time filled by the presence of the now," and no writer in 1776 was more possessed by this presence than Thomas Paine.[27]

A great deal of the force of *Common Sense* comes from its heightened temporal sensitivity. Its publication, Isaac Kramnick reminds us, "could not have been better timed" ("Introduction" to *Common Sense*, 8). The pamphlet came out in January of 1776 in Philadelphia where the Second Continental Congress sat divided over the issue of independence. On the very day it was published a copy arrived in Philadelphia of King George III's speech to parliament in which he declared that the "rebellious war" in the colonies was "manifestly carried on for the purpose of establishing an independent empire" (quoted in Kramnick, "Introduction," 9). ("Had the spirit of prophecy directed the birth of this production," wrote Paine in an appendix to the third edition, "it could not have brought it forth, at a more seasonable juncture, or a more necessary time," *Common Sense*, 113.) Taken together, then, the king's delayed reply and his disloyal subject's timely pamphlet enacted a direct confrontation between the outdated and the immediate.[28]

But a sense of immediacy and of the importance of the moment – the revolutionary "now" – is also apparent within the language of Paine's pamphlet itself. "Now is the seed time of continental union, faith and honor," wrote Paine; "the least fracture now will be like a name engraved with the point of a pin on the tender rind of a young oak; the wound will enlarge with the tree, and posterity read it in full grown characters" (*Common Sense*, 82). "A new method of thinking hath arisen," Paine continues, in the wake of the Battles of Lexington and Concord: "All plans, proposals, etc. prior to the nineteenth of April, i.e. to the commencement of hostilities, are like the almanacks of last year: which though proper then, are superceded and useless now" (82). Paine has an intoxicating sense of this "now." "Every thing that is right or natural pleads for separation," Paine exclaims. "The blood of the slain, the weeping voice of nature cries, 'TIS TIME TO PART" (87). The enemy is "delay": "The present winter is worth an age if rightly employed" (89). The word "now" punctuates Paine's account with an almost aggressive insistence: "Ye that oppose independence now" (99); "Britain being now an open enemy" (85); "The last cord now is broken" (99). Paine wants his listeners to feel the pressure of time, a time heavy with justice: "The present time," he announces, "is that peculiar time, which never happens to a nation but once . . . the *present time* is the *true time* for establishing [union]" (108).[29] For Paine, it seems, the revolution raises the possibility of an experience of the present that in itself guarantees the legitimacy of the political break he so desires.

The provocative insistence of Paine's rhetoric should also remind us, however, that this revolutionary invocation of the present moment meets with a great deal of resistance, not all of it external to the revolution. Paine's own text counters its invocation of revolutionary new beginnings with an equally overpowering invocation of divine consistency. "Where says some is the King of America? I'll tell you Friend, he reigns above" (98). Paine was convinced – occasionally to the point of absurdity – of the revolution's conformity with a higher law: "Even the distance at which the Almighty hath placed England and America," suggested Paine, "is a strong and natural proof, that the authority of the one, over the other, was never the design of Heaven."[30] Paine's words suggest that what we encounter in the heat of revolution is not only a transformative contact with the *new* or the *now* but a dramatic demonstration of the mutual dependency of a discourse of the present and a discourse of the divine: the now cannot be announced without a simultaneous declaration of another order of time, this one eternal and transcendent.

The political moment *par excellence*, the revolutionary now, is also (according to a desperate logic of recuperation) an encounter with divine time.[31] (Seventy-five years later, in an address on the subject of the Fourth of July, Frederick Douglass, at his politically and rhetorically most effective, begins a section entitled, "The Present" in this way: "My business, if I have any here to-day, is with the present. The accepted time with God and his cause is the ever living now" ["What to the Slave," 324].[32])

That the political temporality of the American Revolution should be immediately rewritten as divine temporality should not surprise us. What we encounter throughout revolutionary discourse is one or another attempt to write the revolution into an old story, one or another attempt to inscribe the revolution as a return, a restoration, a renewal, or an adjustment to necessity or to previously existing laws. The American Revolution is legitimized by "the laws of nature and of nature's God," the Declaration of Independence announces; the change of government is grounded in the right of the people to "alter or to abolish" any government that destroys "certain inalienable rights." And all this is taking place "in the course of *human* events" and "among the powers of *the earth*" (my emphases). That is to say, that whatever there is of novelty in this Declaration, in this revolution, it is contained within a world framed by eternal law and absolute power. The Declaration's bravura – we are all quite familiar with this – is composed "with a firm reliance on the protection of divine providence." There is – there must be – nothing new under God's sun.[33]

Indeed, it is quite possible that the very idea of a beginning, the very idea of the new was threatening to many of those who participated in the American Revolution.[34] For there was (and is) something profoundly disturbing about the new: a beginning or a new coming about is a form of creation, and very few Americans in 1776 would have been willing to entertain the full consequences of the idea that people, mere mortals, could create anything. To allow for the possibility of something absolutely new taking place in history, for the possibility of a radical beginning, would be to open up the gates of atheism. Eight years after the end of the War of Independence, John Adams registered discomfort with precisely this element of the revolutionary times he was living through. In the "Discourses on Davila" (1791), Adams reflects, among other things, on recent events in France and in particular on the relationship between revolutionary politics and a matter that "shall barely be hinted at, as delicacy, if not prudence, may require in this place some degree of reserve." He continues:

> Is there a possibility that the government of nations may fall into the hands of men who teach the most disconsolate of creeds, that men are but fireflies and that this *all* is without a father? Is this the way to make man, as man, an object of respect? Or is it to make murder itself as indifferent as shooting a plover, and the extermination of the Rohilla nation as innocent as the swallowing of mites on a morsel of cheese? ("Discourses on Davila," *Political Writings*, 176–94)[35]

For Adams, the violence of atheism is linked, via an intriguing figure, to an experience of time as the brief space of an exemplary mortality – that of the firefly. Taken together, the Declaration of Independence and Adams' sentiments suggest what we have always, to some extent, understood. Namely, that the radicalism of the American Revolution's encounter with historical time was contained by a reassuring and essentially conservative investment in the stability of heavenly law, the safety of divine time, the permanent protection of a divine patriarchy. The revolution's historical intervention would simultaneously put an end to history as such by restoring the eternal and immutable laws of "nature's God."[36]

What becomes apparent in much of the leading revolutionary discourse, then, is the insistent relationship between a rhetoric of the present and that of divine sanction. The aura of the absolutely new or the absolutely present – the "now" – is, in other words, a theological aura.[37] At the same time, however, this same discourse bequeaths to us (despite itself) a way to think about a temporality that we might call *textual*. It is the possibility of a temporality not at one with itself (a temporality, once again, that recalls the duplicity of the absolute monarch's two bodies) that needs to be read out of the revolutionary moment. It is a new understanding of temporality that the revolution gives us to think in the form of what might appear to be its contradictions and inconsistencies. The two temporalities invoked in the revolutionary moment (implied by Jefferson's qualified reference to a "when" that is in the course of "*human events*") can be read as a registration of a difference or deferral within our concept of temporality, a deferral that is related to the possibility of a retroactive revolutionary belonging for belatedly enfranchised citizens.[38] The theological aura of Paine's revolutionary now gives way under political pressure to a textual temporality that would allow for America, in Langston Hughes' words, to "be America again – / The land that never has been yet – ."[39] If Paine and Jefferson, among others, resisted the "fabulous retroactivity" of their own revolutionary intervention it was in part because they were still inclined to associate such temporal disorientation with hereditary monarchism: "While Royalty is harmful from its very nature," wrote Paine, "hereditary Royalty is, in addition, absurd and disgusting." He continues:

Just think of it! Yonder is a man who claims that he has a hereditary right to rule me! Where did he get it? From his ancestors, he says, and from mine. But how could they give him a right they did not possess? No man has power over posterity . . . If we returned to life, we could not rob ourselves of the rights acquired in a second existence; still less could we rob posterity of their rights. ("An Essay," 389)

Paine's tortuous introduction of science fiction here in an attempt to repudiate the absurd temporal violations of monarchism finds something of an antidote sixty-five years later in Abraham Lincoln's "Speech in Reply to Judge Douglas." Ironically challenging Douglas' invocation of a temporally bound Declaration, Lincoln asks: "I understand you are preparing to celebrate the 'Fourth' to-morrow week. What for? The doings of that day had no reference to the present; and quite half of you are not even descendants of those who were referred to that day. But I suppose you will celebrate; and will even go so far as to read the Declaration" (Lincoln, "Speech," 183).[40]

  Whose time, then, is the time of revolution? Which time does the revolution announce? "Let us . . . endeavour if possible," wrote Thomas Paine in 1776, "to find out the *very* time" (*Common Sense*, 100). Which time? The time for revolution; the time *of* revolution? Paine goes on: "But we need not go far, the inquiry ceases at once, for the *time hath found us.*" It is the time of founding that Paine has found *finding* him (and his fellow Americans). Is this the time of late eighteenth-century Americans? Is it "their time," as we would say, the time historians and literary critics are asked to observe at the risk of being anachronistic? But here, right at the very moment that defines their time most memorably, the Americans seem to be at one remove from time. Their time and "the *very* time" are not one. Time hath found them. Like captives awaiting their salvation, the revolutionaries find themselves realized by a time that is not quite identical with their intentions. This too is what it means to be the subject of revolution, and this is the self-different and self-alienated historical subject that literary theory's "present-mindedness" attempts to read. "How do you thank a man," asked Malcolm X in what we need not take as simply a rhetorical question, "for giving you what's already yours?" ("The Ballot," 2547)

REVOLUTIONARY PRESENCE

Spell sb. 3 [Related to SPELL v.3, and perh. directly representing OE. *–espelia* substitute.]
1. A set of persons taking a turn of work in order to relieve others; a relay, relief-gang, or shift.

The rather obscure use of the word "spell" to refer to a kind of substitution (specifically in order to "relieve" someone) harbors a useful hesitation. Most of the supporting examples given by the *OED* suggest that the substitution involved is a temporally limited one. In other words, this use of the word "spell" seems closely related to **Spell** *sb.3* **4. a.** ("A period or space of time of indefinite length"). Hence:

1825 J. NEAL *Bro. Jonathan* II. xviii. 138 One or two . . . were continually offering to give him a "spell" – or a "lift" – or a "turn" [at counting his money].
1829 B. HALL *Travels in N. A.* I. 188 A poor old negro . . . begged to be taken in, and offered to give me a spell when I became tired.

The substitutive "spell" suggests that one will take another's place only for a limited amount of time; the place does not become the substitute's; nothing is lost or given over to the substitute, the "speller." This equivocation (is the substitution a real substitution or a deferral, a temporary aid to the subject in order to secure his permanent occupation of a place?) in fact inhabits most discussions of political representation. Is the political representative there to extend the citizen's political reach, to supplement the physical limitations of the citizen? In this case the representative must not usurp or displace the citizen; he or she must be ready at any moment to give the position of power back, in its entirety, to the electorate. On the other hand, some argue that the representative must be granted full authority over the political voice his electorate has given him. He speaks for the people, but he does not simply say what they would say were they not, shall we say, over-extended. This question, of the representative's "independence" or his "mandate" is, as political scientist Hannah Pitkin observed many years ago, a persistent one. Indeed, she writes, with surprising frankness, the persistence suggests that "there might be a . . . philosophical paradox involved" in the whole notion of representation. "For something to be represented," Pitkin explains, "it must be made present in some sense while nevertheless not really being present literally or fully in fact." This is the paradoxical requirement of representation: "that a thing be both present and not present at the same time" ("Commentary," 40). And once we are talking about things being present and not-present at the same time we have ventured dangerously close to the language of spells and transubstantiated bodies that the democratic revolution had always sought to discard.

"Representation," writes J. G. A. Pocock in an essay on "the American Founding in Early Modern Perspective," was "the one great invention in politics that had been made since antiquity" (Ball and Pocock, *Conceptual Change*, 70). And, Gordon Wood adds, "no political conception was more important to Americans in the entire revolutionary era than representation" (*Creation*, 164). "Representation," said Moses Mather in 1775, "is the feet on which a free government stands"; defending representation as the key component of the new Federal Constitution, James Wilson, one of the most influential members of the Convention, celebrated the principle as "a cure for every disease" (quoted in Wood, *Creation*, 164, 532). "The principle of representation," wrote Madison in *The Federalist Papers*, "is the pivot on which the American republic will move" (*Federalist Papers*, 372). And yet representation is also the source of some of the revolution's most anxious moments. In fact, one version of the revolution begins with a representational crisis. When, during the Stamp Act Crisis of the 1760s, English politicians responded to American complaints by describing the fantastic powers of virtual representation, colonists were understandably incensed. This is how Soame Jenyns defended the English position:

[If representation] can travel three hundred miles [i.e. within England, where not every district had a representative], why not three thousand? If it can jump over rivers and mountains, why cannot it sail over the ocean? If the towns of Manchester and Birmingham, sending no representatives to parliament, were notwithstanding there represented, why are not the citizens of Albany and Boston equally represented in that Assembly? (quoted in Wood, *Creation*, 174–5)[41]

"No taxation without representation," cried the colonists; but not *this* representation. Jenyns' fantastic – almost gothic – representation has to be distanced from the kind of representation that the revolution puts to work in, for example, the text of its annunciation. The Declaration of Independence is delivered by "the Representatives of the United States of America, in Congress Assembled" and signed "in the name, and by the authority of the good people of these colonies." No revolution without representation, this text suggests; in the beginning, there will have been representation.

Nevertheless, the great fear of many democrats in the post-revolutionary era was that representation might compromise the sovereign will of the people. As Gordon Wood has so elegantly demonstrated, this period witnessed an intensification of calls for limits on the autonomy of political representatives, and time limits were among the most important measures advocated by proponents of direct (or at least more direct) representation. The representative, it was said, is not taking the place of the people; he is merely holding the people's place for them for a while; he is lending a hand – not engaging in an active substitution. Inevitably, the problem of representation generated some of the revolution's most interesting rhetorical interventions. Efforts to ensure that political representatives directly articulated the interests of their electorate were described as attempts to "fetter" or put "leading strings" on politicians.[42] Local interests looked "through the eyes" of elected representatives, preventing a broader vision of the national interest.[43] At the same time, those in favor of a more direct democracy felt encouraged by the idea that chosen representatives would be "the breath of our nostrils."[44] In perhaps the most important – because most consequential – discussion of American political representation, *Federalist* no. 10, James Madison refers to the "public views" refined and enlarged by being passed through "the medium of a chosen body of citizens" (*Federalist Papers*, 126). As Garry Wills and others have pointed out, Madison is here using a scientific metaphor to impress his readers with the appropriateness and effectiveness of the representational system he is espousing. But the multivalent etymology of this word (medium) would only lead us to suspect that a great deal of equivocation is being more or less successfully contained by Madison's carefully chosen term. That the word should by the mid-nineteenth century have entered popular usage as a term for those who facilitated exchange with the dead only reminds us of the unsettling implications already harbored by Madison's term in 1787. (Indeed, it is still possible to hear contemporary denunciations of Madisonian representation which claim that the Constitution's theory of representation secured power for a socio-economic elite only by transforming the body politic into a "specter" [see Miller, "The Ghostly Body Politic," and Nelson, *National Manhood*].) In other words, the notion of representation as it has informed political thought from the eighteenth century to our own time carries with it some deeply disturbing implications about democracy's relationship to what Henry Thoreau would

call "the black arts of government."[45] Recent political philosophy has
not eased this concern. One of the achievements of political philosopher
Ernesto Laclau's work has been to articulate clearly and effectively a
post-modern understanding of some key terms in the democratic vocabulary. In "Power and Representation," Laclau turns to the concept of
representation and begins by outlining the basic terms of the "problem":

> The conditions of a perfect representation would be met, it seems, when the
> representation is a direct transmission of the will of the represented, when
> the act of representation is totally transparent in relation to that will . . . Thus
> the opaqueness inherent in any substitution and embodiment must be reduced
> to a minimum; the body in which the incarnation takes place must be almost
> invisible. This is, however, the point at which the difficulties start. ("Power and
> Representation," 290)[46]

Laclau goes on to suggest that if an individual needs to be represented
at all, it is because "his or her identity is an incomplete identity, and
the relation of representation – far from being a full-fledged identity –
is a *supplement* necessary for the constitution of identity" (290). If late-
eighteenth-century democrats worried that representation would compromise the sovereign will of the people, precisely by resurrecting the
ghost of a monarch whose left hand did not know what its right hand
was doing, late-twentieth-century post-Marxists know it is too late: this
sovereign will was compromised to begin with: it comes into being as an
identity in need of supplementation. "There is an opaqueness, an essential impurity in the process of representation," writes Laclau, "which is
at the same time its condition of both possibility and impossibility" (291).

Both the discourse of the revolutionary era and the insights of recent
political philosophy, then, suggest that representation can be registered
as a threat to, as well as an opportunity for, the political subject. One
recent account of the revolution's beginnings finds this originary or constitutive representation of the subject of independence at work in an
insistently visible manner. In his account of popular political rituals and
celebrations in the early republic, David Waldstreicher writes about the
crucial political value of a simultaneously legislative and empirical performance of independence: "On sending out the printed Declaration,
the Congress did not recommend fasting, mourning, bell ringing, or any
other observance. Congress would not – it could not – order the nation
to celebrate its own birth. The new nation could not exist until the people
spontaneously celebrated its existence, until evidence of this nationwide

celebration appeared in print" (*In the Midst*, 30). For Waldstreicher, it is a dual investment in spontaneous public action and in widespread print publication (of both the Declaration and newspaper accounts of popular celebrations) that together constituted the birth of the United States. The new American was immediately the subject of particular times and places (Boston, Philadelphia, Savannah) and of the mass-produced printed document (the Declaration, the newspapers): "The printed description of local display was thus the perfect way to spread nationalism. The same vehicle that reported the local and present-oriented recent past could make the extralocal future self-evident" (*In the Midst*, 34). On a national level and at the outset of the revolution it is no longer possible to discuss the subject of the revolution without recourse to this mutually reinforcing dialogue between the spontaneity of local, bodily outbursts and mass-reproduced, textual representations. The subject in the street is the subject in the newspapers: the revolutionary authenticity of the people who took to the street in New York City is guaranteed by their posthumous appearance in the *Virginia Gazette*'s account of nationwide independence celebrations as well as by their anticipation in the plural voice of the Declaration. In registering the complex original moment of independence, Waldstreicher augments Jacques Derrida's observation about the structure of any meaningful event: it cites itself at the origin; it begins as a unique event *and* as that event's (self-) quotation: "Every sign," Derrida writes, "linguistic or nonlinguistic, spoken or written (in the current sense of this opposition), in a small or large unit, can be *cited*, put between quotation marks" (*Limited Inc.*, 12). But this is also to say that citationality is constitutive of a sign: "This citationality, this duplication or duplicity, this iterability of the mark is neither an accident nor an anomaly, it is that . . . without which a mark could not even have a function called 'normal.' What would a mark be that could not be cited? Or one whose origins would not get lost along the way?" (12). If this idea seems in its abstract form one of those mystical anachronisms that literary theory foists on historiography, Waldstreicher's work suggests that a careful look at the empirical events of the past produces no less complex a theoretical conclusion. What would a revolution be that could not be cited? Or whose origins would not get lost along the way?

The political subject of the simultaneously textual and empirical, inventive and cited Declaration of Independence is far from being "ordinary." His or her location within the state will, from this moment on, be a matter of some concern and confusion. Is the independent American a paper subject? A legal fiction? A rhetorical construction? Or is the independent American only to be found "out of doors" or in the street? (Is the new American, to anticipate my next chapter, to be found in his body politic or his body natural?) Will the revolution resolve itself into anarchy or into a repressive state bureaucracy, a legal dictatorship? The revolution in fact initiates a radical deconstruction of this opposition at precisely the same time as it heightens the intensity with which these terms will be deployed in political argument. The Declaration, the street celebrations, and the newspaper accounts are different versions of an attempt to speak the uncompromised voice of the revolutionary subject. What the events of July 1776 demonstrate is the extent to which these authoritative, originating performances required the supplement of each other. In the summer of 1776 the subject of revolution is born again and again, prematurely and retrospectively, in a performance driven as much by a revolutionary commitment to the possibility and justice of a presentation uncompromised by mediation as it is by an implicit recognition of the political efficacy of multiple, mutually reaffirming representations. Political debate in the post-revolutionary years will often take the form of pitting the defenders of "men in the street" against the supporters of the law, or the structures of state power. This opposition will sometimes take the form of a direct confrontation between a discourse invested in the authenticity of the body (its gestures, its voices, its expressions and effusions) and a discourse that derives authority from the anonymous efficiency of the printed word. But the simultaneous investment in both forms of revolutionary expression in the founding moment will remind us in what follows that these frequently oppositional political discourses often distract attention away from their similar investments in the possibility of accessing the unmediated wisdom of the legitimate revolutionary voice.

DEMOCRATIC SOVEREIGNTY

What would it mean, finally, to question the sovereignty of "the people"? How would one go about articulating a *democratic* resistance to the authority of "the people?"[47] Any compromise of the foundational legitimacy of the Declaration's "good People" is, it would seem, a neo-monarchical act. To suggest that "the people" are constitutively lacking in their status as foundational agents of democracy is, for many, to align a post-humanist, post-Marxist political philosophy with the constitutive other of the American Revolution, that is to say, with monarchism. But is it possible to imagine a deconstruction of popular sovereignty that would nevertheless remain post-monarchic and democratic?

Post-Marxist discussions of constitutive ruptures in the democratic social space can be traced back to specific aspects of the constitutional establishment of the United States. The "true distinction" of the American governments, wrote Madison in *Federalist* no. 73, "lies *in the total exclusion of the people in their collective capacity*, from any share in [government]" (*Federalist Papers*, 373). Odd as this isolated claim may sound (particularly when we recall that parades – such as the one in Philadelphia – organized to celebrate ratification of the Constitution featured "a framed copy of the Constitution over the words 'THE PEOPLE'" [Silverman, *A Cultural History*, 583]), what Madison successfully argued here was that the people's power under the Federal Constitution was guaranteed precisely by taking them out of any *particular* branch of the government. From now on, said Madison, every elected official would be a representative of the people, precisely because the people were nowhere present (in their particularity) within the offices of government. The topography of the American political system would hereafter be remarkably (deceptively) simple: the people in their empirical particularity and entirety would be forever separated from a government that would be entirely inhabited by representatives. The ballot box would mark the point of the divide. In order to describe this central achievement of the founders, Gordon Wood is forced to introduce a term that in another context might sound suspiciously gothic, or, indeed, post-modern:

Americans had retained the forms of the Aristotelian schemes of government but had eliminated the substance, thus divesting the various parts of government of their social constituents. Political power was thus *disembodied* and became essentially homogenous . . . Politics in such a society could no longer simply be described as a contest between rulers and people, between institutionalized orders of the society. The political struggles would in fact be among the people themselves, among all the various groups and individuals seeking to create inequality out of their equality by gaining control of a government divested of its former identity with the society. It was this *disembodiment* of government from society that ultimately made possible the conception of modern politics and the eventual justification of competing parties among the people. (Wood, *Creation*, 604, 608)

To have recourse to the word "disembodied" to describe what it was that the Federal Constitution succeeded in achieving for modern politics is to acknowledge, once again, the ambivalent dimension of this version of democratization.[48] What post-Marxist political philosophy gives us to contemplate in terms of the "constitutive incompletion of the social" (Laclau, "Deconstruction," 48) is here opened up in the moment of the

American Revolution via a radicalization of the concept of representation and an institutionalization of a rupture between the "body" of the sovereign populace and those who speak in their name (those who *spell* for them). [49] The people's access to sovereignty passes through an experience of disembodiment that, not surprisingly, left some suspicious, some uncomfortable, and others transfigured.

On the other hand, the democratic subject has often been treated as if his or her defining feature was a common transparency to the political eye. The democratic subject is the subject of the crowd, whose passions are all on the surface, who has no secrets and who exists in a society of people who are all alike, as if equality had simplified the citizen and put an end to dissimulation. But here and there we will find other versions of the democratic sovereign. "The people," wrote Thomas Jefferson thirteen years after the Declaration of Independence, "cannot assemble themselves."[50] The people, in other words, are irreducibly disassembled. To participate in this dissembled subjectivity is – to return to where I began – to find oneself straddling the cardboard wall (what Madison might have called the "parchment barrier") of the Haitian voting booth: head "poked" out, at odds with a writing one cannot refuse, and at the same time watching, guarding, and shouting – "almost in unison" – with the guardians of democracy: "You have to decide for yourself!" Inside and outside, watching without being seen, writing anonymously to your citizen-self: this is what it is to be a subject of the American Revolution; this is what it is to be a subject of the spell of democracy.

CHAPTER I

Monarchophobia: reading the mock executions of 1776

> In metaphorical terms, the colonials killed their king in 1776.
> (Edward Countryman, *The American Revolution*, 125)

> The body is with the king, but the king is not with the body.
> (William Shakespeare, *Hamlet* IV.ii 29–30)

Philip Freneau was the poet laureate of American anti-monarchism. As early as 1775 (in "A Political Litany"), he was calling for delivery from "a royal king Log, with his tooth full of brains," (Freneau, *Poems*, III, 141), and in the aftermath of the war he put as much effort into reminding his readers of what had been left behind as into imagining what was to come. For Freneau, the United States were fundamentally post-monarchic:

> Forsaking kings and regal state,
> With all their pomp and fancied bliss,
> The traveller owns, convinced though late,
> No realm so free, so blest as this –
> The east is half to slaves consigned,
> Where kings and priests enchain the mind.
> ("On the Emigration to America," in Freneau,
> *Poems*, II, 280)[1]

Twenty years later, in the wake of the French Revolution and with Thomas Paine's *Rights of Man* by his side, Freneau remained passionate about the object of patriotic loathing:

> With what contempt must every eye look down
> On that base, childish bauble called a crown,
> The gilded bait, that lures the crowd, to come,
> Bow down their necks, and meet a slavish doom.
> ("To A Republican With Mr. Paine's Rights of Man,"
> in Freneau, *Poems*, III, 90)

Freneau's political theatre always had a place for the prince's crown. The rejected crown in "To A Republican With Mr. Paine's Rights of Man" remains capable of drawing the poet's eye – and that of the contemptuous populace – even in disgrace: every eye looks down on what once had captivated them. Monarchism had certainly not disappeared from the world in 1795, but one might have thought that in the United States, in 1795, there would be little need to reiterate the message of 1776. Instead, Freneau celebrates his republic with an insistent refrain: "Without a king, we till the smiling plain; / Without a king, we trace the unbounded sea" (91). In fact, "To A Republican" has more to say about kings than about republics. It cannot take its gaze away from the king even after nineteen years of independence. And the final line of the poem, hesitating between prophecy and prayer, suggests that this will be the eternal condition of the American republic:

> So shall our nation, formed on Virtue's plan,
> Remain the guardian of the Rights of Man,
> A vast republic, famed through every clime,
> Without a king, to see the end of time.
>
> (91)

To the end of time, the United States will be "Without a king." One could almost begin to suspect that this is a poem that mourns, that does not want to forget, that feels the weight of a loss. Philip Freneau does not want to let go of his absent king.[2]

The pre-revolutionary struggle between colonial governments and the British parliament involved parties who both claimed allegiance to the crown of England, who both signed themselves in the king's name and who both celebrated their British subjecthood. This intra-national political struggle became a revolution when – and only when – Americans turned against the crown. The American repudiation of George III, Hannah Arendt suggested in 1963, was also a "rejection on principle of monarchy and kingship in general" and, thus, it constituted what Arendt claims was, "perhaps the greatest American innovation in politics as such" (*On Revolution*, 129, 153). At the same time, however, it is important to acknowledge that as long as the revolutionaries defined themselves with respect to this monarchic other, they were participating in an event and a political structure that we would still have to call "colonial." We know this, because we have witnessed many "revolutions" since 1776 that turned out to have been "uprisings" or "rebellions," mere disturbances by a group of disaffected individuals within a single state. In order for the revolt to have been a revolution (in order for there to be a post-revolution) something had to happen to the absolutely antagonistic relationship between the revolution and its monarchic other. There had to be, in other words, a redistribution – I will call it a translation – of the structures and characteristics of monarchism within the new political order.

"The great social antagonists of the American revolution," writes Gordon Wood in his Pulitzer prize-winning study, *The Radicalism of the American Revolution* (1991), "were not poor vs. rich, workers vs. employers, or even democrats vs. aristocrats." "They were," he continues, "patriots vs. courtiers – categories appropriate to the monarchical world in which the colonists had been reared" (*Radicalism*, 175). In the years before 1776, American anti-monarchism was fueled by a growing frustration with the abuse of royal patronage by would-be courtiers in the colonies, an abuse which increased with the accession of George III in 1760. Wood writes: "Americans steeped in the radical whig and republican ideology of opposition to the court regarded these monarchical techniques of personal influence and patronage as 'corruption,' as attempts by great men and their power-hungry minions to promote their private interests at the expense of the public good and to destroy the colonists' 'balanced constitutions and their popular liberty' " (174–5). As early as 1750, Jonathan Mayhew could be heard proclaiming that "Nothing can well be imagined more directly contrary to common sense, than to suppose that *millions* of people should be subjected to the arbitrary, precarious pleasure *of one single man*" ("Discourse," 406). And in his 1765 "Dissertation on the Canon and Feudal Law," John Adams, never one to mince his words, praised the Puritan settlers of New England for seeing clearly that "popular powers must be placed as a guard, a control, a balance, to the powers of the monarch and the priest, in every government, or else it would soon become the man of sin, the whore of babylon, the mystery of iniquity, a great and detestable system of fraud, violence, and usurpation" (*Political Writings*, 9).[3]

Nevertheless, the political force of anti-monarchism in the revolutionary era is out of all proportion with American attitudes towards monarchy before 1776. "Despite overwhelming evidence of George III's complicity in the policies that were driving them toward revolution," writes Peter Shaw, "Americans of all classes on the patriot side sustained their loyalty to the king throughout the period from 1760 to 1776" (*American Patriots*, 14). He continues: "The king's name was loudly upheld and his health drunk enthusiastically at the earliest Stamp Act demonstrations, the dedication of Liberty Trees, Stamp Act Repeal Ceremonies, and subsequently at virtually every anti-British demonstration up to 1776.

During this period his birthday continued to be celebrated with similar enthusiasm throughout the colonies" (14). The repeal of the Stamp Act in 1766 was celebrated by Americans as the work of the king, intervening in his proper sphere as protector of the rights of ordinary Englishmen, and in 1768 George was looked to as the colonists' best hope of repealing the Townshend Acts (which George had, of course, approved). What is striking about American attitudes toward monarchism, then, is how suddenly the King of England became the focus of disaffection, and thus how quickly a rebellion turned into a revolution. The crown's final disappointing response to one of the many petitions outlining the colonists' grievances arrived in Philadelphia in January of 1776 (although it had been written in August of 1775). "By declaring the colonies in a state of rebellion ["open and avowed rebellion"] and committing the monarchy to vigorous military measures to force the colonies to yield to parliamentary authority in August 1775," Jack Greene explains, "George III convinced most American leaders that he was now, if he had not been all along, at the head of the plot to deprive the colonies of their liberties" (Greene, *Colonies to Nation*, 3). Within a very short space of time, this sentiment became the driving force behind the movement for independence. "Government by kings," wrote Thomas Paine in January of 1776, "was the most prosperous invention the Devil ever set on foot for the promotion of idolatry" (*Common Sense*, 72). And by July of the same year, a very particular sense of the monarch's injustices serves to beef-up the body of the Declaration of Independence. "The history of the present king of Great Britain," states the Declaration, "is a history of repeated injuries and usurpations, all having in direct object the establishment of an absolute Tyranny over these States. To prove this let Facts be submitted to a candid world." There then follows a lengthy list of specific grievances against George III culminating in the charge that "A Prince, whose character is thus marked by every act which may define a Tyrant, is unfit to be the ruler of a free people."

Thus, when American patriots took to the street to celebrate independence they produced one of the most visible manifestations of their revolution in the extravagantly humiliated and executed body of a mock king. On the occasion of the public readings of the Declaration of Independence, only a few years after the king had been celebrated in colonial toasts, effigies of George III were (for the first time) hanged and given mock funerals throughout the colonies. New Yorkers pulled down the gilt equestrian statue of George III that had been commissioned after the repeal of the Stamp Act, and sent it in pieces to Litchfield,

Connecticut, where it was molded into cartridges for the use of revolutionary soldiers.[4] Abigail Adams, writing to her husband in Philadelphia,
described the proceedings in Boston: "After dinner the King's arms were
taken down from the State House and every vestige of him from every
place in which it appeard and burnt in King Street. Thus ends royall
authority in this State, and all the people shall say Amen" (*Book of Abigail
and John*, 148). Newspaper accounts of a mock funeral for George III
in Savannah, Georgia claimed that the interring of the king before the
court house attracted "a greater number of people than ever appeared
on any occasion before in this province" (quoted in Waldstreicher, *In the
Midst*, 33–4). As David Waldstreicher puts it, "From being the great protector who legitimized the execration of other (British) enemies, George
III became the soul of Britain itself, reconstituted as *the* enemy. His funeral
became the national birthday" (*In the Midst*, 30).

The American turn against George III was swift and decisive, then,
but it nevertheless fell short, as commentators have since been quick to
point out, of actual regicide. The American revolutionaries "metaphorically" killed their king, we are reminded, and for this reason, perhaps,
their revolution would always be lacking. One of the earliest and most
scandalous expressions of American anti-monarchism was delivered by
Patrick Henry in the form of a famously elliptical warning in the Virginia
House of Burgesses in 1765: "Tarquin and Caesar each had his Brutus,"
said Henry, " – Charles the First his Cromwell and – George the
Third . . . may profit by their example" (quoted in Fliegelman, *Declaring
Independence*, 104). Henry was interrupted, so legend has it, by gasps
and anticipatory outcries from House members who, like most of their
fellow colonial subjects, were far from ready to turn against their distant sovereign. For the first, and not the last time, the King of England
narrowly avoided execution in the colonies. Indeed, while the French
Revolution had its Louis XVI and the Russian Revolution its Czar
Nicholas II, the American Revolution never got to "have" its George III.
As far as the revolution was concerned he was "not quite all there." And
this is perhaps one of the reasons why the American Revolution has not
entered the imagination of the West with anything like the dramatic force
of the French. At the center of the American Revolution is an absence
of precisely that figure with whom the revolution seemed to be doing
away. And what could be less spectacular than a revolution by proxy?
The American revolutionaries had to make do with effigies, so the story
goes, and when compared to the spectacle of the guillotine or the Russian
Royal Family lined up and shot in their palace, can anyone be forgiven

for thinking of the American Revolution as puppet theatre? Having determined that the king and their rejection of him was at the heart of this revolution, we might be tempted to pity the colonials their need to make do with an effigy, as if even in revolution they were mocked by the king's obliviousness. What can we make of this ambiguous revolutionary inheritance: the centrality of the monarch and the monarch's execution for the revolution, on the one hand, and the humbling absence of the flesh and blood body of the deposed monarch on the other? What does it mean to be the political subject responsible for and produced by this attack on a virtual monarchic body? What, in other words, are the implications of Edward Countryman's suggestion that "in metaphorical terms, the colonials killed their king in 1776"? Prompted by these questions, I want to suggest not only that the turn against George III was central to the American Revolution, but also, that the public execution of the king's effigy, far from being the sign of this revolution's impoverished relation to real political intervention, provides us with the most appropriate and most suggestive point of entry into the originality of the American break with England. And I will begin by asking this question: what if the mock body interred in Savannah and all over the colonies in July of 1776 was not just a stand-in for the king's body? What if it was the king's other body?[5]

THE KING'S TWO BODIES

The discourse of English monarchism since at least the seventeenth century had produced another way of thinking about what it was that colonial Americans were doing away with. As Ernst Kantorowicz explains it in his classic study, *The King's Two Bodies*, crucial changes began to take place in the European understanding of monarchical power in the wake of the Reformation. "The new territorial and quasi-national state," Kantorowicz writes, "self-sufficient according to its claims and independent of the Church and the Papacy, quarried the wealth of ecclesiastical notions ... And finally proceeded to assert itself by placing its own temporariness on a level with the sempiternity of the militant church" (Kantorowicz, *The King's Two Bodies*, 207). The primary method for achieving this sempiternity was the concept, deployed increasingly by Elizabethan lawyers, of the relationship between the king *body natural* and the king *body politic*. The Catholic church's attempts to realize Christ's presence first in the eucharist then in the members of the church itself presented monarchism with a blueprint for establishing a relationship between secular political authority and immortality.[6] Kantorowicz quotes from crown lawyers who had been called upon in 1562 to decide on a matter concerning the granting of land by the child-king Edward VI. The lawyers agreed:

> that by the Common Law no Act which the King does as King, shall be defeated by his Nonage. For the King has in him two Bodies, viz., a Body natural, and a Body politic. His Body natural (if it be considered in itself) is a Body mortal, subject to all Imfirmities that come by Nature or Accident, to the Imbecility of Infancy or old Age, and to the like Defects that happen to the natural Bodies of other People. But his Body politic is a Body that cannot be seen or handled, consisting of Policy and Government, and constituted for the Direction of the People, and the Management of the public weal, and the Body is utterly void of Infancy, and old Age, and other natural Defects and Imbecilities, which the Body natural is subject to, and for this Cause, what the King does in his Body politic, cannot be invalidated or frustrated by any Disability in his natural Body. (quoted in Kantorowicz, *The King's Two Bodies*, 7)[7]

The notion articulated here, whereby the *arcana imperii*, or "mysteries of the state" becomes detached from the *arcana ecclesiae* and is put to work in the service of a deified monarch, was part of what Michael McKeon calls a "flowering" of absolutist doctrines of royal sovereignty around the end of the Tudor period (*The Origins of the English Novel*, 178). But what the English Puritans (and later Americans like John Adams) realized was that this notion also had radically destabilizing potential. Without the concept of the king's two bodies, Kantorowicz writes, "it would have been next to impossible for the [revolutionary Parliament of 1642] to . . . Summon, in the name and by the authority of Charles I, King body politic, the armies which were to fight the same Charles I, King body natural" (*The King's Two Bodies*, 21). As seventeenth-century historian Peter Heylyn put it, parliament sought to "destroy Charles Stuart, without hurting the king."[8] Parliamentarians argued – somewhat ingeniously – that their challenge to the king was *not* treason precisely in so far as their actions were directed at the body of Charles Stuart: "treason is not treason as it is [i.e. because it is] against [the king] as a man, but as a man that is a king, and as he hath relation to the kingdom, and stands as a person entrusted with the kingdom and discharging that trust" (*Remonstrance of Both Houses*, in Kenyon, ed., *The Stuart Constitution*, 243). Parliament declared that their actions had "*the stamp of Royal Authority, although His Majesty . . . do in his own Person oppose or interrupt the same*" (*Declaration of the Lords and Commons*, quoted in Kantorowicz, *The King's Two Bodies*, 21).[9] The interesting thing about this argument is the extent to which it sets up a virtual king whose survival authorizes activity that would otherwise be known as treason. This king, the one the parliamentarians did not kill in 1649, "*stands as* a person [entrusted etc.]" and is the equivalent of a "*stamp* of Royal Authority"; in other words, this king is a representational body, the body of the stamp, the mark, the substitute, the representation. We could, following Slavoj Žižek, call this virtual king a "sublime object" ("that other 'indestructible and immutable' body," Žižek writes, "which persists beyond the corruption of the body physical... this immaterial corporeality of the 'body within the body' gives us a precise definition of the sublime object," *Sublime Object*, 18).[10] It is this virtual body of the king that the parliamentarians of the English Civil War explicitly claim to have left alone, thereby preserving their actions from the charge of treason. Under the heat of its disarticulation by the parliamentarians, therefore, the concept of the king's two bodies reveals a peculiar correlation between the authority-preserving power of immortality and the very threat to monarchism contained in the idea of a political authority carried entirely by representational structures of legitimacy. Immortality, that is to say, opened a rupture in the ideology of absolutism that it was meant to preserve.

Writing as *Novanglus* in 1774 and 1775, John Adams followed a similar line of attack to that of his English Puritan predecessors by first distinguishing between the king's two bodies and then asserting that while the king body natural might hold land in America the king body politic could not. Thus "no homage, fealty, or other services can ever be rendered to the body politic, the political capacity, which is not corporated but only a frame in the mind, an idea. No lands here, or in England, are held of the crown, meaning by it the political capacity; they are all held of the royal person, the natural person of the king" (*Political Writings*, 78–9). Here again the concept of the king's two bodies is taken at its word and used to legitimate a challenge to English rule. But in Adams' formulation we can see the signs of a crucial American difference. For if the parliamentarians in the 1640s directed their explicit antipathy towards the "body natural" of Charles Stuart, Adams here, speaking for the colonies, is engaged in a quarrel with "the body politic... which is not corporated but only a frame in the mind, an idea." The American Revolution, coming within a year of the *Novanglus* letters, will follow Adams' lead and celebrate the Declaration of Independence with an outbreak of public mock-executions: in killing the effigies of George III, these revolutionaries could be said to have been killing the "frame in the mind," the king body politic that has no natural body. The American Revolution was a revolution – was "treason" (following parliamentarian logic) – precisely in so far as it failed to direct its revolutionary public violence against the body natural of George III. The American Revolution realized itself in a turn against (even as it was also an important acknowledgement of) the political power of the English monarch's constitutive non-presence, his virtual body. From this perspective it is possible to think of the American Revolution, its original and radical intervention, as the revolution that the Cromwellians could only dream about: the revolution against the figural authority of the King of England, the revolution that would ignore the body of the prince precisely in order to challenge the whole structure of monarchic power.[11] It was precisely in killing the non-fleshly figure of monarchy that the colonists rejected monarchism altogether: the American republic begins with an execution of metaphor.[12] American regicide was a direct attack on monarchism's appropriation of divine authority; it rejected the divine body of monarchism's hereditary line. Those effigies, oddly enough, were meant to remind everyone that humanity is a mere effigy of the divine that perpetually tries to forget or conceal its lack of divinity. The execution of effigies was a perfectly appropriate event to establish a Puritan as well as an anti-monarchical revolution. The revolutionary executions were thus also founding acts of a political philosophy invested in the institution of bodiless (or disembodied) political authority, and the absence of the body from this scene of execution/founding is thus entirely appropriate.

But if there is a sense in which the absence of the king's real body was crucial to these revolutionary celebrations, we also have to think about what it was, precisely, that the revolutionaries were burning. For in burning effigies they were also attacking the mere stuff of the body, the mortal materiality that men share with objects. How will the United States come to think of this symbolic substitution? What is the particular significance of the effigy's role in the American founding? I want to approach this question by looking at how one American writer thought of the revolution's relationship to monarchism sixty years after independence.

THE MONARCHIC HIEROGLYPHIC

Half-way through "Self-Reliance" (1841), Ralph Waldo Emerson pauses to produce this remarkable paragraph:

The world has been instructed by its kings, who have so magnetized the eyes of nations. It has been taught by this colossal symbol the mutual reverence that is due from man to man. The joyful loyalty with which men have everywhere suffered the king, the noble, or the great proprietor to walk among them by a law of his own, make his own scale of men and things, and reverse theirs, pay for benefits not with money but with honor, and represent the law in his person, was the hieroglyphic by which they obscurely signified their consciousness of their own right and comeliness, the right of every man. ("Self-Reliance," 38)

Emerson here offers an original reading of monarchism, one that begins by appearing to rehabilitate the symbolic value of the prince. Emerson is willing to look to monarchism not just to provide a target for patriotic contempt, but for instruction. As the passage continues, however, it becomes clear that it is the relationship between the prince and his subjects (what we might call the political subjectivity of monarchism), that Emerson wants to characterize. It is with their "joyful loyalty," Emerson suggests, that the subjects of monarchism "obscurely signified their consciousness of their own right . . . the right of every man." The monarchic subject is one whose sense of his own and others' political rights takes a detour through the body of the prince. The movement from monarchism to republicanism is thus also a movement of clarification within a semiotic economy. The political subjectivity of the acquiescent monarchist was a "hieroglyphic," writes Emerson; democratic subjectivity was always, he implies, the opaque signified of this archaic signifier. Given this understanding, we are encouraged to read the break with monarchism as, simultaneously, a break with the very order of the hieroglyph. The age of subservience to noblemen has passed along with the age of the hieroglyph, and Emerson's use of the word "hieroglyphic" here cannot but remind us of the etymological relationship between democracy and demotics. Democratic subjectivity, Emerson's analogy suggests, belongs to the order of the demotic signifier. Democracy replaces the hieroglyph of monarchic subjectivity with a demotic citizenship.

  Emerson's explicit claim, then, is that in a democracy the object of democratic reverence, the citizen himself, will coincide with the subject who reveres. There will be no more "obscure" signification of men's rights because those who "joyfully" suffer the sovereign people to "walk among them by a law of [their] own" are the self-same members of the sovereign people. There will no longer be a gap, a deferral, a detour, separating the political subject from the political sovereign. The movement towards this kind of political order, Emerson suggests, corresponds to a movement beyond the order of the hieroglyphic. But is this model, the model of a one-to-one relationship between the citizen as subject and the citizen as sovereign, the model of the demotic signifier? In fact, it might be more accurate to consider Emerson's model here as corresponding to that of the "pictograph" with its suggestion of a one-to-one relationship between the concept signified and the simple signifier. The democratic subject, according to Emerson, is a walking pictograph of his own significance, a pictograph "within which the being of the subject distinguishes itself neither from its act nor from its attributes" (Derrida, *Of Grammatology*, 279).[13] If we draw Emerson's analogy out, therefore, we are led to consider the idea that the relationship he imagines between the subject of democracy and the object of democratic reverence, which is to say the self-doubling relationship of the citizen as source of and subject to the law's authority, is not simply post-hieroglyphical: it is outside of all language as disruption, detour, opacity, or deferral.

Emerson's invocation of a radical break with the order of the hieroglyph thus intimates a radical break with the order of the signifier in general.[14] Monarchism, in this scheme of things, becomes the historical name for the interruption of the political sign, the failure of the political signifier to transcend its own material noise. Emerson's version of the American Revolution participates in a powerful desire to record the historical development of a perfected, which is to say transparent, writing and a perfected political subjectivity. This movement finds in monarchism all the excessive material weight of the insistent signifier. Monarchism becomes the historical name for all that comes between mankind and the grand signifieds of divinity and truth. The prince, consumed by what Freneau called his "pomp and fancied bliss" ("On the Emigration," *Poems*, II, 280) is the embodiment of a luxury that, as John Adams wrote, "effaces from human Nature the Image of the Divinity" (*Book of Abigail and John*, 217). A revolution against this monarchism derides all the signs of the prince's participation in the logic of the hieroglyph, including all his excessive ornamentation, his visual signifiers of wealth and power, his luxury, his excesses of money, time, and even pleasure. The monarch comes to stand for the hieroglyph, the signifier in all its corrupt, earthly, gaudy materiality (hence Freneau's "gilded bait" or "childish bauble called a crown" ['To A Republican"]). In this position the monarch can serve as a defining other to a whole range of disparate revolutionary ideologies: the common-sense populism of early Thomas Paine and the democratic-republicans; the enlightened federalism of James Madison, the Puritanism of John Adams and Timothy Dwight, the scientific rationalism of Thomas Jefferson, or the agricultural essentialism of a St. John de Crèvecoeur.

To read Emerson's passage, then, is to see how the ideology of the revolution's break with monarchism refuses to think through the post-revolutionary inhabitation of structures of power and authority that democracy shares with monarchism. And thus, this transcendental figuration of the democratic revolution as a break with the order of the hieroglyph and the opacity of the signifier finds a literal enactment in the public events of July 1776 themselves. For it was not, to repeat, the flesh and blood King George who was executed by the revolutionary Americans, but George in effigy. And how better to represent monarchism's relationship to the earthbound materiality of the signifier than in the form of dead stuff – the rags and straw of an effigy? It was not just that the colonials killed their king "in metaphorical terms"; it was also the king's privileged relationship to the order of the metaphor, the profane substitution, that the revolutionaries were attempting to rid themselves of even as they danced around their straw man.[15] Americans, whatever else they might be said to have been doing, were also engaged in a public repudiation of the materiality of the signifier when they burned George III's dummy representations. The scandal of monarchism, by 1776, was its shameless embodiment of the material detour that mankind had to take through representation in order to claim or recognize its own rights, its own "comeliness." The revolutionaries were also, we ought to remember, proto-transcendentalists.

AMERICAN MONARCHISM

Thus, following the lead of Emerson and Kantorowicz, we can begin to see how complex the revolution's regicide really was. On the one hand, the monarch had come to figure the corruption of materiality (with his gaudy visibility, his hereditary superiority, his interruption of mankind's self-realization), and hence the American break with this order was indicated by the public destruction of mocked matter; on the other hand, the American revolution differentiated itself from the English Civil War of the previous century by rejecting not just the mortal, vulnerable, fleshly body of one corrupt king, but by rejecting the trans-individual order of monarchism in general, by rejecting the king's "invisible" and "immortal" body. In this case, the absence of the king's real body from the scenes of American regicide was crucial: the mock bodies represented, that is to say, the king's other body, the invisible, immortal "body politic." With their mock executions the revolutionaries were engaged in a critical act of what we would now call historical materialism. The other body, the body that monarchic absolutism had claimed for its kings, was, said the American Revolution, a material, political, earthbound body in disguise. The artifice of the effigy here coincides with the radically political aspect of the revolutionary intervention: it is precisely *as* a representation that the effigy works to politicize monarchic charisma. Artifice and politicization are inseparable in this founding moment. (This is a structure I will return to below.) The revolution's effigies demythologized the immortal body of monarchism even as their reproducibility helped produce the transcendent political body of the United States. Thus, as they watched their mock kings burn all over the ex-colonies, patriots were witnessing the destruction of one transcendental discourse (the discourse of the monarch's immortal body) and the hegemonic intervention of another (the discourse of republicanism's transcendence of monarchism's debased materialism). Moreover, we cannot forget that in order to accomplish this transfer of power, the revolution also had to betray itself: in making mock kings and treating them like real people (taunting them, torturing them, burning them, burying them) the revolution engaged in precisely that idolatrous over-valuation of the merely material that would seem to have characterized monarchism. The King of England was never more alive in America, we might provocatively suggest, than when he was paraded, humiliated, abused, and interred all over the country in 1776. The new nation brought itself into being by giving itself a very uncanny monarch: a monarch conjured out of mere matter, a monarch produced – and reproduced – by street theatre, a monarch to be buried on American soil, a monarch, in other words, who was given the capacity for resurrection in the very moment of his repudiation: a ghost-monarch for a new nation. "We commit his political existence to the ground," went the words of one mock funeral oration for the king, "corruption to corruption – tyranny to the grave – and oppression to eternal infamy, in sure and certain hope that he will never obtain a resurrection, to rule again over the United States of America" (quoted in Hazelton, *The Declaration of Independence*). 1776 was a year of exorcisms in the colonies; which is to say, a year of conjurings: the mock funeral was, to quote Jacques Derrida talking about other times and places, "a matter of a performative that seeks to reassure but first of all to reassure itself by assuring itself, for nothing is less sure, that what one would like to see dead is indeed dead" (*Specters of Marx*, 48).[16] In eighteenth-century English culture, Robert Blair St. George points out, the official use of effigies "had long been recognized as a way to exalt and commemorate individuals who had died in the service of their country" (*Conversing by Signs*, 251). But their inverted use to mock or parody was also an established practice. St. George writes, "[as] memorials of living people, effigies were commonly believed to have sympathetic magical powers. They were thus related to the cloth poppets used by witches to afflict their victims; their potential was very 'real'" (251).[17]

In one of the moments of its founding, then, the United States demonstrates a very complex and ambivalent relationship towards monarchy and towards structures of political representation. If, at this same moment, Americans were celebrating the end of mankind's self-alienation in the structures of a monarchical representation, *and* founding themselves via a crucial deployment of representation (the mock king), we have to consider the possibility that what announces itself from one perspective as the revolution against monarchic materialism simultaneously presents itself as a new economy of the relationship between the subject of political power and the material signifier. Viewed from this perspective, the revolution could also be said to participate in a defense of the order of the hieroglyph in the face of its corruption at the hands of an individual – the monarch – who insists that he and he alone has transcended the order of the signifier and that he has combined the contingent materiality of the hieroglyph and the eternal ideality of the signified truth in his monarchic body. In the revolutionary resistance to the singular, hereditary association of reverential right and freedom with one man, we can detect a desire to restore – by democratizing – the mediation of the hieroglyph. Emerson precedes his remarks on the monarch with a reference to the transfer of "lustre" from kings to "gentlemen." These "gentlemen," Emerson's lines intimate, would become their own hieroglyphics, heirs to a lustre that proceeds from the capacity to embody a universal right, a lustre that is coterminous with the enigmatic duplicity of a subject who is both outside the law (he moves by a "law of his own"), and at the center of the law (the law would be "represented" "in his person."). In other words, Emerson's lines help us to articulate one of democracy's founding uncertainties: is it the body of the monarch that American democracy rejects (the particular bio-historical body of the royal bloodline that carried the weight – all the excess weight – of a political hieroglyphic) or the charisma – the black magic – of hieroglyphic representation itself? Is it the "King's real, or his stamped face," to borrow from John Donne, that democracy seeks to forget? The sacrifice of the mock monarch in 1776 substitutes the violence of a literal regicide for an almost heretically figural or materialist gesture which, by treating rags and sticks like a man, announces the beginning of a political order that will find many more uses for material representations. The mock executions remind us from the start that the revolution did not succeed in transcending the order of the signifier any more than it succeeded in escaping, for once and for all, the spell of monarchism. The democratic citizen's political subjectivity (his institutionalized self-reliance) is hieroglyphically structured, just as was his monarchic subjectivity, which is to say that Emerson's remarks, rather than suggesting a rupture, might be used to suggest a redistribution – a shifting – within the obscurely signifying economy of political subjectivity. What, we would then want to ask, came to take the place (either in a scapegoated or a venerated capacity) of the monarch in the post-revolutionary United States? How did democratic citizens signify their consciousness of their "right and comeliness"? How did post-monarchic political culture figure the relationship between empirical "men" and the subject of "right"? What new detours attempted to erase the distance that had been collapsed into the "lustre" of the monarch? The revolutionary mock kings (the objects that spelled for the king) were the first of many stand-ins, inaugurating a whole politics of the stand-in (the representative) even as they attacked the debased nature of any stand-in, of any material that comes between man and the divine.

MONARCHOPHOBIA'S DISPLACEMENTS

In the eleventh of Hector St. John de Crèvecoeur's *Letters From an American Farmer*, we are introduced to John Bertram (a fictional version of the botanist, William Bartram) on his homestead in Pennsylvania. He is another of the book's examples of what it means to be a successful American. Here is how the narrator describes dinner time on the farm:

We entered into a large hall, where there was a long table full of victuals; at the lowest part sat his Negroes; his hired men were next, then the family and myself; and at the head, the venerable father and his wife presided. Each reclined his head and said his prayers, divested of the tedious cant of some and of the ostentatious style of others. (*Letters*, 188–9)

While the narrator goes on to stress the community's differences from the Old World ("I never knew how to use ceremonies," says Bertram, "they are insufficient proofs of sincerity"; and again, "We treat others as we treat ourselves," 189), it is clear that what is celebrated is a divinely ordained structure of hierarchical authority whose patriarchal legitimacy is only emphasized by the distinct lack of pomp or extravagance.

For a moment, however, this American ideal (no "tedious cant," no "ostentatious style") is threatened from the outside: towards the end of the meal in the great hall, the narrator thinks he hears the sound of "a distant concert of instruments" (190). "However simple and pastoral your fare was, Mr. Bertram," he remarks, "this is the dessert of a prince; pray what is this I hear?" (190–1). But Bertram reassures him: "It is of a piece with the rest of thy treatment," he explains, the "music" is merely "the effect of the wind through the strings of an Eolian harp" (191).

This scene presents us with a version of American monarchophobia, an almost paranoid sensitivity to what is figured as monarchic luxury ("the dessert of a prince"). The example suggests, however, that anti-monarchism and egalitarianism are not the same thing. Those who admire the ordered hierarchy of the independent American farmer are troubled not by (or at least not only by) the spread of democratic politics but by the possibility that their society could become infected with monarchic excess, the luxuries and trappings of wealth and power. Crèvecoeur's narrator fears all those performances of wealth and authority that figure the excessive power of the king, or, in this instance, the power of the independent farmer. A significant gap opens up between the monarch's (or the independent farmer's) authority (legitimate, pre-eminent, and divinely sanctioned) and the trappings of power, those objects, conventions, and practices that convey or represent the monarch's (or the patriarch's) authority.

The Eolian harp on Bertram's farm is a device for producing music without performance, but the momentary unease it produces in Crèvecoeur's *Letters* alerts us to the half-hidden idea that this harp is in fact only the conveyor of a performance at one remove. The harp has been crafted and judiciously positioned in order to give the American listeners the illusion of a natural (or divine – Eolian from *Aiolos*, Greek god of the wind) performance. Everyone on the farm, it would appear, is comforted by the idea that there is a non-human origin for the music, that it comes from nature or God. American sovereignty, the harp announces, is blowing in the wind. A human origin for the music would disrupt this fantasy and force everyone to consider the historical production of the patriarch's wealth and power. (The visitor to the farm is finally reassured that "It appears to be entirely free from those ornaments and political additions which each country and each government hath fashioned after its own manners," 199.) As art, in other words (as opposed to nature), the music of the harp would also constitute a political signifier. As in the case of the mock kings discussed above, artifice reveals itself in this instance to be inseparable from a politicizing gesture, a gesture that always threatens to question power's attempts to ground itself outside of history. The Eolian harp's music is the ghostly hum of a monarchism that the independent American farmer cannot seem to leave behind.[18]

While the fantasy of post-monarchic authority it helps to sustain seems relatively benign, the harp's placement on the border between the cultivation of the homestead and the wilds of the woods reminds us that it is also located at the site of (and no doubt also standing in for) those Americans who first occupied the land Bertram has come to own.[19] And indeed, any device or character that can be figured as inhabiting this border space – the border between white civilization and nature – is in danger of being appropriated for the management of revolutionary monarchophobia. The fantasy registered by Bertram's Eolian harp – that nature "herself" provides the American with his monarchic trappings – is also at work in the aggressive revolutionary appropriation of the Native American as the new nation's monarchic progenitor.[20]

John Leacock's famous song "The First of May, to St. Tammany" (from his patriotic wartime play "The Fall of British Tyranny" [1776]) is an extended toast to a Native American chief who, as Carla Mulford suggests, serves to identify white revolutionaries with an original American "in order to propagandize republicanism as a peculiarly American right" (in Lauter, ed., *Heath Anthology*, 842).[21] But what is most striking about the song is its unabashed celebration of Tammany's monarchic status. "A king, tho' no tyrant was he"; Leacock writes, "His throne was the crotch of the tree." He rules, of course, "without statutes or book" and he "reason'd most justly from nature," but he is a king nevertheless. Beneath the tree and without books he is clearly an emblem – and a monarchic emblem – for the revolutionary "people out of doors." As such, Tammany gives a body (albeit a cynically appropriated body) to what is implicit in much revolutionary rhetoric: the idea that the people make up the monarchic body of republicanism. King Tammany is a particular kind of monarch, of course, one who lacks any of the trappings of monarchic power and wealth. All the symbols of his status are resolutely "natural" (the crotch of a tree, etc.). His is a kingly demeanour, a kingly authority, and a kingly wisdom, but there is nothing to suggest that this sovereignty has anything to do with the work of man. He does not even consult a book – his very laws emanate from the forest. He does not even need to speak. And, perhaps most important of all, he is insistently dead. Tammany, that is to say, belongs to a tradition of invoking the silent, regal, and deceased Native American Indian to suggest a kind of natural American nobility. This invocation reaches its apex (or nadir?) in Cooper's 1826 novel, *The Last of the Mohicans*.[22] In Cooper, as in the poetry of Philip Freneau, monarchy, far from being dismissed, is in fact refigured, via the Native American, as natural, silent, and spectral – spectral because always presented as long since departed or, as in the case of Cooper's Mohicans, because marked in advance by imminent and unavoidable extinction.[23] If King George was only "metaphorically" executed, to use Edward Countryman's phrase, in the course of an actual rejection of his monarchy, Native Americans were actually executed while their metaphorical monarchism was repeatedly – one might say desperately – deployed. The constitutive role played by monarchism as the other of revolutionary republicanism is remarked in a displaced and therefore distanced fashion by the tradition of invoking a native American nobility. The full effect of this disavowed invocation *requires* the death of the Native American.[24] The Indian (spelling here for the English monarch) provides the deceased body out of which a spectral American monarchism can be summoned and put to work for republicanism. The phantasmatic monarchism of these displaced and destroyed natives allowed revolutionary Americans to claim a lost monarchism while simultaneously figuring that monarchism as the violent and threatening other of revolutionary ideology. And while the idea of an ancient American nobility required the passing away of the Indian, the threat of his savage nobility justified it. Monarchophobia is another name for the ideology of Indian-hating.[25] It is through the Indian that the revolution attempts to import the charisma of monarchism's immortality and thus its powerful appearance of having transcended politics and history. The Native American's noble legitimation of the Euro-American's revolution shares something, that is to say, with Charles I (body politic)'s legitimation of the execution of Charles I (body natural).[26] The native's nobility is always the product of a spectral existence – it is a post mortem charisma. It was precisely this feature of monarchism, this form of its power, that revolutionary ideology remained under the spell of even as it sought to exorcise it from the new order. The demonization of Native Americans was not just a political reprisal against figures such as Joseph Brant who were accused of massacring innocent patriots, but part of a logic that saw the noble savage as always also a figure for the savage noble. The revolution wanted the same transcendental legitimacy that monarchism had so perniciously claimed for itself. But the monarch had attempted to bind this transcendence to his own person; the revolution had to reject this heresy even as it appropriated the power that it offered.

The princely Native American and Bertram's Eolian harp signify some of the anxiety generated by America's post-revolutionary relationship to monarchism. One way of trying to account for the treatment of the Native American in revolutionary and post-revolutionary America is to read this treatment in the context of republicanism's disavowel of its relationship to monarchism. Seeing democracy as a form of monarchy, a translation of monarchy rather than as its binary other, would also mean renouncing the revolution's desperate claim to a natural, transhistorical, trans-political legitimacy. The demythologization of the Native American and the deconstruction of the opposition between democracy and monarchism, I am suggesting, could proceed in tandem. Initiating such a project, we could do worse than return, once again, to those Independence Day street celebrations. The troubling relationship between republican monarchophobia and republican racism is given a compelling prefiguration in this description of an Independence Day effigy:

At Huntington, Long Island [patriots] took down the old liberty pole (topped with a flag dedicated to liberty and George III) and used the materials to fashion an effigy. This mock king sported a wooden broadsword, a blackened face "like Dunmore's [slave] Virginia regiment," and feathers, "like Carleton and Johnson's savages." Fully identified with the black and Indian allies his generals had enlisted to fight the Americans, wrapped in the Union Jack, he was hanged, exploded, and burned. (Waldstreicher, *In the Midst*, 31)

This figure, the English monarch as Native American as African, is hardly one that we have inherited as a revolutionary icon.[27] Historians like David Waldstreicher can remind us of the specific events in pre-revolutionary history that would lead to the construction of such a figure, but we are left with an excess of association. We cannot contemplate this revolutionary object without asking after the ways in which the European monarch, the Native American, and the African could be brought together in the early American political imagination.[28] We are hardly predisposed to think of the most privileged of political figures (the European monarch) and the most marginalized subjects of eighteenth-century America as inhabiting any of the same political positions, and yet in the early United States there are ways in which they do.[29] Monarchophobia, the name I am giving to the complex structure of ambivalent responses to monarchism that can be found in the dominant discourse of revolutionary America, also has a racist legacy. Challenging revolutionary monarchophobia, in other words, would also

mean re-materializing and re-historicizing the white male body of revolutionary ideology and thereby challenging the revolution's hierarchization
of this body over all those bodies it deemed marked on their surface by
historicity and contingency, starting with the king's.[30] Monarchophobia,
that is to say, is also one of the discourses of white mythology.[31]

THE MONARCHIC VOICE

The prince, in Emerson's formulation, mediates the relationship between
individual men and "their own right and comeliness, the right of every
man." In its most effective moment, this mediation, Emerson was willing
to admit, could be experienced "joyfully": that is what it would mean
to be a good subject of monarchism. But the mediation can also be
registered as an interruption or an impediment: the letter that kills the
spirit. Post-monarchical political culture plays out these same dynamics
in response to various attempts to mediate the relationship between
individual citizens and the general rights they claim. Towards the end of
Common Sense, Paine imagines what is – even for the routinely histrionic
Paine – a quite extravagant piece of democratic theatre. Looking into
the future, Paine imagines a ritual crowning of the new nation's charter
of laws. This is how he puts it:

Let a day be solemnly set apart for proclaiming the charter; let it be brought
forth placed on the divine law, the word of God; let a crown be placed thereon,
by which the world may know [that so far as we approve of monarchy], that in
America, THE LAW IS KING. For as in absolute governments the king is law, so in
free countries the law *ought* to be king; and there ought to be no other. (*Common
Sense*, 98)

This would be strange enough (a crown on top of a charter on top of a
bible), but then as if to respond to an unspoken word of caution, Paine
adds: "lest any ill use should afterwards arise, let the crown at the conclusion of the ceremony be demolished, and scattered among the people
whose right it is" (98). It is hard to imagine this ritual actually taking place
in post-revolutionary America, but the fantasy of the charter (the Constitution) as a monarchic substitute is not simply Paine's eccentricity. One
might compare Paine's crown here with the crown conjured up forty-
five years later in a fourth of July address given by the then Secretary of
State John Quincy Adams in 1831. "The Declaration of Independence,"
proclaimed Adams, "was the crown with which the people of United
America, rising in gigantic stature as one man, encircled their brows, and

there it remains; so long as this globe shall be inhabited by human beings
[!], may it remain, a crown of imperishable glory!" (*Voices of the American
Revolution*, 192). These suggestions – Paine's and Quincy Adams' –
work to reduce the historical materiality of the founding documents,
in order to give them some of the immortal charisma of monarchic absolutism. The examples may be crude, but their impulse is not eccentric.
Michael Warner's *The Letters of the Republic*, for example, traces a political
investment in the effective anonymity of print in the revolutionary era, an
anonymity that, when successful, offers Americans the fantasy of a direct
access to the objective, impartial, disinterested voice of political reason –
a fantasy fed by the printed text's evacuation of its own relationship to
human production (for the pamphleteers and printers Warner discusses,
"the very printedness of [public] discourse takes on a specially legitimate
meaning, because it is categorically differentiated from personal modes
of sociability. Mechanical duplication equals publishing precisely insofar
as public political discourse is impersonal" [*The Letters of the Republic*, 39]).
The printed text participates in the fantasy of truth speaking through a
language that has dispensed with the mediatory noise of the body. Print's
mechanical uniformity has a rhetorical effect, in other words, that helps
to give the ideas expressed the force of a wisdom that is indistinguishable
from the eternal laws of nature (the stars of the stars and stripes served
a similar purpose: stars were a privileged example in the late eighteenth
century of empirical objects that conformed to absolutely consistent and
predictable *laws* of motion and attraction). Printed text produces a meta-
individual, trans-historical effacement of the signifier, an effect that coincides with its uniformity, its reduction of particularity, its participation,
in other words, in the same reduction of signification's material presence that can be recognized in the movement from the hieroglyph to
the alphabet.[32] Print culture represents one way in which the American
Revolution translated the ideology of the monarch's body politic, that
ungraspable, immortal, and avowedly trans-historical conveyor of political authority (the king body politic, Elizabethan lawyers wrote, "is
a Body that cannot be seen or handled," Kantorowicz, *The King's Two
Bodies*, 7) into the democratic force of disembodied legitimation.[33]

At the same time, however, scholars of the revolutionary period have
noted an increasing investment in the spoken voice as a medium that
could offer direct access to the truth of affect, sincerity, and feeling. As
Jay Fliegelman has pointed out, guides to public speaking in this period
offered readers the possibility of circumventing the interruptions that always seemed to accompany any linguistic attempt to express the heart's

truth. In the work of Adam Smith, James Burgh, Thomas Sheridan, John Rice, and others, Fliegelman traces a discourse on language in the eighteenth century that, in its extreme form, gestured towards the possibility of a communication "utterly independent of words" (Fliegelman, *Declaring Independence*, 30). In this tradition, as Fliegelman explains it, "[speaking] becomes less a form of argumentative or expository communication than a revelation of 'internal moral dispositions' and passions registered by vocal tones, physical 'exertions,' and facial expressions that are received in unmediated form by the sympathetic 'social' nature of the auditor" (*Declaring Indepence*, 3). But while the oratorical revolution and the revolution of Warner's print culture may seem to be entirely at odds, their simultaneous significance for the revolutionary era begs us to recognize their mutual determination. The oratorical fantasy mobilized the body's extra-linguistic signifiers (gestures, sounds, expressions, tears) for rhetorical purposes, much as print culture deployed the extra-linguistic rhetoric of the printed page's physical appearance. Both discourses give us powerful examples of post-revolutionary attempts to recapture the political and rhetorical force of the monarch's body politic. Print culture's rhetorical invocation of the analogy between mechanical duplication and natural law's eternal consistency is every bit as sentimental, in other words, as oratorical culture's exploitation of the analogy between the body's physical and emotional interiority (the spontaneous gesture as evidence of the heart's truth or of an internal spasm).[34] Print culture and oratorical culture, it is quite clear, are mutually determined oppositions within the same discursive field: alternative cultural fantasies of the circumvention of the signifier's gaudy and secular-historical materiality. Their construction as antitheses, then and now, only helps to distract attention from their shared limitations. The sanctification of the founding documents and the fetishization of the great public speaker translate the monarchic function for republicanism: they both participate in an effort to speak in a divine voice. Post-monarchical politics inherits the difficulty that monarchism had – to a certain extent and for limited periods of time – found a way to manage, that is to say, the fundamental political problem: how to reconcile the subject of the State to the irreducibly alienated form in which he or she experiences his or her political rights.

These tensions are all on view in the *Autobiography* of Benjamin Franklin. One of the distinguishing features of the monarch, according to Emerson, was that he moved among men "by a law of his own" (Emerson, "Self-Reliance," 38). This sense of a self-given law receives a different articulation in the gesture of a private "giving-of-the–law-to–oneself."

That is one of the most compelling aspects of Benjamin Franklin's proto-democratic self-writing in the *Autobiography*. Consider Franklin's famous table of virtues ("Eat not to dullness/Drink not to Elevation" etc.) that is accompanied by a prayer in his notebook asking God to "Increase in me that Wisdom which discovers my truest interests; Strengthen my Resolutions to perform what that Wisdom dictates" (*Autobiography*, 96). Franklin, in his dreams, would be the subject of a law of his own, although this law is characteristically depersonalized as the work of an invisible dictator – "Wisdom." What Franklin discovers, however, in the course of his moral experiment, is what de Tocqueville (as we shall see) would call the "thick darkness" of a certain interior *mise-en-abîme*:

For something that pretended to be Reason was every now and then suggesting to me, that such extreme Nicety as I exacted of myself might be a kind of Foppery in Morals, which if it were known would make me ridiculous; that a perfect character might be attended with the Inconvenience of being envied and hated; and that a benevolent Man should allow a few Faults in himself, to keep his Friends in Countenance. (*Autobiography*, 99)

This moral aporia (it is immoral to be perfectly moral) is suggested by "something that pretended to be Reason," an enigmatic usurper of the "Wisdom" that would dictate his "truest interests." This voice puts immediate relationships between men before abstract moral concepts. Franklin plays out a conflict, here, between his status as a member of mankind (his exterior relations) and his isolated (interior) relationship with transcendental categories like morality or virtue. His character proceeds from – is structured around – an irresolvable tension between what he registers as transcendental and what he recognizes as socio-historical codes of behavior. Indeed, Franklin's *Autobiography* demonstrates repeatedly the irreducible effect of the social (man in general) on the particular (Franklin). He is crossed by a social character that has everything to do with the burgeoning hegemony of democratic political structures. The self that Franklin writes (and this is a self that his memoirs helped, generically, to invent) is a democratic self insofar as its depthless interiority corresponds to an aporetic (and thus persistent) crossing of the solitary and the social. The solitary man (defined by his relationship with the transcendental as God, morality, or virtue) keeps up a productive relationship with the social (most often registered as the eye of social evaluation, the force of reputation, the politics and diplomacy of general approval). The external magnificence of the monarch has been translated, under the effects of a democracy that was advancing throughout the eighteenth century in

America, into the rich interiority of a subject worthy of autobiography. That Franklin should so repeatedly, and so intriguingly analogize this subjectivity with the practices of writing only helps us to draw the link back to Emerson's metaphorical schema in the passage from "Self-Reliance." Hence, Franklin writes of his attempt at moral perfection: "As those who aim at perfect Writing by imitating the engraved Copies, tho' they never reach the wish'd for Excellence of those Copies, their Hand is mended by the Endeavor, and is tolerable while it continues fair and legible" (*Autobiography*, 99). Michael Warner argues that the most salient point about Franklin is his exploitation of the depersonalizing negativity of print culture. "The paradox," Warner writes, "is that the personal is founded on and valued within the pure reproduction of the social, not, as is usually assumed, the other way around" (*The Letters of the Republic*, 87). In a note to this passage Warner also suggests that Franklin regularly displays a "habit of subdividing the self out of existence. The self that not only denies itself but further applies that denial is scarcely recognizable *as* a self" (190 n.15). But it is precisely the "paradoxes" and seeming aporias of the Franklinian "self" that produce the enigma of subjectivity that drives the autobiography. It is the *non-sense* of Franklin's interiority that marks the democratic inheritance of monarchic lustre, monarchic arbitrariness, monarchic unreasonableness. The monarch was not, after all, only a symbol of man's "right and comeliness." For Thomas Paine, as we noted above, the king was above all a symbol of an infuriating paradox ("There is something exceedingly ridiculous in the composition of monarchy; it first excludes a man from the means of information, yet empowers him to act in cases where the highest judgement is required" [*Common Sense*, 69]). It is as a subject of the paradoxical back and forth between the individual and the social, the particular and the technologically reproducible, that Franklin exemplifies a democratic subjectivity which, I want to stress, is also the appropriated and transformed subjectivity of Paine's "ridiculous" monarch.

This democratic subjectivity was given one of its earliest descriptions by Alexis de Tocqueville for whom the monarch who "magnetized the eyes" (Emerson) was replaced by the equally absorbing "man alone":

The poets of democratic ages can never, therefore, take any man in particular as the subject of a piece ... I am persuaded that in the end, democracy diverts the imagination from all that is external to man, and fixes it on man alone ... Looking at the human race as one great whole, they easily conceive that its destinies are regulated by the same design; and in the actions of every individual they are led to acknowledge a trace of that universal and eternal plan on which God rules our race ... (de Tocqueville, *Democracy in America*, 180)

De Tocqueville is the first poet of democratic man: he is America's French Whitman:

I need not traverse earth and sky to discover a wondrous object woven of contrasts, of infinite greatness and littleness, of intense gloom and amazing brightness, – capable at once of exciting pity, admiration, terror, contempt. I have only to look at myself. Man springs out of nothing, crosses time, and disappears forever in the bosom of God; he is seen but for a moment, wandering on the verge of two abysses, and there he is lost. (182)

De Tocqueville's two abysses here seem at first to refer to the time before and after any individual's birth and death. But de Tocqueville's remarks address a subject who vascillates between two other abysses: the abyss of particularity (the "infinite greatness" of "myself") and the abyss of man in general ("the human race as one great whole" whose "destinies are regulated by the same design"). What de Tocqueville records in his comparison between monarchism and democracy is the emergence of a new sovereign whose identity takes the form of an indissociable but never quite identical coincidence of the general subject of rights and laws (mankind, the people, the nation) and the individual citizen. "In democratic communities, where men are all insignificant and very much alike," wrote de Tocqueville, "each man instantly sees all his fellows when he surveys himself" (*Democracy in America*, 180). "Instantly," de Tocqueville writes, thereby alerting us to the temporal anxiety that underlies this idealized – but no less useful for all that – description of democratic man.[35]

De Tocqueville stresses the extent to which this turn to man as a subject of contemplation is coterminous with a renewed sense of the impenetrable obscurity of the human heart. Democratic authors, he suggests, will not "seek to record the actions of an individual, but to enlarge and to throw light on some of the obscurer recesses of the human heart" (*Democracy in America*, 183). He reasons that this is because actual democratic, equal individuals are not interesting in and of themselves as individuals but as subjects of democracy. Their clothes, behavior, language, and actions are familiar to all. The surface equality of individuals in democracy, however, produces the "hidden depths" of mankind's "inner soul" (183): "the nature of man is sufficiently disclosed for him to apprehend something of himself, and sufficiently obscure for all the rest to be plunged in thick darkness, in which he gropes forever, – and forever in vain, – to lay hold on some completer notion of his being" (183). The mysteries of state, that is to say, have been replaced by the mysteries of the democratically shared human heart. De Tocqueville's democratic subject is not a subject of clarity and light, not the subject who has transcended the semiotic obscurity of the monarchic symbolic economy. Rather, de Tocqueville recognizes, in wonderfully suggestive terms, the new architecture of signification and obscurity, blindness and insight, that democracy initiates. It is in this sense that it might be worth playing with Emerson's schema: if monarchic subjectivity participates in the order of the hieroglyph, democratic subjectivity participates in that of the alphabetic sign. But this alphabetic sign would be a demotic only insofar as this term indicates a correspondence, rather than a radical rupture, between the order of the hieroglyph and that of the alphabetic sign. Like the alphabetic sign, the democratic individual (following de Tocqueville) has a minimum of surface interest (the democratic individual's "language, dress...daily actions...are not poetical in themselves...they are too familiar to all those to whom the poet would speak of them" (*Democracy in America*, 182). The hieroglyph's material extravagance has been displaced, however, onto the "hidden depths" of man's "inner soul." This is an economic, not an absolute, transformation of signification. The democratic subject inherits the monarch's all too visible extravagance and theologico-political mystique (his aura or "lustre" as Emerson put it, but also his arbitrariness, his unreasonable power) as an interiority demanding a reading no less reverential and endless than the worship that the monarch demanded of his subject's "magnetized eyes."

When Jonathan Mayhew declared, in an early and provocative instance of American anti-monarchism, that "Nothing can well be imagined more directly contrary to common sense, than to suppose that *millions* of people should be subjected to the arbitrary, precarious pleasure of *one single man*" ("Discourse," 406) he had in mind the single man of the throne. But something of the relationship between monarchism and democracy emerges when we listen to these lines again in the aftermath of the revolution. From a not illegitimate perspective, the democratic revolution succeeded (would succeed) by subjecting millions of people to the "arbitrary" pleasures of (each) single man (and woman). Sovereignty, be it monarchic or popular, names this subjection to the arbitrary at one or another location in the political structure. Indeed, the correspondence urges us to recognize that a negotiation with something arbitrary that we experience as coming from outside us (be it the outside of the distant monarch or the outside of all those single others) is constitutive of the political. The monarch, as Mayhew's words remind us, served revolutionary Americans by appearing to gather the force and uncertainty of this arbitrariness at the site of one convenient figure. It is the monarch (and thus monarchism) that subjects us to arbitrariness (with all its precariousness and its discomfiting "pleasure"). But the revolutionary public celebrations of independence, organized around the reproduction and multiple performances of the Declaration of Independence, the representation of events in the newspapers, and, most strikingly, in the use of effigies, allows us to construct American democracy around an original encounter with substitutions that have a crucial relationship with an irreducible arbitrariness (not to mention pleasure). If it was "in metaphorical terms" that the colonials killed their king in 1776, then it is also true to say that metaphor plays a crucial part in the founding of American independence, and hence American democracy. The revolutionary people who burned and hanged George III in effigy simultaneously produced themselves as the effigies of a new sovereignty. The first independent Americans were "mock" revolutionaries, "mock" sovereigns, "mock" democrats (not unrelated, therefore, to what Mayhew described as that "mock martyr," Charles I ["Discourse," 420]). And this, I want to insist, was not a matter of a false beginning or a momentary hesitation on the way to a realization of full political presence. This performative political subjectivity is constitutive for democracy, even if it has been persistently resisted in the name of a desire for constative certainty that leaves its traces in the form of all those who have been branded with the mark of an incomplete political identity (the three-fifths of a person that the United States Constitution invented, for example, in one of the most telling examples of a displacement of anxiety about democracy's constitutive dispersal of the self-sufficient singularity of its citizens[36]). The democratic revolution bequeaths to its subjects the monarch's relationship to arbitrariness, to pleasure (intimately related as it is with the artificial, and thus with the performed, the literary) and to the precarious (read: historical – subject to unpredictable change). This bequeathal was appropriately registered by way of a democratic street theatre in which the people celebrated the constitutive substitutability of their new democratic identity (they will only experience democratic subjectivity as the experience of being substitutable for all those other subjects of the "inalienable" rights of "men"). The effigy that spells for the monarch had always been a doubled popular device (used for celebration or execration, for the dead and the living); in 1776 that duplicity remains. Were the people in the streets celebrating or lashing out in desperation against their new-found substitutability? Were they celebrating or publicly trembling in the face of an accession to power that would only ever be experienced as an accession to the "ridiculous" and precarious subjectivity of the prince?

CHAPTER 2

Crèvecoeur's revolutionary loyalism

> I resemble, methinks, one of the stones of a ruined arch, still retaining that pristine form which anciently fitted the place I occupied, but the center is tumbled down.
>
> (J. Hector St. John de Crèvecoeur, *Letters From an American Farmer*, 211)

In "The Force of Law," an essay on Walter Benjamin's study of political violence, Jacques Derrida writes of the "deconstruction of [a] network of concepts in their given or dominant state" in this way:

> In the moment that an axiom's credibility (*crédit*) is suspended by deconstruction, in this structurally necessary moment, one can always believe that there is no more room for justice, neither for justice itself nor for theoretical interest directed toward the problems of justice. This moment of suspense, this period of *époché*, without which, in fact, deconstruction is not possible, is always full of anxiety, but who pretends to be just by economizing on anxiety? And this anxiety-ridden moment of suspense – which is also the interval or space in which transformations, indeed juridico-political revolutions take place – cannot be motivated, cannot find its movement and its impulse (an impulse which itself cannot be suspended) except in the demand for an increase in or supplement to justice, and so in the experience of an inadequation or an incalculable disproportion. ("Force of Law," 955, 957)

That the moment of juridico-political revolutions might be an "anxiety-ridden moment" for those who speak for the revolution is often obscured by the performance of determination, conviction, and clear-sightedness that the successful revolutionary rehearses. "The sun never shined on a cause of greater worth," wrote Thomas Paine, one of the most forceful examples of a confident revolutionary (*Common Sense*, 82). One of the most compelling inscriptions we have of such anxiety, however, comes from J. Hector St. John de Crèvecoeur's *Letters From An American Farmer* (1782), a text that establishes itself early on as the work of a profound admirer of eighteenth-century American liberties and of the opportunities available to poor Europeans who emigrate to the colonies. Crèvecoeur's pre-revolutionary narrator articulates a proto-republican ideology that fails to prepare us for the anxiety that he displays in the face of the revolution. This anxiety inscribes Crèvecoeur's text with a revolutionary suspense that, taken together with the decision that follows upon this moment of suspense, offers us a quite original allegory of revolution in the guise of an anti-revolutionary outburst.

CRÈVECOEUR'S BAFFLING REVERSALS

Michel-Guillaume-Jean de Crèvecoeur was born into petty nobility in Caen, Normandy, in 1735. His father was a country gentleman, "well bred and reasonably well off," who spent most of the year on the family estate that Michel-Guillaume would be expected to inherit (Allen and Asselineau, *An American Farmer*, 2). But around the age of eighteen, Michel was sent to England, perhaps after falling out with his father, and he did not return to France for another twenty-five years. From England, he sailed to Canada in 1755, where he enlisted in the French colonial militia. He served as a surveyor and cartographer during the French and Indian War and was wounded in the battle of Quebec in 1759. He then sold his commission and took the very unusual step of emigrating to New York State. There he adopted the name James Hector St. John and traveled extensively in the wilderness of northern New York and Vermont as a surveyor and Indian trader. He became a naturalized citizen of New York in 1765 and continued to explore the Atlantic seaboard, the Ohio valley, and the Great Lakes regions. In 1769 he married an American (Mehitable Tippet) and bought 120 acres of farmland in Orange County, New York. At the same time he began writing essays and sketches on America. Between 1769 and 1778 Crèvecoeur farmed, traveled, wrote, and fathered three children with Mehitable.

Orange County was not a good place to be in 1776. Crèvecoeur found his farm attacked by Indians, New York Torys, and, once his refusal to participate in the revolution became known, by angry patriot neighbors. In 1778 he applied to the American authorities for permission to travel to France by way of New York City (his motives are unclear, but he took his eldest boy with him and it is suspected that he wanted to ensure the boy's legitimate right to inherit the Crèvecoeur estate; Mehitable and the two other children remained with friends in New York. She did not survive an attack on Crèvecoeur's farm house and the children were taken to Boston where Crèvecoeur finally met up with them in 1784). Arriving in

New York City on his way to France, Crèvecoeur was promptly arrested by the occupying British forces as an American spy. (Although, as Everett Emerson notes, the manuscripts Crèvecoeur was carrying included what the British general, James Pattison, described as "a sort of irregular Journal of America," including remarks that tend "to favor the side of [the British] Government and to throw odium on the Proceedings of the Opposite Party, and upon the tyranny of their Popular Government" (quoted in Everett Emerson, "Hector St. John de Crèvecoeur," 45). Crèvecoeur finally made it to England in 1781, where he sold the manuscript of his most famous work to Davis and Davies, who published the first edition in London in 1782.[1] By the time he reached France the American war was over and he was already beginning to become known as the author of the very popular *Letters*. In France, Crèvecoeur put together a different selection of letters and published them, in French, in 1784 (*Lettres d'un cultivateur Américain*).[2] Indeed, the *Letters* established Crèvecoeur as one of late-eighteenth century Europe's favorite authorities on the New World. The book encouraged Enlightenment references to America as the workshop of social, political, and agricultural experimentation and fed romantic images of America's wild beauty, sublime expanse, and unprecedented freedom.[3] Crèvecoeur was appointed French Consul to New York, New Jersey, and Connecticut and returned to the United States in 1783. He spent much of the remainder of his life traveling between the United States and France, serving in various diplomatic positions, establishing friendships with the likes of Jefferson, Madison, and Franklin, attending the pre-revolutionary salons of Count de Buffon, Madame d'Houdetot, and others, and helping as much as any one individual to strengthen political, cultural, and intellectual ties between France and the United States. In 1789 he was elected to membership in the American Philosophical Society, and played a big part in promoting and reporting the triumphant tour of the Marquis de Lafayette through the United States in 1784. He returned to Europe in 1790 and died in France in 1813.

The *Letters* are written in the voice of James, a Pennsylvania farmer, not unlike Crèvecoeur, but, nevertheless, and false advertisement of sincerity notwithstanding ("The following letters are the genuine production of the American farmer whose name they bear etc. etc." *Letters*, 35), a fictional character. The twelve letters are addressed to a learned Englishman who has recently returned to Cambridge after a brief stay in the pre-revolutionary American colonies.[4] The Englishman requires more information about America, and James, the insistently "humble" farmer, is flattered that he should have been asked to perform such a task. After an introductory letter in which James describes, in some detail, the circumstances surrounding his decision to honor the Englishman's request, James goes on to describe the general situation of the colonial farmer in two enthusiastic missives: "On the Situation, Feelings, and Pleasures of an American Farmer" and "What is an American?" In subsequent letters we read descriptions of Nantucket, Martha's Vineyard, Charles Town, South Carolina, and Pennsylvania, as well as detailed descriptions of snakes, humming-birds, honey-bees, and a host of other natural wonders. While there is much of interest in these chapters, what makes the *Letters* an intriguing rather than merely a pleasant work of literature, is the sudden intrusion of the revolution into the world of the letters and James' disconcertingly pessimistic registration of this event. Everything about the first eleven chapters of the *Letters* leads us, on a cursory reading, to expect a rousing celebration of the war for independence, but instead, in a final chapter entitled "Distresses of a Frontier Man," Crèvecoeur's farmer laments what he calls "this unfortunate revolution" (*Letters*, 204), and resolves to abandon his farm and retreat, with his family, to an Indian village. The contrast between James' celebration of American liberty in the preceeding chapters and his condemnation of anti-monarchic revolution in the final chapter (what Thomas Philbrick refers to as the *Letters'* "baffling . . . reversals of position," [*Hector St. John de Crèvecoeur*, 68]) has left many critics puzzled.

Writing after the revolution, Benjamin Rush listed the motives that had actuated those Americans who refused to support the war for independence.[5] Many loyalists were so, he wrote, for religious reasons (either they were too attached to the Church of England or, like some Quakers and Episcopalians they feared the power of a Presbyterian United States); some wanted to protect the power and office they enjoyed under colonial government, and others feared the termination of a lucrative commercial relationship with Britain. These socio-economic motivations have been analyzed in some detail by twentieth-century historians.[6] These same historians have also noted that a significant proportion of the colonial population simply hoped for peace and felt, as did shopkeeper John Ross of Philadelphia, that "Let who would be king, he well knew that he should be subject" (quoted in Nelson, "The Tory Rank and File," 287). Benjamin Rush mentions another category of loyalist, however, one that has received less attention, perhaps because it falls outside the realm of the more popular socio-economic enquiry and instead calls for an application of political philosophy (or indeed literary theory). Some loyalists, Rush writes, resisted the revolution out of "an attachment to kingly government" (quoted in Richard D. Brown, *Major Problems*, 272).

Letters from An American Farmer proceeds from the perspective of one who, for all his admiration for colonial liberty nevertheless will become tormented by his sense of attachment to the King of England. The *Letters* contain glowing accounts of the freedoms available to all who emigrate to pre-revolutionary America ("Where is that station," asks James, the fictional author, "which can confer a more substantial system of felicity than that of an American farmer possessing freedom of action, freedom of thoughts, ruled by a mode of government which requires but little from us?" (*Letters*, 52). James' early letters celebrate America as a country of men who are "strangers to those feudal institutions which [had] enslaved so many" (42), and they frequently contrast what the New World has to offer with the degradation of Europe – where the poor "sweat and work for the great" and are "obliged to give so many sheaves to the church, so many to your lords, so many to your government, and have hardly any left for yourselves" (84). We should not be surprised to find such sentiments in a book by one who would become a good friend of some of the leading revolutionaries and would spend much of the second half of his life promoting the United States in his native France. What is surprising, however, and what gives this book some of its lasting fascination, is that its narrator, James, the Pennsylvania farmer, refuses to support the revolution. In a letter entitled "Distresses of a Frontier Man," Crèvecoeur's farmer laments what he calls "this unfortunate revolution" (204), that has (in the words of the preface to the first edition of the *Letters*) "deformed the face of America," and occasioned "a rupture between the parent state and her colonies" (35). "The climate best adapted to my present situation and humour," writes the despondant James, "would be the polar regions . . . The severity of those climates, that great gloom where melancholy dwells, would be perfectly analagous to the turn of my mind" (200).

In other words, Crevecoeur's book presents us with a character hesitating before the revolution, a character who perhaps exemplifies a distinction made by Hannah Arendt: James exhibits the "desire to be free from oppression" but not "the desire for freedom as the political way of life." The former, Arendt explains, "could have been fulfilled under monarchial – though not under tyrannical, let alone despotic – rulership," while the latter, the desire for "freedom," demanded "the formation of a new, or rather rediscovered form of government. It demanded the constitution of a republic" (*On Revolution*, 33). The final letter repudiates a revolution that, as one commentator puts it, was "a necessary fight to rid Americans of the very kinds of tyranny Crèvecoeur castigates in [the larger part of] his book" (Plumstead, "Hector St. John de Crèvecoeur," 218). In his own attempt to account for this change of heart, James confesses to a "fear of innovations, with the consequence of which I am not well acquainted" (*Letters*, 203).[7] But this is by no means the whole story. James is also reluctant to join the patriotic cause because of what he calls "the respect I feel for the ancient connexion" (204). This is the connection with England, the "mother country" (although, as we shall see, it is with the father that England is most importantly associated in the *Letters*), and it is a connection which seems to ground and guarantee all the freedoms that the New World has to offer. Crèvecoeur's farmer wants to believe that feudal tyranny has been sufficiently restrained by the colony's pre-revolutionary system of wise laws and distant monarchic protection. The farmer's ideal world is one of "repose," a static and entirely satisfying world that has apparently been achieved in pre-revolutionary America.[8] Thus, Larzer Ziff figures the author of the *Letters* at the intersection of two historical periods:

> *Letters from an American Farmer* embodies a culture at the turning point: written by a farmer yet still requiring the patronage of a great man; glorifying a natural harmony yet still depending upon imperial politics for its maintenance; asserting the ability of the yeoman to express his life yet still deploring the incursion of the represented into the world of the real. Its charm and energy derive from the coherence of a viewpoint ... situated between new world and old ... (*Writing in the New Nation*, 33)

In this account, James represents a stage on the way towards a full endorsement of revolutionary values. His lingering attachment to Old World ideas, we are led to believe, will exclude him from the historical emergence of American republicanism. James is simply not modern enough. In one of the most careful studies we have of the *Letters'* politics, Myra Jehlen seems to come to a similar conclusion. The system of laws that guarantees liberty and independence to the independent farmer appears not to be at odds with what James calls the "ancient connexion" to England. In fact monarchy – at a distance – would seem to be an essential component in maintaining this American freedom. Jehlen writes:

> "*At a distance*": the phrase was all-important to Crèvecoeur, it was the key to his outlook. If we recall that he defined personal identity entirely in terms of self-possession and property, it becomes evident that he must have viewed

external authority *per se* as inevitably problematical. It had to be all-inclusive and absolute: it also had to be non-interfering, indeed non-engaging. Across a dangerous ocean, thousands of miles away, the crown of England was the best solution imaginable. It was "the law at a distance" incarnate. ("J. Hector St. John Crèvecoeur," 218)

Thus Jehlen concludes, anticipating Larzer Ziff, that Crèvecoeur, "may be seen as representing an intermediate stage in the evolution of America's liberal political philosophy" (222). Jehlen's attempt to answer the question of Crèvecoeur's politics, however, is more nuanced than this claim suggests, as the second part of her concluding sentence somewhat surprisingly indicates: Crèvecoeur "may be seen as representing an intermediate stage in the evolution of America's liberal political philosophy," she writes, "*or as a case in point for its paradoxical nature at any stage*" (222). This would seem to be a crucial equivocation. Either Crèvecoeur represents an immature politics or his work captures something persistent within American political philosophy. Jehlen's hesitant conclusion supports the idea that Crèvecoeur's James is, intriguingly, both behind and ahead of his time. The *Letters'* inscription of a resistance to revolution within a discourse that celebrates liberty and independence marks it as a unique vantage point from which to consider the American Revolution as more than just a clash of two political positions (the loyalist reactionaries and the patriotic revolutionaries). It is James' hesitation that will be most instructive here. What does he hold onto in holding back from the revolution? Could it be that James sees (perhaps more clearly than most) what precisely will make the revolution *revolutionary*? The *Letters* suggest that American liberty and American anti-monarchism are not one and the same thing. This is an important insight, since what it suggests is that James sees a relationship between individual liberty and the monarchic function that was threatened by the revolution. The *Letters*, I will argue, register a far more profound sense of the implications of post-monarchism than most revolutionary rhetoric was willing to entertain. James, as the first eleven chapters of the *Letters* make clear, might have supported the execution of Charles I (the execution carried out in the name of "Charles I, body politic"), but he is horrified – in 1776 – by the mock-executions of King George III.

Furthermore, if James' resistance corresponds to a sharp sense of the deep implications of the revolution, we should not be surprised to find a fascinating allegory of revolution and founding coinciding with the *Letters'* apparent neutrality. Crèvecoeur's book, I will show, proposes revolution in spite of itself; in fact, it is precisely with his resistance to the revolution that James figures the revolutionary act. As if, that is to say, one cannot represent what is revolutionary about the revolution from within the revolution's own discourse about itself. For after all, it is not really as a loyalist that James refuses to join the revolution, but as a disaffected individual, one who, following an important strand of the modern revolution, seeks above all else to begin again, outside of the history of men's confrontations, outside of politics, in the "unconverted wilderness" of a just beginning.

Myra Jehlen calls Crèvecoeur an anarchist because his primary investment is in what she calls "the political integrity of the individual": "His definition of self-determination was thus more radical or more absolute than that which is commonly implied by democracy, because he could see in the accommodations of majority rule no advantages but only a loss of freedom for each individual" ("J. Hector St. John Crèvecoeur," 221). She calls him a "monarcho-anarchist," however, because this investment seems to necessitate the presence – albeit the distant presence – of a monarch. The independent yeoman farmer, such as James, needs the absolute authority of the monarch in order to "keep each man free of his equals" (217), and thus, Jehlen writes, "monarchy was for him the corollary of social equality" (222). "His opposition to the American Revolution," Jehlen disconcertingly suggests, "was grounded in the principle that all men are created equal – and that so should they remain" (222). If this is one of those paradoxes of American political philosophy that Jehlen suggests can be found in Crèvecoeur's work, perhaps we can try to reformulate it. For Crèvecoeur, the American Declaration of Independence offered, above all, a threat to individual independence. Individual sovereignty, that is to say, was threatened by the transfer of political power from a monarchic to a republican political system. Democracy offered the people political power even as it dissembled their individual sovereign integrity. Even if it was in the mode of anxiety and indeed resistance, Crèvecoeur's James here suggests a reading of the revolution that is entirely compatible with post-modern approaches to the democratic transformation. His "paradoxes," to quote Jehlen, become our insights.

How exactly does the *Letters'* idealized state of politico-economic independence participate in a monarchic ideology? How, that is to say, does the book's understanding of sovereign individual integrity participate in a monarchic logic? And how is it, finally, that while the revolution appears in the *Letters* as the event that will radically disable this ideology (of patriarchal, monarchic, we might even say *deistic*, sovereignty),

Crèvecoeur himself is finally able to come to terms with the revolution? Could it be that Crèvecoeur's "monarcho-anarchism," to use Jehlen's term, finds a place in post-revolutionary America because its leading architects were themselves reluctant to institute the radical rupture that James' panic anticipates? Even the "distress" of this fictional American is less disjunctive than we might think in post-revolutionary America: a tone of pessimism and disappointment runs through the later writings of the founding generation that has something in common with that of Crèvecoeur's dejected farmer. Benjamin Rush, for example, wrote of his "deep regret" and described himself as a "stranger" in the new nation. "Only by considering the people of his home state, Pennsylvania, 'deranged upon the subject of their political and physical happiness,'" notes Gordon Wood, "could he contain the anger and contempt he felt" (*Radicalism*, 366). James' proposed retreat into the wilderness at the end of the *Letters* could even be said to anticipate, in certain respects, the fate of the founders, who finally inhabited a private sphere that for many must have felt like exile. "All, all dead," wrote Jefferson in 1825, "and ourselves left alone amidst a new generation whom we know not, and who knows not us" (quoted in Wood, *Radicalism*, 368).

Coming to terms with the politics of the *Letters*, then, involves making a distinction between monarchism as a particular example of a political system invested in the fantasy of self-possessed, sovereign independence (an independence guaranteed, even as it is compromised, by the monarch's power to mediate all conflict between individual subjects), and monarchism as the name for any political ideology that demonstrates an investment in the fantasy of sovereign individuality. While the leading American revolutionaries eventually showed no hesitation in separating themselves from the former, that is to say, from the King of England, I think we must consider the possibility that they did so because they had found a way to reinscribe sovereign self-possession within a post-monarchical political ideology. Crèvecoeur's narrator, on the other hand, hesitates in the face of the revolution because the revolutionary break appears to him as a far more radical departure: a philosophical revolution into the unknown (what he calls the revolution's "innovations," *Letters*, 204). From this perspective, James' revolution would be the radical revolution that the founding fathers never experienced (or only experienced in their nightmares). The revolution that James resisted, in other words, was the post-modern revolution that contemporary political philosophy wants to suggest was always haunting the modern revolution of the founders: James recognized the constitutive nature of a political gap left by the absence of the king, a gap that revolutionary rhetoric (in the years immediately following the Declaration of Independence) had successfully and reassuringly filled in. Post-modern political philosophy, however, identifies the political institution of this gap (the king's absence) as the founding point of modern democracy. Thus, Claude Lefort describes the "revolutionary and unprecedented feature of democracy":

> The locus of power becomes *an empty place* ... it cannot be occupied – it is such that no individual and no group can be consubstantial with it – and it cannot be represented. Only the mechanisms of the exercise of power are visible, or only the men, the mere mortals, who hold political authority. We would be wrong to conclude that power now resides *in* society on the grounds that it emanates from popular suffrage; it remains the agency by virtue of which society apprehends itself in its unity and relates to itself in time and space. But this agency is no longer referred to an unconditional pole; and in that sense, it marks a division between the *inside* and the *outside* of the social, institutes relations between those dimensions, and is tacitly recognized as being purely symbolic. (Lefort, *Democracy and Political Theory*, 17)

The democratic revolution, according to this analysis, would seek to replace the body of the prince not with another body – not even the body of the people, or the body of science (nature), but with a functional absence. We can hear an inarticulate registration of precisely this political transformation when the author of the *Letters* despairs that the only place on the globe appropriate to his state of mind "would be the polar regions ... The severity of those climates, that great gloom where melancholy dwells" (*Letters*, 200). James' polar isolation prefigures the unsettling lack that features so prominently in post-Marxist conceptions of democracy – what Ernesto Laclau and Chantal Mouffe call "the radical indeterminacy which democracy opens up" (*Hegemony and Socialist Strategy*, 188).[9] James' colonial independence was monarchically structured, and as such, depended on the position, however distant, of the King of England.[10] But this dependence, no matter how distant it might have seemed, was always at work, threatening to make itself apparent in the life of the self-sufficient farmer (hence his discomfort with market relations, with profit, excess, law, and, as we shall see, writing – anything that forced him into a relationship of temporal or political self-difference). The figure of the king absorbed all of James' colonial anxiety about the individual's mediated or prosthetic independence; the revolution, on the other hand, promised to radicalize and return to all America's subjects the political dependence that had been so successfully contained by the "ancient connexion." The democratic citizen, as James/Crèvecoeur seemed to suspect more than most, would become the independent site of an originary self-supplementation: the subject of a freedom ever after indissociable from a forceful auto-authorization.[11]

THE "ANCIENT CONNEXION"

The tension that precipitates the crisis of the *Letters'* final chapter is antic-ipated by a tension throughout the text between descriptions of indepen-dence that emphasize the moral achievement of an honest, industrious freedom, and descriptions of independence as the effect of a trick of the pen – the magic of law. It is this tension that the king (and his var-ious paternal stand-ins) works to reduce in his capacity as the figure in whom legal power and extra-legal, divine righteousness come together. The king (or good father) performs the reassuring coincidence of the political and the moral. Revolution, then, is the name for an experience of the breakdown, or suspension, of this assurance. It is, ultimately, the relationship between law and justice that the king (and his paternal stand-ins) contains and that revolution proceeds by re-posing as a structurally undecidable relationship. The moment of anxiety-ridden revolutionary suspense is also the moment of a familial crisis, a moment of patriarchal crisis and of crisis over generation and inheritance. With this in mind, I want to turn for a moment to Crèvecoeur's various father figures.

James' reference to the "ancient connexion" with England alerts us to what it is about monarchy that James values most: its indication of a connection outside of present history, a connection that transcends local political association. The king who is repeatedly referred to as the "good father" sustains a model of union that emphasizes the familial over and against the political. This connection is neither transitory nor contingent. England is "the mother country," "the great nation of which we are a part," and the "ancient connexion" without which the farmer feels adrift in a world of "innovations" (*Letters*, 203–4). (Thus he is loathe to believe that England has really been less than just to her "distant conquests." He writes, "I shall not repeat all I have heard because I cannot believe half of it," 203.) The King of England is the good father, and his patriarchal example can and should be followed by the "manly" and independent American farmer. One of his great remaining hopes, James tells us at the end of letter II, is that he may live to give each of his children a farm and teach them to be "like their father, good, substantial, independent American farmers" (65). Independence, in James' description, is the in-dependence of a monarch, owner of his land, his produce, his animals, and, of course, his "negroes," who, he tells us, "are tolerably faithful and healthy" (53). "The instant I enter on my own land," James writes, again with a useful lack of self consciousness, "the bright idea of property, of exclusive right, of independence, exalt my mind" (54, *sic*). "What should we American farmers be without the distinct possession of that soil?" (54) James asks, and the answer is obvious.[12] The revolution threatens the independent patriarchal farmer, then, and it is this threat that occasions James' unpatriotic melancholy. Moreover, as Jay Fliegelman has so persuasively demonstrated, James was not wrong to recognize an anti-patriarchal element in the discourse of the revolution: "a call for filial autonomy and the unimpeded emergence from nonage echoes throughout the rhetoric of the American Revolution," writes Fliegelman. "At every opportunity Revolutionary propagandists insisted that the new nation and its people had come of age, had achieved a collective maturity that necessitated them becoming in political fact an independent and self-governing nation" (Fliegelman, *Prodigals and Pilgrims*, 3–4).

But if the *Letters* celebrate (and fear for) the moral superiority of an industrious independent farmer, they also register the importance of more explicitly political aids to independence. As we saw in the discussion of Andrew, the "simple Scotchman" (in the introduction to this book), "the indulgent laws" (*Letters*, 90) also play a part in the making of an American. In fact, the discussion of Andrew is full of equivocation on this question of the relationship between moral and political factors in the achievement of independence. Andrew's exemplary advance in his new home proceeds, we are initially informed, "not by virtue of any freaks of fortune," but by "the gradual operation of sobriety, honesty, and emigration" (*Letters*, 90). This last term, of course, jars somewhat with those that precede it (there is nothing inherently virtuous about "emigration"), and it does so not only because we are also told that Andrew left Scotland with no advance stake in any property in the New World (indeed, although James assures us that Andrew's success is not attributable to any "freaks of fortune," his decision to emigrate was quite rash: with no advance stake in any American property, Andrew's hopes rested "entirely upon chance" [95]), but also because it introduces a specifically political dimension into Andrew's success. "Honesty," "vigor," and "the benignity of government," James will later remark, are what allow the new American to thrive (94); to his land will be "annexed" "every municipal blessing" (83). Virtue proceeds, in the farmer's analysis, from what he calls "that manly confidence which property confers" (94), and property, in turn, is guaranteed by the law that Andrew experiences as one of the "mysteries" of American freedom. One source of American freedom, then, is the law that secures dominion; but this faceless law is insistently juxtaposed with the figure of the good father whose benignity, sobriety, and example is inherited by the "fortunate" son. Hence, Andrew's success is also attributed to his "honesty" and "sobriety" and it is as a kind of adopted son of James that he succeeds so admirably in the New World.

James knows all about such paternal relationships, of course, because he himself is the primary model for this patriarchal story of American liberty. It is James who reminds us (and who is regularly reminded by his unnamed wife), that his good fortune in large part results from his father's wisdom and foresight.

My father left me three hundred and seventy-one acres of land, forty-seven of which are good timothy meadow; an excellent orchard; a good house; and a substantial barn. It is my duty to think how happy I am that he lived to build and to pay for all these improvements; what are the labours which I have to undergo, what are my fatigues, when compared to his, who had everything to do, from the first tree he felled to the finishing of his house . . . By a long series of industry and honest dealings, my father left behind him the name of a good man; I have but to tread his paths to be happy and a good man like him. (52–3)

But the insufficiency of this paternal model as an account of American freedom is indicated, albeit in a rather passive form, by the resistance written into the words used to describe James' obedience. Even without a knowledge of Crèvecoeur's fraught relationship with his own father we could detect some tension in this passage. "It is my duty to think how happy I am" writes James, and it would seem to be necessary for his wife to remind him of this duty from time to time. James is in debt to – and in this way continues to feel the presence of – his father and that "good name" he left behind him. This sanctified father who began (mythically?) with nothing and bequeathed everything, leaves James unburdened by financial debt (and thus burdened, paradoxically, by his father's solvency and economy), yet clearly feeling the weight of that good name. Importantly, however, that good name is not the name made by writing (the signature). As James' wife keeps trying to remind him, while trying to dissuade him from writing the letters in the first place, writing indicates, among other things, "idleness and vanity" and "had [your] father spent his time in sending epistles to and fro [he] never would have left thee this goody plantation, free from debt" (48).

This tension between a recognition of the debt to patriarchy (the debt to particular virtuous individuals, and thus to "ancient connexion" be it familial, monarchical or divine) and a celebration of the wonders of sound politico-legal policy is paralleled by another aspect of the *Letters*. "The eruption of physical conflict at the close [of the *Letters*]," writes Larzer Ziff, "is an externalization of irreconcilable differences within the writer's position rather than the intrusion of public events into an otherwise felicitous private life. These differences exist as a conflict between what is valorized in the writing and the act of writing itself" (*Writing in the New Nation*, 22). Ziff continues: "Once the happy farmer becomes the writing farmer he disrupts the harmony he intends to celebrate. If he can abstract himself from his everyday presence and assume a practice that is traditionally that of another class, then despite his political loyalty to the British system he is manifesting the cultural circumstance that disrupts it" (29). James' decision to take up the pen and write down his observations on life in the New World represents a curious and indeed risky excursion, and it is his wife, once again, who is most aware of this fact. James' letters are written in response to a request from a friend, Mr. F.B., who is described as a "great European" and who had once visited James on his farm in Pennsylvania. His hesitation, however, is provoked by his wife's opposition. "If thee persistest in being such a foolhardy man," she says, "for God's sake let it be kept a profound secret among us" (*Letters*, 47). She repeats this charge two more times in her short speech: "Let it be as great a secret," she says, "as if it was some heinous crime . . . how would'st thee bear to be called at our country meetings the man of the pen?" (48,49). James' wife draws on at least two concerns in resisting his writing. On the one hand, such activity indicates, as we have already seen, "idleness" and vanity (James' father did not waste his time writing); on the other hand, writing also suggests political aspiration and an unsettling desire for a change in the *status quo*. Writing, James' wife explains, suggests "vain notions not befitting thy condition." "Some would imagine," she says, "that thee wantest to become an assemblyman or a magistrate . . . I had rather be as we are, neither better nor worse than the rest of our country folks" (48). James is manifesting, in other words, what Arendt would call the emergence – as if by accident – of a desire for public, political freedom rather than simply the desire for private liberty. James' wife makes quite clear that the tension between farming one's own land and entering into the public world of writing is linked to the tension between filial obediance and political republicanism: James' father would not have taken up the pen, would not have risked appearing to want to change his or anybody else's station in his static, hierarchical, pre-revolutionary world.

Crèvecoeur's biography tells us that for unknown reasons he left his native France (Normandy) around the age of eighteen and went to England (biographers Allen and Assineau speculate that it was because of a break with his father). Many years later Crèvecoeur's father tried to gather his whereabouts in America in a letter that indicated the extent to which communication had broken down between the father and his eldest son. Crèvecoeur, in the meantime, had married a Protestant, an act that would probably have incensed the father who had sent his son to Jesuits for his early education. Crèvecoeur had, it is clear, cut himself off from his landowning father at an early age and proceeded to make his own way in England, France, and the American colonies. And yet his writing is full of reverence for the figure of the good father. Not only are we reminded that James, the fictional author of the *Letters*, owes his happiness to his father (when in fact Crèvecoeur had bought and farmed his own land), but other fathers are praised in the highest terms. In "An Happy Family Disunited by the Spirit of Civil War," a sketch first published in Dennis Moore's recent *More Letters from an American Farmer*, a particular, unnamed, rural patriarch (the oldest man in the county) is compared to "one of those beautiful Elms often left by the Cultivator, to shade their meadows": "He has long stood the admiration of his neighbours [&] the most distinguish'd pattern of perfection." (Moore, *More Letters*, 3). (In the version Moore gives us, however, there is an interesting deletion: comparing the patriarch to one of his elms, that was planted to provide shade, Crèvecoeur adds that the elms were also left to "ornament their fields" (3). This less utilitarian purpose was then struck through by Crèvecoeur, once again indicating a hesitation with regard to the dangerous supplementary effect of ornamentation as a sign of success and power.) The praise of this father figure is hyperbolic and extensive, and it modulates into a celebration of fathers in general. "But for the courage of our fathers, we should not be at this day possessed of extensive fields, of rich meadows, of large Barns & convenient houses . . . They have laid the foundation of our welfare, a pathetick lesson which I often bring to my mind, the effects of which my children likewise shall feel" (5). It is clear that Crèvecoeur is highly invested in a fantasy of the father that is full of a fascinating ambivalence. The man who had cut himself off from his own father imagines an ideal father, but almost always at the same time as he reflects on the death of this father. In this instance, he passes quickly from a reflection on the debt he owes to his father to these comments on his father's burial site:

the Orchard where my father lies buried, shall not pass into other hands, who regardless of his Ashes, might wantonly till a spot, on which nothing ought to grow but the grass of Nature [in order] to render it still more respected & ~~more~~

awful I have planted it close with Locusts which the greediest possessor can hardly ever destroy, their Roots shall surround his Ashes, & their shade add still something to the gloom, with which a [Ye] sight of that place always inspires me. (*Letters*, 5)

Crèvecoeur's fathers, in other words, are idealized and buried simultaneously; their charisma seems linked to their death. Indeed, a latent hostility arises almost every time a father figure is mentioned in Crèvecoeur's work. As paternal fantasies, Crèvecoeur's images share something with the veneration of George Washington (who is first referred to as "Father of his Country" in 1778). "The mythologization of Washington as founding father," writes Jay Fliegelman, "enthroned the antipatriarchal values that made up [revolutionary] ideology" (*Prodigals and Pilgrims*, 199). But crucial to the success of this apparently paradoxical figure (founding father of anti-patriarchalism) is Washington's famous sterility. In a world in which the right to pass on one's property to the next generation was valued as a cornerstone of freedom, Washington's sterility represented another kind of death in life, a death that in its own way constituted Washington's unintentional sacrifice on behalf of his American children. Fliegelman writes: "Washington's sterility freed America permanently from the hereditary monarchy that some Federalists, if Republican propaganda may be believed, wished to make from the the Washington line. Through his 'great example' Washington himself and not his generation would remain America's parent" (*Prodigals and Pilgrims*, 200). As with Crèvecoeur's father figures, Washington's importance was probably greatest in the ground – that virtuous American soil. Some resolution is brought to Crèvecoeur's "Happy Family Disunited by the Revolution" ... when the narrator persuades the warring family,

to erect a Vault to deposit [the father] in, to the End that when engaged in that mournful occupation, the [sentiments] it will inspire them with may have a powerfull Tendency towards softening their hearts, & to reunite them all at least in that reverence, in that respect which they so justly owe to the ashes of so good so venerable a father – (*More Letters*, 19).

The father figure is he who, starting from nothing and without recourse to writing, lays the foundation for that which will continue to be united around his corpse. Crèvecoeur's fathers are ghostly; they are never more powerful than when laid in their grave, and it is in this respect that the father resembles the monarch: they both inhabit or embody a power that exceeds their life above ground: the king is dead, long live the king.

It is this patriarchal, monarchic power that America offers its citizens in the democratized form of a legal life after death. Andrew, the simple Scotchman, is the beneficiary of a kind of translation of monarchic authority. The letter of the law does for Andrew what patriarchal virtue and wisdom did for James' father. Andrew's "dominion" will extend beyond his death. This politico-legal mystery, this necessarily written mystery, acknowledges the power of a republic to legislate the life (that is to say the reborn life – life after death) that the feudal subject only recognized in his king. But while Crèvecoeur's James seems to acknowledge this translation, he does not do so without some reservation. This American "mystery" needs to be contained, for James, within the frame of the only acceptable immortality, that of the king. The figure of the king, and the "ancient connexion" represented by the figure of the king, serves to conceal any rupture that might become apparent between law as the product of political history and law as the extra-political voice of justice. In lamenting the revolution's anti-monarchism, Crèvecoeur detected, and was made most anxious by, the possibility of a revolt against the figure of the father, the fantastic father, such as a very distant King George might represent. In addition to the real threats to his property that he witnesses, James also responds on some level to an attack on his phantasmatic patriarchalism, an attack that is simultaneously a literal reminder of what he himself has done in cutting himself off from his father in France.

Given this scenario, the break with monarchy, constitutes, for Crèvecoeur's farmer, something like an attempt to kill what is already dead: an attempt to kill a very important ghost. This is disconcerting to say the least. A break with the phantasmatic monarch opens up the prospect of what James fearfully calls "innovations, with the consequence of which I am not well acquainted" (*Letters*, 204). It is here that I want to see James with his unique apprehension as a witness to another kind of revolution, a revolution that inhabited what we have come to think of as the modern revolution. James was ahead of the game; he panicked in the face of a revolution that did not quite arrive. He saw the irreducible political gap opened up by the disappearance of the ghost-monarch, the phantom-father; he anticipated what post-Marxist political philsophers like Ernesto Laclau have called the "constitutive incompletion" (Laclau, *New Reflections*, 71) of the democratic social order. James' registration of this constitutive absence takes the form of panic: indeed, he is on the verge of the kind of madness that Charles Brockden Brown will figure so memorably in his novel of pre-revolutionary hysteria, *Wieland*. James writes:

I am convulsed – convulsed sometimes to that degree as to be tempted to exclaim, "Why has the Master of the world permitted so much indiscriminate evil throughout every part of this poor planet, at all times, and among all kinds of people?" . . . Life appears to be a mere accident, and of the worst kind . . . Thus, impiously I roam, I fly from one erratic thought to another, and my mind, irritated by these acrimonious reflections, is ready sometimes to lead me to dangerous extremes of violence. (*Letters*, 209–10)

The key words here are "indiscriminate" and "accident." It is a radically unsettling encounter with contingency, or with what we could call history untethered from any teleological horizon, that James describes. His language not only recalls Theodore Wieland and Edgar Huntly in Brockden Brown's novels, but also John Adams in the "Discourses on Davila," where he rejects with horror what he sees to be the radical Jacobinian implication that "men are but fireflies and that this *all* is without a father" (Adams, *Political Writings*, 193). For Adams, too, such an idea is inseparable from a descent into indiscriminate violence ("[it] is to make murder itself as indifferent as shooting a plover" [193]). What James does not seem to have noticed, however, is that while he was panicking, the founding fathers were already filling that revolutionary gap with what the Declaration of Independence called the laws of nature, or "nature's God." The revolution, wrote Thomas Paine, responds to "the weeping voice of nature;" from now on nature (which is always God's nature) will be the "touchstone" of legitimate political action (*Common Sense*, 87, 88). The people of the United States, the Declaration explains, are assuming the station "to which the laws of nature and nature's God entitle them." They are endowed "by their creator" with "inalienable rights." The revolution, in this reading, merely goes over the monarch's head and appeals to the supreme monarch, the Christian God, he whom John Adams referred to as "the great legislator of the universe" (quoted in Arendt, *On Revolution*, 185). As I have suggested above, the Declaration's appeal to "God," "the creator," or "the laws of nature and of nature's God" as source of the justice that legitimates this revolution is in tension with that same document's reference to "the course of human events" in which political rupture "becomes necessary." Human historical and political decisions and actions, on the one hand, and divine order on the other, are always in danger of becoming unhinged in the careful construction of the Declaration's opening lines. Similarly, the Enlightenment's translation of divine omniscience, the reference to "self-evident truths," remains in tension with what Arendt sharply reminds us is this phrase's deceptively political supplement: "We *hold* these truths to be self evident"

(*On Revolution*, 193–4).[13] The revolution did not want to be seen to be abolishing the role of that which, outside of politics, nevertheless gives a grounding legitimacy and permanency to politically achieved rights and liberties. What it concealed, in other words, was the inherent arbitrariness that informs all beginnings (Arendt, *On Revolution*, 206). In this respect, as I have already suggested, the principle of a monarchic political position remains intact in the discourse of the founding, even as the revolution- aries contested a particular, historical arrogation of this principle. Given this understanding, it is possible to detect James' hesitation about the radical anti-monarchism of the revolution running through the thought and writing of all the leading revolutionaries.[14] Hannah Arendt writes:

we can hardly avoid the paradoxical fact that it was precisely the revolutions, their crisis and their emergency, which drove the very "enlightened" men of the eighteenth century to plead for some religious sanction at the very moment when they were about to emancipate the secular realm fully from the influences of the churches and to separate politics and religion once and for all. (*On Revolution*, 185–6)[15]

If James is ambivalent about revolution, then ("Shall I discard all my ancient principles, shall I renounce that name, that nation, which I held once so respectable? ... On the other hand, shall I arm myself against that country where I first drew breath, against the playmates of my youth, my bosom friends, my acquaintance" [*Letters*, 204–5]), he is so in a most illustrative way. And nowhere is he more melodramatically ambivalent than in his final fantasy of starting over.

BEGINNING AGAIN

In his final letter, James resolves – although the narrative ends before we get to see this resolve acted upon – to abandon white America and take up residence in the wilderness among the Indians. This decision gives the *Letters* a touch of drama and wonder that must have particularly appealed to Crèvecoeur's European audience. At the same time, the decision has struck many readers as rash and impractical, an idea that says more about the character's (or the author's) desperation than it does about any coherent response to the situation James finds himself in.

But James' decision follows, in certain respects, from his puzzling re- luctance to give up on the ancient connection with England. The onset of war with Britain dissolves the fantastic, extra-political qualities of one father figure and leads James to seek another. "Must I, then, bid farewell to Britain, to that renowned country? Must I renounce a name so ancient and so venerable? Alas, she herself, that once indulgent parent forces me to take up arms against her" (*Letters*, 209). Unwilling to take up arms, James does the next best thing, in his opinion, and turns to "Nature," "that great parent" (207).[16] Nature is also outside of, or in a privileged relationship with that which remains outside of politics and human history. And it is an outside–of–politics that James desperately seeks: "Self-preservation is above all political precepts and rules," he concludes, and thus, "I will revert into a state approaching nearer to that of nature, unencumbered either with voluminous laws or contradictory codes" (211).[17]

In the midst of the War for Independence, James abandons all allegiance and anticipates retreating into the wilderness, which is also to say, the space of the Native American. If we read this in the terms James gives us, it is a retreat out of politics, out of history even, certainly out of the revolution. On the other hand, what James' resolve reminds us is that the wilderness and its native inhabitants have always been a crucial part of the American political landscape. James' invocation of the wilderness and the Indians here is no less fantastic (and no less political) than his invocation of the "ancient connexion" with the King of England (or his invocation of what he calls the "mysteries" of American liberty, referring to the legal production of posthumous authority.) In fact, James' decision to move his family, while it follows from his nostalgia for monarchism, is at the same time the *Letters'* inscription of the revolutionary strike for independence. And like the larger political struggle that occasions this text, James' move even has its own Declaration: "Lest my countrymen should think that I am gone to join the incendiaries of our frontiers, I intend to write a letter to Mr. _____ to inform him of our retreat and of the reasons that have urged me to it" (219). James gives up on the fantastic royal parent and turns instead to nature in a move that is directly replicated in the Declaration of Independence and much of the most powerful rhetoric of the American Revolution. James' conception literalizes much of the rhetoric that Americans inherited from a tradition of natural rights philosophy. References to the "immutable laws of nature," or "the unalienable and inestimable inheritance, which we derived from nature" could be found in petitions produced by local and national delegations throughout the 1770s. The invocation of nature had become a commonplace in late-eighteenth-century political discourse, but with James' decision to move his family to the unnamed Indian village we are presented with a unique literalization of that political cliché.

Just as James seems to have had a particular investment in the actual –
though distant – presence of the monarch as the symbol of ancient rights
and privileges, so he seems resolved to literalize the connection with
nature that the American revolutionary leaders were largely content to
put to abstract rhetorical use. James' wilderness is the empirical "out
of doors" that Thomas Paine invoked as the space where the most legitimate political authority originated and could be exercised. But it is
also the site of a curious folding of democratic space – the space of
healthy revolutionary sunlight – into the secret space of what Philip
Freneau called "the unsocial Indian" ("On the Emigration," *Poems*, II,
280). In this respect, the move out of doors is also a movement out of
the public eye, recalling the movement of the secretive Constitutional
Conventions that I will discuss in chapters three and four. James writes,
"when once secluded from the great society to which we all belong, we
shall unite closer together, and there will be less room for jealousies and
contentions" (*Letters*, 225), a remark that bears comparison with the ways
in which delegates sometimes spoke of the Constitutional Convention in
Philadelphia. James' fantasy anticipates Benjamin Franklin's invocation
of unanimity in the speech in the convention that I will discuss at more
length in the next chapter. At the same time, his comment reminds us
once again of the relationship between secrecy (here, "seclusion") and a
founding unity.

One way of emphasizing nature's function as a space outside of
politics is by diminishing the political profile of those peoples who
are considered coterminous with nature: Native Americans. Nature,
as it appears in Jefferson's Declaration (or in Paine's writing) is always tenantless, but this cannot be the case in James' proposed excursion. Crèvecoeur's letter exposes the extent to which the rhetoric
of nature as source of entitlement depended on its association, in
America, with her "immediate children." The Native American supports
James' conception of a space outside of politics, a space that guarantees the possibility of starting again, outside of history.[18] The Indians, James writes, "most certainly are much more closely connected
with Nature than we are; they are her immediate children: the inhabitants of the woods are her undefiled offspring" (*Letters*, 215). ("The
charm of the Indian to me," Thoreau would write, "is that he stands
free and unconstrained in nature, is her inhabitant and not her guest,
and wears her easily and gracefully" [quoted in Pearce, *Savagism and
Civilization*, 148]). They are also, in James' fantastic conception, "strangers
to our political disputes," and have "none among themselves." In the

wilderness village he intends to retreat to, he writes, "Not a word of politics shall cloud our simple conversation" (*Letters*, 225–6). This notion – that the Indians knew no politics – was commonplace, and for Jefferson it was even a source of some philosophical uncertainty: "I am convinced," he wrote in 1787, "that those societies (as the Indians) which live without government enjoy in their general mass an infinitely greater degree of happiness than those who live under the European governments." At the same time, writing from Paris, Jefferson told Madison that "It is a problem, not clear in my mind," that the condition of the Indians in this regard "is not the best" of all possible forms of society.[19] Outside of politics, the Indians are also importantly outside of history as the history of unpredictable human political conflicts and transformations. Contrasted with this political history is a fantasy of time as progressive evolution (time de-historicized because it is governed by a rationality – progress – that is outside of time), a fantasy to which the American Indian has already become centrally important, as this passage from Jefferson reveals with wonderful clarity:

Let a philosophic observer commence a journey from the savages of the Rocky Mountains, eastwardly towards our sea-coast. These he would observe in the earliest stage of association living under no law but that of nature, subsisting and covering themselves with the flesh and skins of wild beasts. He would next find those on our frontiers in the pastoral state, raising domestic animals to supply the defects of hunting. Then succeed our own semi-barbarous citizens, the pioneers of the advance of civilization, and so in his progress he would meet the gradual shades of improving man until he would reach his, as yet, most improved state in our seaport towns. This, in fact, is equivalent to a survey, in time, of the progress of man from the infancy of creation to the present day.[20]

The wilderness, then (and the Indian village is its corollary), is the space of new beginnings outside of history. An escape from time as human production is sought in the Indian as the figural guarantor of a meta-historical logic governing history. For James, going back to the Indian means starting again: he will teach them to farm instead of hunt ("It is the chase and the food it procures" that makes people wild! [*Letters*, 220]), and he will introduce laws about trading with white men, regulate their trade, and encourage respect for elders (221–2). "I . . . Go," he writes with an ominous sense of his own authority, "determined industriously to work up among them such a system of happiness as may be adequate to my future situation" (226). His decision to move to the Indian village follows a reflection on the ruin that he wants to rebuild: "I resemble, methinks, one of the stones of a ruined arch, still retaining that pristine form which

anciently fitted the place I occupied, but the centre is tumbled down"
(211). But he goes on: "I can be nothing until I am replaced, either in the
former circle or in some stronger one. I see one on a smaller scale, and at
a considerable distance, but it is within my power to reach it" (211). Thus
he introduces his decision to move to Indian country as the intention to
rebuild, to build a stronger circle of stone to replace the monarchical,
Anglocentric political structure he has now given up for good. James
retreats out of politics but at the same time into the space of political
foundation.

One of the oddities of the *Letters* is that its final set of images, those
of the familial retreat into the wilderness, are never realized – they are
left suspended, as it were, in a space of anxious imagining that only
serves to emphasize the phantasmatic work that the wilderness and the
Native American would do for revolutionary Americans. Nature seems
to fulfill the function of what Ernesto Laclau calls a "floating signifier"; it
is, in other words, "the name of an absent fullness" (*Emancipation(s)*, 94).
The wilderness that James contemplates is in fact the post-revolutionary
United States, the space of new beginnings and new systems that will
not only prove disastrous for Native Americans but will pose a series of
threats to the stability and authority of the revolution's ruling classes.
Although James' wilderness is a retreat and a place from which to start
again outside of politics, it is also a frightening and unpredictable space:
James and his family, he writes, are to become "members of a new and
strange community" (*Letters*, 212). He tries to reassure himself about what
he calls this "metamorphosis" (222): "These changes may appear more
terrific at a distance," he tells himself, "than when grown familiar by
practice" (213). But there are clearly dangers involved in this new beginning. "I cannot but recollect what sacrifice I am going to make, what
amputation I am going to suffer, what transition I am going to experience" (215).[21] Imagining the prospects for his children, James also
figures the threats to a nation that enters into revolution. The children
of the revolution will be introduced to the charms of the space of new
political and social possibilities, and these charms will put them at odds
with the very father figures who have led them into this space. The danger that James returns to repeatedly is that his children will be lost to the
Indians: "the apprehension lest my younger children should be caught
by that singular charm ["some great intoxication among the Indians"]"
is one that "startles" James (213); "I dread lest the imperceptible charm of
Indian education," he writes a little later, "may seize my younger children
and give them such a propensity to that mode of life as may preclude

their returning to the manners and customs of their parents" (219). The idea that the space of new beginnings could also produce beginnings that the founder cannot control is given one of its most powerful images in the threat of miscegenation (a blood alliance between his daughter and an Indian) that is, for James, the most terrifying figure for an encounter with the space of revolutionary origins.[22] Such a union, James writes, is "disagreeable, no doubt, to Nature's intentions, which have so strongly divided us by so many indelible characters" (222). James' protestation suggests that we know nature's intentions by her writing on the bodies of whites and Indians. The socio-historical and biological differences between ethnic groups are like the differences between texts. Intermarriage here suggests that these texts can be reinterpreted. And indeed James seems at other times excited by the prospect that he and his children will become part-Indian: "According to their customs, we shall likewise receive names from them, by which we shall always be known. My youngest children shall learn to swim and to shoot with the bow" (219). Like Cooper's Hawkeye, forty years later, however, James' children will learn from the Indian, but they will have "no cross in their blood": for although he respects "the simple, the inoffensive society of these people in their villages," James writes, "the strongest prejudices would make me abhor any alliance with them in blood" (222).

If the native threatens a miscegenation that figures, in my schema, the excessive democratization of post-revolutionary America, the native's relationship to a kind of luxury and superfluity (recall the "desserts of a prince") anticipates the post-revolution's democratization of an archaic materialism. "Perhaps you would not believe that there are in the woods looking-glasses and paint of every colour; and that the inhabitants take as much pains to adorn their faces and their bodies, to fix their bracelets of silver, and plait their hair as our forefathers the Picts used to do in the time of the Romans. Not that I would wish," he writes, "to see either my wife or daughter adopt these savage customs" (220). The space of the revolution is also the space of an encounter with dangerous ornamentation, the ornamentation that is also associated with figurality and thus with the material and earthbound as original and generative. Savage vanity is thus one of the displaced names for James' recognition that the logic of supplementarity is already at work in the founding moment. In the beginning there will have been ornamentation.[22]

Whatever else it may do, then, the space of revolution introduces a radical uncertainty into the experience of those who pass through it.

And this is perhaps the mark that a revolution has taken place. Seeking a space outside of a particular politics and a particular history (even as they designate it outside of all politics, the space of timeless nature or nature's God), the revolutionaries also find a space of instability and unpredictability that opens up crises of legitimacy and a challenge to all idealisms, all transcendent values. Thus it is that James' Indians are always doubled in their natural pre-political simplicity by those Indians who are unnaturally violent, "monsters left to the wild impulses of the wildest nature" (207). Located at the site of an imaginary fullness (the fullness of a pure origin) the Indians are always in danger of being appropriated either as the de-politicized "children" of this original space, or demonized as the sources of the excesses and impurities that revolutionary idealism does not want to recognize already at work in this fantastic original moment. The mutual determination of James' idealization of the Indians with his aggressive antipathy towards them thus not only recalls the democraphobia of the early republic (the widespread resistance to the politicization of the "mob" existing simultaneously with a pervasive revolutionary invocation of the sovereign "people"), but also repeats the ambivalence we discovered in his attitude towards father figures. As source of an absolute and unequivocal legitimacy outside of politics, these figures (the monarch, the good father, the people, the Indian) are simultaneously the site of a founding violence that cannot be contained within any schema. These figures generate an idealization that is indistinguishable from the kind of aggression that for the Native American made the post-revolutionary United States one enormous graveyard.

I have tried to suggest that James' breakdown in the final chapter of Crèvecoeur's *Letters From An American Farmer*, while it can be shown to be the culmination of a tension at work in other parts of the book, nevertheless inscribes the aporia of revolution (the revolution's suspension of law in the name of justice) in the form of an experience of maddening contingency: "I fly from one erratic thought to another, and my mind, irritated by these acrimonious reflections, is ready sometimes to lead me to violence" (210). As such, James' madness also figures the madness of the revolution's own failure to be at one with itself in the moment of its taking place. Moreover, I have suggested that this madness (and the "extremes of violence" that he ominously hints at as accompanying this moment) resolves itself only by appropriating the Native American and the "wilderness" space of the native village. Literalizing the revolutionary investment in a concept of nature that was never disconnected from its association with the "native" people who were its "children," James demonstrates the lines of continuity that link the revolution's displacement of a crisis of law and justice (which is simultaneously the revolution's failure to think through the concept of sovereignty) onto the body of the Native American. Rather than being late-eighteenth-century America's best example of an anti-revolutionary text, then, Crèvecoeur's *Letters From An American Farmer* is one of the most ominous examples we have of the revolution's anxiety-ridden need to displace a founding confrontation with the structural undecidability of the democratic state.

CHAPTER 3

Citizen subjects: the memoirs of Stephen Burroughs and Benjamin Franklin

> In a popular Government, the political and physical power may be
> considered as vested in the same hands, that is in a majority of the
> people, and consequently the tyrannical will of the sovereign is not
> to be controuled by the dread of an appeal to any force within the
> community.
>
> (James Madison to Thomas Jefferson, 1788)[1]

STEPHEN BURROUGHS' NOTORIETY

In 1786, the small town of Pelham, Massachusetts counted among its inhabitants both Daniel Shays and a fraudulent preacher named Stephen
Burroughs. While the fame of the former grew out of his "open" challenge to the authority of the State, Burroughs earned his notoriety by
presenting various false faces to the people of western Massachusetts.
Born in 1766 in South Killingly, Connecticut, Burroughs, the only son of
a Presbyterian clergyman, spent most of his childhood in Hanover, New
Hampshire. After an interrupted enlistment in the continental army
at age fourteen, he received education from a Connecticut minister
and at Dartmouth College in Hanover, from which he was expelled
in his sophomore year. He spent the 1780s in various parts of New
England trying to make a living without falling afoul of the local authorities. He was involved in, or accused of (among other things) preaching
under false pretences, passing counterfeit coin, and, when employed as
a schoolteacher, of sexually assaulting his female pupils. The *Memoirs
of Stephen Burroughs* were first published by Benjamin True in Hanover,
New Hampshire in 1798, and a second installment appeared in 1804.
But the most popular of the many versions was an 1809 "Sketch of the
Life of Stephen Burroughs . . . " that went through numerous reprintings
throughout New England from 1810 to 1818. According to Philip Gura
in the introduction to the most recent edition, there had been more

than twenty-five reprintings of the *Memoirs* by 1840 (Gura, "Foreword," xx–xxi).

Robert Frost was the first (in 1924) to suggest that Stephen Burroughs' *Memoirs* should be placed on the shelf next to Benjamin Franklin's *Autobiography*. "Franklin will be a reminder of what we have been as a young nation in some respects," he writes, "... Burroughs comes in reassuringly when there is question of our not unprincipled wickedness, whether we have had enough of it for salt" (Frost, "Preface to the 1924 Edition," in Burroughs, *Memoirs*, v–viii). And curiously enough, Burroughs' and Franklin's memoirs overlap at a crucial point in their publication history. Franklin's book largely documents his experiences in colonial America, although the manuscript was begun in 1771 and completed between 1784 and 1790. One year after Franklin's death a French version of his memoirs appeared in Paris, and an English translation of this edition appeared in London in 1793. An American edition, however, was not published until 1818. Thus, both Franklin's and Burroughs' memoirs found their greatest American audience in the wake of the War of 1812.[2]

But beyond their generic compatibility, and the suggestion that their texts might shed light on the cultural politics of the United States in the aftermath of the "second war of independence," what more can we say about the relationship between these two memoirs? In what respects are both men representative Americans? How can the two figures, taken together, help to inform our understanding of American revolutionary, or post-revolutionary subjectivity? Burroughs' and Franklin's memoirs share a similar investment in the American character responsible for – and shaped by – the break with England and with monarchism. Franklin's is the story of the proto-republican American written from the perspective of the revolution, while Burroughs' is the story of the neo-revolutionary American subject written in the difficult early years of independence. Yet at first glance they could not be more different. Franklin tells the story of an almost infuriatingly smooth rise from "the Poverty and Obscurity in which I was born and bred" to "a State of Affluence and some Degree of Reputation in the World" (*Autobiography*, 3), while Burroughs describes his life as "one continued course of tumult, revolution and vexation" (*Memoirs*, 1). Nevertheless, the two narratives present a number of compelling parallels. Both, to begin with, are framed as letters (Franklin's to his loyalist son, William; Burroughs' to a friend, John Griffin, for whom Burroughs' character is an "enigma" [*Memoirs*, 1]). Both tell of New England boys with little formal education who broke with their families at an early age and attempted to make it on their own in the world. One reader, citing its "falsifying rhetoric, and its subversion of the dominant social ideals of its time," has recently suggested that Burroughs' narrative be thought of as utilizing the "strategies and themes" of the traditional Spanish Picaresque (Jones, "Praying Upon Truth," 32–50). But Burroughs' narrative shares its other Picaresque elements (the tale's origin in a break with the father and the central character's penchant for tricks and disguises) with Franklin's story of exemplary civic responsibility.[3] Who is the exemplary subject of the American Revolution? Who has more to tell us about the vicissitudes of citizenship? These are the questions I want to consider in the pages that follow.

I want to think about Franklin and Burroughs by paying close attention to a handful of crucial scenes in their texts. Both writers encourage such an approach by introducing early childhood memories as exemplary character sketches. Franklin's, which he singles out "as it shows an early projecting public spirit," involves a scheme to steal building supplies at night from a construction site in order to build a fishing wharf on the swamp for the local boys. The next morning, Franklin recalls, "inquiry was made after the removers; we were discovered and complain'd of; several of us were corrected by our fathers; and tho' I pleaded the usefulness of the work, mine convinc'd me that nothing was useful which was not honest" (*Autobiography*, 10). Burroughs opens his narrative with an event which, he writes, "had a decided influence in giving a tone to the character which I sustain at this time, and in directing the operations of my after life" (*Memoirs*, 4). The principle antagonist in the story is "a neighbour of my father" who owns "a fine yard of watermelons." "One night," writes Burroughs, "he took his stand in a convenient place for watching, unknown to anyone" with the intention of discovering who it was that had been stealing his watermelons. Burroughs (whom we suspect of being the thief – although he does not tell us this) remarks that "Accident made me acquainted with the old man's situation, and suspecting his intention, I went to a son of his, a young man of about twenty, and told him I saw a man in the watermelon yard, whom I suspected to be the thief, and advised him to go cautiously to the yard, and peradventure he might catch him" (4). In due course, the boy is seen by the father, who mistakes him for the thief and beats him severely before finding out his mistake. "This scene of merriment," Burroughs writes, "I enjoyed to the full," presumably because he, like the old man before, occupied a "stand in a convenient place for watching, unknown to anyone" (4). Burroughs presents the story with some effort at apology, but clearly relishes it, and in so doing implicitly identifies himself with (even as he deceives) the authoritarian father figure whose power to inflict excessive punishment he so ingeniously manipulates.[4]

In many ways, then, these early stories – long remembered – evidence a shared investment in anti-authoritarian impulses that can be reappropriated as evidence of healthy American initiative and native independence. Burroughs, in particular, has been described by recent readers as an example of individual freedom and revolutionary resistance to dominant authority figures in the post-revolutionary United States.[5] In all Burroughs' schemes, writes Larzer Ziff, there is "a deliberate aim to discomfit authority"; Burroughs' brand of ingenious deception, Lawrence Buell writes, "might be regarded as a folk counterpart of the comparatively 'learned' or 'scholarly' cast of New England culture...but as antagonistic to the establishment conception of what counts as intellectual prowess"; Daniel A. Cohen, who includes the *Memoirs* in his study of New England crime literature, claims that Burroughs' autobiography "actually implied a sweeping rejection of traditional dogmas and hierarchies in favor of an egalitarian social order based on natural reason and fraternal benevolence"; and Jay Fliegelman suggests that Burroughs, in his *Memoirs*, counters post-revolutionary pessimism and conservatism by holding on to an "image of freedom and unlimited opportunity." "In its shamelessly self-interested way," Fliegelman continues, the *Memoirs* reads "as a plea to the new nation to embrace the new age of deception and invention." Finally, Christopher Jones writes:

Stephen Burroughs' narrative undercuts most of the key institutional powers struggling to assert themselves: the first colleges, the defensive churches and declining ministers, the early courts, the first prisons, and even the first libraries . . . The *Memoirs* does not represent a post-Revolutionary world in confident opening of democracy, but one that is provincial, overzealous, and hypocritically conservative in its attempt to assert religious, legal, and political truth.[6]

Burroughs, it would seem, lends himself to rehabilitation as a figure for democratic resistance and individual freedom. But I want to come back to consider how and at what price this becomes possible, because one also does not have to look far to find evidence in Burroughs' narrative to support Robert Gross' claim that "despite his repeated imprisonment by the same government that had suppressed the backcountry, the Dartmouth dropout never shed his identification with the cosmopolitan elite" ("The Confidence Man," 315). (Such an identification can be heard at work in the opening chapter of his *Memoirs*, where Burroughs digresses to offer some advice on teaching and parenting which he says will "habituate our youth to submit to good and wholesome laws, without being in danger of that restless turbulent disposition, which so frequently distracts the government of a Commonwealth" [8].)

Taking Burroughs at his word, then (and thus according his childhood anecdote a certain privilege as a source of information about his character), I want to think about the scene in the watermelon patch in more detail before turning to some of the other events in Burroughs' memoir that earned him his notoriety. While Franklin remains attached to his childhood story because "it shows an early projecting public Spirit" (*Autobiography*, 10), Burroughs claims no such mitigating interpretation. The corresponding affect in the Burroughs story can be found in the "scene of merriment" which he "enjoyed to the full" (*Memoirs*, 4). Burroughs' pleasure is solitary (he observes alone and in secret) and spectatorial. (The enjoyment of this "scene" is, perhaps, linked to what Burroughs goes on to describe as the "very pernicious" "romantic scenes" which he developed a passion for in the course of his early attachment to novels [5].)[7] Burroughs introduces the story about the watermelon patch as "my first entrance on the stage of life" and as evidence of a "volatile, impatient temper of mind" and an "insatiable" "thirst for amusement" (3). What the boy likes to do, it would seem, is to set up scenes for himself (and sometimes others) to watch and enjoy. He enjoyed "making [others – especially "my superiors"] appear in a ludicrous situation, so as to raise a laugh at their expense" (3). Burroughs puts himself out of sight and sets others up on an invisible stage upon which they can be observed and laughed at in their ludicrousness or their pain. It is quite clear that this entertainment involves a fantasy of power for the young man. But what kind of power is it?

The Stephen Burroughs of the watermelon patch is not interested in wronging an injustice or establishing a new order of things. What he seems invested in is a scene in which the law (figured by the father) finds itself (figured by the father's son) subject to its own violence. The law, we might even say, is forced to confront its own capacity for injustice here, and this, some might argue, constitutes the proto-progressive, or at least somewhat recuperable, aspect of Burroughs' mischief. Burroughs fools the law (here represented by the property-owning father) in the name of an idea of justice that condemns – simply by demonstrating – the law's intimacy with violence. This is the Stephen Burroughs who is celebrated by readers like Daniel Williams as "revolutionary": "Through its disruption

of traditional values and perceptions, through its insistence on the relativ-
ity of all values and perceptions, [Burroughs' book] challenged readers
to consider the subjective nature of their comprehension" (Williams,
"In Defense of Self," 113). What Williams is suggesting here is that
Burroughs, whatever the particular nature of the disruption he initiates,
can always be read as a figure for a just subjectivity, for a particularity, specificity or individuality that is ignored or abused by what gets
called "authority" (Ziff), "the establishment" (Buell), and "traditional
dogmas and hierarchies" (Cohen). Burroughs, in other words, demonstrates an investment in justice as, in Jacques Derrida's words, "infinite,
incalculable, rebellious to rule and foreign to symmetry, heterogenous
and heterotropic" ("Force of Law," 959). As such, Burroughs pro-
vokes readings that narrate – or allegorize – an antagonism between
this idea of justice and that law which is "stabilizable and statutory,
calculable, a system of regulated and coded prescriptions" (Derrida,
"Force of Law," 959). Stephen Burroughs comes to be thought of as
"revolutionary," "democratic," or "independent" in so far as he demonstrates a resistance to law and authority even if that resistance is carried
on in the name of nothing more than what he calls "merriment" (or what
we might call "the pursuit of happiness").[8]

Having failed to make a career in the military or at sea, and having
already made a bad reputation for himself in his home town as a trick-
ster and a thief, Burroughs finds himself penniless and alone, "an outcast
among mankind" (*Memoirs*, 47). Lack of funds or connections cuts off all
the career paths he can think of, yet he is in dire need of an income.
The answer comes in the form of an address: "There is one thing, said
contrivance, which you may do; and it will answer your purpose; –
preach!" (48). He takes on a pseudonym, travels down the Connecticut
river to a part of the country in which he can be sure he is unknown
and presents himself to a local minister as a clergyman in need of a
congregation. The education he has received from his father allows him
to convince this minister that he is indeed a trained and orthodox clergyman, and as a result he procures a letter of recommendation that
finally secures him employment in the town of Pelham, Massachusetts.
Burroughs' ability to perform the role of clergyman depends in large
part on his use of a number of sermons that he had previously stolen
from his father. However, he cannot dispel an air of curiosity that follows
him, and when a member of the congregation "who had wondered at
my always being prepared to preach" notices that the manuscript of one
of the sermons looks "too old to be lately written" (54) the community

becomes alarmed. They test Burroughs by asking him to preach on an assigned line of scripture at very short notice, but he succeeds in improvising a convincing sermon and thus holds on to his precarious position. Before long, however, the truth of his deception is made known to the community by visitors who recognize Burroughs, and he is forced to flee.

How does Burroughs defend himself in this instance? In a move that will become familiar, Burroughs puts his defense into the mouth of an anonymous well-wisher who appears to help Burroughs after he has been cornered in a barn by the Pelhamites. This "bystander" asks: "why need you make any difficulty? he preached well – you paid him well – all parties were satisfied, and why need you now be uneasy? What signifies what he called his name?" (71). The last question here is crucial: "What signifies what he called his name?" We all recognize this kind of justification; it proceeds from, and draws upon, a persistent tendency to distrust formal structures wherever they may seem to limit the formless freedom of truth, wisdom, or ability. The question itself reminds us that this sort of complaint always has some relationship to a more general resistance to language as that which forces the spirit into conventional or historical molds of signification. In this specific instance, what the defense says is "who cares whether or not the man is a formally, institutionally qualified and recognized preacher if he preaches well enough for us?" "Under these circumstances," Burroughs writes, "whether I ought to bear the name of imposture, according to the common acceptation, is the question" (67). In place of the rule of law, Burroughs argues, the autonomous and self-regulating sphere of social acceptation ought to be the standard of legitimation.[9] Another key word in Burroughs' defense is "circumstances," and it is with a recourse to the singularity of circumstances that Burroughs defends himself throughout the *Memoirs*. "I know the world will blame me," he writes, but "they are not capable of judging upon the matter, with any propriety, because they ever will and ever must remain ignorant of the particular causes which brought these events into existence" (67). Such an argument once again participates in a criticism of the injustice of law in general, a criticism that focuses on the law's inability to adjust itself to the particularity or individuality of any experience. The abstractions of judgments made at an (unrecoverable) distance from the events in question, such a criticism asserts, can only be countered by a narrative (a memoir) that nevertheless may only serve to, in Burroughs' words, "justify my conduct to myself" (67). In making the case for circumstantial, particular determination of the legitimate or just, Burroughs contests formal, conventional, and politically established determinations. To be a minister, Burroughs pragmatically argues, is not to be the bearer of an institutional certificate of authenticity, but to perform as a good minister in a specific situation. Like any good revolutionary, Burroughs rejects the authority of law in general in favor of a justice that resists formal representation.

The same argumentative structure recurs when Burroughs tells the story of his involvement in a famous case of counterfeiting. After failing in a venture involving the transmutation of copper into silver, Burroughs joins a friend in purchasing a quantity of counterfeit silver dollars made by the infamous coiner, Glazier Wheeler. He is caught in the act of trying to purchase goods with one of these coins and thereby launches himself into what will be an extended and painful confrontation with the legal system. When it comes to his counterfeiting exploits, Burroughs once again lets others advance the justifications he would like to be able to benefit from. His friend Lysander puts the case in an attempt to persuade the apparently reluctant Burroughs to join him in the purchase and utilization of a large amount of false coin. "I know the law speaks in general terms," Lysander begins, "because it cannot descend to particulars, there being such an infinity, as to put it beyond the power of man to comprehend the whole in a system; therefore, general principles must direct us in our interpretation of law" (82–3). In accordance with this approach, Lysander emphasizes the "spirit" of the law as that which ought to be attended to, and that "spirit" seems to be intimately associated with an appreciation for "circumstances." "The whole nature, design and spirit of law is to protect each other from injury; and where no injury is intended, nor in fact done, the whole essence of law is attended to" (82). This sounds very much like Burroughs, though it is here put into the mouth of his friend. These remarks on the "spirit" of law conclude by suggesting that under present circumstances, the key consideration ought to be the "undue scarcity of cash [which] now prevails," a fact that justifies the actions of any person who helps to "increase the quantity of cash, [and] does not only himself, but likewise the community, an essential benefit" (84). Lysander's argument here appeals to the very economic facts that lay behind the eruption of Shays' rebellion, and his call for the restitution of a "due proportion between representative property and real property" (84) borrows the terms of those grievances noted by convening farmers in the counties of western Massachusetts in the mid-1780s.[10] Perhaps here we might find a way to articulate Burroughs' solidarity with a popular form of resistance to entrenched New England political and economic power. In agreeing to help Lysander pass the coins, Burroughs would seem to have been engaging in an act of rebellion parallel to the activities of Shays' farmers.

But Burroughs' subsequent arrest for passing counterfeit coin does not endear him to the people of Pelham or to any other group of discontented citizens. He is denounced by Pelhamites as "the greatest villain in the world" (89) and his counterfeiting is considered to be merely one more example of his dangerous propensity for deception. (Indeed, Burroughs' attitude towards the people of Pelham demonstrates anything but solidarity with their marginalized position.[11] He describes the mostly Irish Presbyterian population of the town as "A people generally possessing violent passions, which once disturbed, raged, uncontrolled by the dictates of reason; unpolished in their manners, possessing a jealous disposition; and either very friendly or very inimical, not knowing a medium between those two extremes" [52]. Burroughs' only other published text, which appeared in the same year as the *Memoirs*, was a short "sermon" purporting to be the text of the speech delivered to the people of Pelham who had chased him out of the town.[12] The sermon adopts a parodic, Old Testament style to narrate a story that conflates elements of Burroughs' own persecution by the Pelhamites with references to the suppression of Shays' rebellion by the forces of General Lincoln [the "Lincolnites" in Burroughs' biblical telling]. In a style reminiscent of Federalist political parody and utilizing a racial stereotyping familiar to readers of Brackenridge and others, Burroughs mocks the people of Pelham not only because their Scottish/Irish accents prevent them from pronouncing "faith" in the "correct" manner, but also for their attempt to engage in issues of social transformation.[13] "We will leave assembling ourselves together to talk politics," he has the chastened Pelhamites announce at the end of the sermon, "and follow our occupation of raising potatoes" [340][14].) In their attempt to introduce counterfeit money into the Massachusetts economy, Burroughs and his associates might appear to have something in common with the Shaysites, whose dire shortage of credit they explicitly claim to be addressing; but the hostile response they generate suggests that for the hard-pressed people of western Massachusetts, the counterfeiters have more in common with those agents of the crown who, during the revolutionary war, introduced counterfeit currency into the rebellious colonies in order to undermine the system of continental paper money.[15] The counterfeiters presume to act with a kind of sovereign authority, effecting an arbitrary introduction of counterfeit money into the system of legitimate tender and attempting to "induce the world to deem it so."[16] In other words, it is in the act of rejecting formal legitimacy (the legitimacy of State-issued money, the legitimacy of a recognized minister, the legitimacy of general laws) that Burroughs encourages his association with rebellion and revolution on the one hand, *and* with a quasi-sovereign self-aggrandizement on the other.

In the second half of the eighteenth century in France, Foucault writes, "protests against the public execution proliferated." The spectacle itself was, for eighteenth-century reformers, "dangerous," because "it provided a support for a confrontation between the violence of the king and the violence of the people" (*Discipline and Punish*, 73). "In this violence," according to [the reformers], "tyranny confronts rebellion; each calls forth the other. It is a double danger" (*Discipline and Punish*, 74). Burroughs' formative story is right at home in this classical paradigm, since, as I have been suggesting, the *Memoirs* regularly participate in the confrontation between tyranny and rebellion that Foucault's eighteenth-century reformers recognized in the public execution. The sovereign force of the authoritative father, or of the law, is directly confronted by the rebellious force of the notorious Stephen Burroughs. But if Burroughs' *Memoirs* give us the classical erotics of sovereign violence (the monarch and the rebel in open combat) what are they doing here – in post-revolutionary, republican America? Does the popularity of the *Memoirs* testify to an odd wave of juridico-political nostalgia in the early republic? And how is that Burroughs, if he is perpetually drawn towards a pre-modern scene of antagonistic power relations, can be appropriated – even today – as a figure for freedom or popular autonomy? The real enigma of Burroughs' character in other words, is his simultaneous participation in marginal-democratic *and* elitist-conservative post-revolutionary rhetoric. He exhibits the racism and anti-populism of a Fisher Ames or a Samuel Miller, even as he embodies everything that conservative discourse assigned to the chaotic spread of democratic values in the new nation. Hence, the confusion in contemporary critical accounts of Burroughs' political significance for the early republic. Was Burroughs an unfortunate revolutionary or a bungling reactionary? Defending himself against the charges of rape brought against him while teaching school in Charlton, Massachusetts, Burroughs reproduces a letter from a "gentleman of high respectability, and an old practitioner of law" (*Memoirs*, 212), supporting the not guilty verdict. The lawyer writes (once again serving Burroughs as a mouthpiece): "When we find a private person injured by a public body, many circumstances are combined to lead the candid mind astray in the investigation of such a subject... Popular clamor will be raised against the injured person; this is like the noise of the waters of Niagara; this swallows up the small voice of the individual" (217). The salient terms here once again reproduce a familiar discourse on justice: justice demands attention to the individual; justice is at odds with the "public body" (in part because as "body" the public is already at a material remove from the ethereal essence of personhood); justice is almost silent (it stands little chance against the "clamor" of popular speech).[17] What begins to emerge from a close analysis of Burroughs' text, I would suggest, is a repeated encounter with a claim on justice that is inextricable from a presumption of sovereign authority and power. Burroughs figures a resistance to mediation in the name of an individual self-empowerment that can be read *either* as revolutionary *or* as despotic. What we are in fact reminded of in the story of Stephen Burroughs is Jay Fliegelman's comment on the Declaration of Independence's "paradoxical" castigation of the unmasked George III: "Tyranny thus becomes defined not only as the abuse of power but more fundamentally as the principle of a free and independent will. . . . By demonizing George, the Declaration stigmatizes individual willfulness at the same time that it articulates an ideology of individual liberty. Independence is thus carefully separated from, and paradoxically made antithetical to, free will" (*Declaring Independence*, 144). "The Declaration," to repeat, "stigmatizes individual willfulness at the same time that it articulates an ideology of individual liberty." What Fliegelman calls a "paradox" in the Declaration of Independence recurs in our reading of Stephen Burroughs' *Memoirs*, where it presents itself as the impossibility of separating, for once and for all, the sovereign violence of arbitrary power from the individualizing demand for justice. It is impossible to say conclusively whether a text like Burroughs' (and its example will be echoed throughout the American literary tradition) represents the spirit of a valuable anti-authoritarianism – a valuable refusal to over-estimate the law and a valuable lesson for the law about its fallibility and its own relationship to violence (not to mention a representation of individual initiative, cunning, and bravery) or, whether what we are shown is a thirst for sovereign violence that escapes any attempt to appropriate it for a positive political or moral agenda. Burroughs, here and throughout his memoir, usefully figures an undecidability that I will, perhaps counterintuitively, call revolutionary (Burroughs, you will recall, referred to his life as "one continued course of tumult, *revolution* and vexation" (*Memoirs*, 1, my emphasis.) His resistance awaits reappropriation within a discourse that would grant it a retrospective legitimacy or a retrospective conformity with a justice that law had failed to address.

Calling Burroughs revolutionary, however, also means rethinking what we mean by this word in an American context. Burroughs' persona, I suggest, helps us to understand the difference between the revolutionary subject and what Etienne Balibar calls the "Citizen Subject" of modern democracy. Balibar writes:

> The citizen can be simultaneously considered as the constitutive element of the State and as the actor of a revolution. Not only the actor of a founding revolution, a *tabula rasa* whence a state emerges, but the actor of a *permanent* revolution . . . the actor of such a revolution is no less "utopic" than the member of the abstract State, the State of the rule of law. (Balibar, "Citizen Subject," 54)[18]

To call Stephen Burroughs a revolutionary figure is thus to explain his continuing appeal to a democratic imaginary while registering his limitations as a model of the democratic subject. The narrator of the *Memoirs of Stephen Burroughs* gives readers access to the "utopic" revolutionary citizen (he who eludes the status of pure juridical subject imposed upon him by the law), and hence his fascination (a fascination he will share with all those other outlaw heroes of American literature). But where should we look for a similarly exaggerated portrait of the "no less 'utopic' . . . member of the abstract State, the State of the rule of law"?

BENJAMIN FRANKLIN'S EXEMPLARY SUBJECTIVITY

Michael Warner has given us the best account to date of the figure for whom, as Warner puts it, "the personal is founded on and valued within the pure reproduction of the social, not, as is usually assumed, the other way around" (*The Letters of the Republic*, 87). For Warner, it is Franklin's professional relationship to the growth of print culture in eighteenth-century America that explains his particular identification with "a social erotic . . . freed from the localization of the personal, the bodily, the corruptible" (87). Warner explicitly links Franklin's pursuit of "print negativity" with the republican political principles of civic virtue that Warner wants to claim as central to the American Revolution: "In Franklin's career the virtuous citizen of the republic attests to his virtue by constituting himself in the generality of letters . . . his career is designed at every point to exploit the homology between print discourse and representative polity. He cashes in like no one else on the resource of negativity. The logic of his career is the logic of representation" (96).

Franklin, and this is something we have long known, demonstrates a remarkable tendency to identify with the force of language. Franklin's

Autobiography refers repeatedly – using a printer's term – to the "*errata*" of his life; at one point he imagines his own reincarnation in the form of a "second edition" complete with an author's corrections; and his self-penned epitaph (which he enjoyed passing out) referred to his dead body as "the Cover of an old Book, Its Contents torn out" (*Writings*, 91). Hence, as Warner puts it, "although Franklin has been (at least since Weber's *Protestant Ethic and the Spirit of Capitalism*) the exemplary figure of modernity, his exemplary modern subjectivity can be read as a very special cultural articulation of printing" (*The Letters of the Republic*, 75). What made Franklin unusual was his early and consistent tendency to see the returns that would accrue to the autonomous subject on the other side of a depersonalizing detour through print's anonymity.

Franklin's delight in textual invisibility is apparent in the following scene from "Poor Richard Improved" (July 7, 1757, marking twenty-five years since the first "Poor Richard" Almanack). Franklin's most famous alter ego tells the story of encountering a group of people awaiting an auction of merchant goods. The crowd call on one Father Abraham to address them on the question "what think you of the Times?" The old man then gives a long speech that is essentially a "Poor Richard's Greatest Hits." Richard himself listens attentively without, of course, revealing himself to anyone, and then comments that "my Vanity was wonderfully delighted with it, though I was conscious that not a tenth Part of the Wisdom was my own which he ascribed to me, but rather the *Gleanings* I had made of the Sense of all Ages and Nations" (*Writings*, 1302).

One might discount Richard's invisibility in this scene if it were not that a rupture between particular, identifiable presence and the persuasiveness of Poor Richard's maxims had long been (and continues to be) a vital part of their force. Poor Richard intuits (and his readers would have gone along with this) that the success of Father Abraham's speech depends on Richard's remaining anonymous in the crowd. But then a strange thing happens. The crowd, we are told, having listened to the sermon, then proceed to conduct themselves at the auction directly contrary to the advice given. Richard himself, however, heeds the advice given by this quoted performance of his own quotations: "I resolved," he writes, "to be the better for the Echo of it; and though I had at first determined to buy Stuff for a new Coat, I went away resolved to wear my old One a little longer" (1302–3). Two curious dynamics are at work here. First, we come to realize that as successful subjects of Franklin's text we have been identifying, although we may not have realized it, not with the crowd of listeners but with Poor Richard himself. We sneer at the crowd's imperviousness to rules of wisdom and identify with the solitary man of sense. But this Richard is an odd figure. He is the figure capable of hearing his own words come back at him as if for the first time. He becomes the subject of the echo of his own maxims – and we ideal readers follow suit. Before our eyes, the author has disappeared leaving only a disembodied and highly persuasive set of moral and economic rules. What we are in fact witnessing is a memorable example of what Michael Warner calls "the submersion of the personal in a general reproduction" (*The Letters of the Republic*, 89).[19]

But let us look closer at Franklin's relationship to secrecy. Students are regularly surprised, and not a little disappointed, to find that Franklin devotes so little space in his memoirs to his sexual life. Towards the end of the first part of the *Autobiography*, Franklin mentions his first brush with marriage. In a handful of very matter-of-fact sentences Franklin explains that although the "girl" in question was "very deserving," the financial terms of the union were not acceptable to him and so the match came to an end (74–5). He soon discovers that "the Business of a Printer being generally thought a poor one, I was not to expect Money with a Wife unless with such a one, as I should not otherwise think agreeable." The situation is urgent, however, since, "In the mean time, that hard-to-be-govern'd Passion of Youth, had hurried me frequently into Intrigues with low Women that fell in my Way, which were attended with some Expense and great Inconvenience, besides a continual Risk to my Health" (75).[20] Thus, before the paragraph is out, a wife (Miss Deborah Reed) has been found. "She prov'd a good and faithful Helpmate," writes Franklin, "assisted me much by attending Shop, we throve together, and have ever mutually endeavoured to make each other happy" (76).

The account of Franklin's sexual life is, in other words, strikingly condensed and ultimately suggests an impatience to get on with the real story he wants to tell. And indeed, it is hard not to be struck by the palpable increase in pleasure expressed by Franklin in the following paragraphs. And what is the source of this pleasure? His introduction of the subscription library in Philadelphia in 1730:

About this time our club meeting, not at a Tavern, but in a little room of Mr. Grace's set apart for that purpose; a proposition was made by me that since our books were often referr'd to in our disquisitions upon the queries, it might be convenient to us to have them all together where we met, that upon occasion they might be consulted; and by thus clubbing our books to a common library, we should, while we lik'd to keep them together, have each of us the advantage of using the books of all the other members, which would be nearly as beneficial as if each owned the whole. (76–7)

From the success of this venture Franklin goes on to propose a subscription library (The Library Company of Philadelphia) which became, in his proud words, "the Mother of all the North American Subscription Libraries now so numerous." Franklin continues: "It is become a great thing itself, and continually increasing. These libraries have improv'd the general conversation of the Americans, made the common tradesmen and farmers as intelligent as most gentlemen from other countries, and perhaps have contributed in some degree to the stand so generally made throughout the colonies in defense of their privileges" (77). It is not too much to say, I believe, that Franklin gets the equivalent of an erotic charge out of the way in which his library is founded and functions. There is a kind of magic involved when a group of individuals (men, of course) get together and by collective action succeed in making something from nothing (in this case, their collaboration somehow produces more books for everyone, "*as if* each owned the whole"). The activity – and here Franklin's language helps us out – is certainly reproductive: Franklin's initiative produced the "Mother" of all libraries, and the progeny are still increasing. The very idea of the library thrills Franklin: it is insistently social and self-dispersing – it is only by relinquishing some degree of individual proprietorial control that one can come to gain access to a shared profit. The library thrives on the impossibility of separating individual from social enrichment. Seen from an angle that would have been very clear to Franklin and his early associates, the library raises the intriguing possibility of borrowing your own property, a kind of rupture in proprietorial self-presence that is quintessentially Franklinian.

But there is another element to the library venture that Franklin himself clearly wanted to remember. The last line of the first part of the *Autobiography* is a note Franklin writes to himself about what he should remember to address next: "My manner of acting to engage the People in this and future undertakings" (77). And despite not having access to this manuscript when he begins the second part thirteen years later, he remains true to his word and writes in more detail of how he went about encouraging people to subscribe to the new library:

The Objections and Reluctances I met with in Soliciting the Subscriptions, made me soon feel the impropriety of presenting one's self as the Proposer of any useful Project that might be suppos'd to raise one's Reputation in the smallest degree above that of one's Neighbours, when one has need of their Assistance to accomplish the project. I therefore put myself as much as I could out of sight, and stated it as a Scheme of a *number of friends*, who had requested me to go about and propose it to such as they thought Lovers of Reading. In this way the Affair went on more smoothly, and I ever after practis'd it on such Occasions; and from my frequent Successes, can heartily recommend it. (87)

Not for the first or last time, Franklin deploys a certain secrecy in order to persuade the public. The public, Franklin realizes, responds far better to proposals that, in one way or another, do not proceed *directly* from any individual speaker. In this case, Franklin merely ventriloquizes the proposals of "a *number of friends*," but as we know, Franklin was just as apt to use print anonymity or pseudonymity to elicit public support (as, for example, in his "Modest Enquiry into the Nature and Necessity of a Paper-Currency," and his 1767 anonymous pamphlet ventriloquizing a British respondent to colonial grievances in such a way as to ridicule the British position and expose their injustices). Franklin's publications deployed an enormous number of pseudonyms from Poor Richard and Father Abraham, to the King of Prussia and Polly Baker.[21] Moreover, in each case he was simultaneously drawing on a force of anonymity that his invented characters both announced and concealed. Language, particularly printed language, has an authority all its own, and Franklin more perhaps than anyone in eighteenth-century America enjoyed this fact. Print's metonymic relationship to the public (as the stuff of mass reproduction and with a uniformity that could always figure equality) gave it a persuasive authority in a proto-democratic society that Franklin never lost sight of. Indeed, as the story of Poor Richard's encounter with his own words suggests, the persuasive authority of words was something Franklin not only enjoyed manipulating but something he enjoyed being self-subjected to. If one of the achievements of the democratic revolution was to replace bodies at the center of state power (the body of the king; inheritable royal blood) with structures of representation, written law, and elected positions, then Franklin gives us an unforgettable example of an individual who was particularly at home with this kind of disembodied authority. To say that Franklin, as he says of himself, is "public spirited" is to say that he identifies – in an unusually intense manner – with the anonymous bodiless structures and devices of the State.[22]

The character of Benjamin Franklin is invested in ways of dispersing the self in language, then, but this is not to say that he remains unaware of the returns of power occasioned by this dispersal. "The present little sacrifice of your vanity," he writes (and I will be returning to Franklin's use of this word "sacrifice" below), after commenting on the efficacy of anonymity, "will afterwards be amply repaid. If it remains a while uncertain to whom the Merit belongs, some one more vain than yourself will be

encourag'd to claim it, and then even envy will be dispos'd to do you justice, by plucking those assumed feathers, and restoring them to their right
owner" (87). Once again, Franklin realizes an investment in the authority of a disembodied legitimating force, here named "Envy." Franklin's
perpetually re-solved dilemma is to gain something like sovereign approval in a post-monarchical world. Franklin sought out ways to allow
the public (or a representative public voice) to exercise (or feel that it
has exercised) its autonomy over individuals in the course of recognizing
a particular individual. What he discovered – to his advantage – was
that the sovereignty of public opinion is preserved and supported by the
anonymity and authority of print. In this respect the print revolution
(if we can call it that) radicalized an experience generated by writing in
general: the experience of writing as both a medium for exercising the
will and as an experience of the self's distancing from the self, the self's
loss in writing. Franklin, peculiarly capable of identifying his subjectivity
with the medium of print (as the story of his epigraph makes very clear),
anticipated the returns available to one who was at ease with the self-
disrupting aspect of writing and print. The result was that this resolutely
anonymous, public-spirited, ventriloquizing man of multiple disguises
and pseudonyms became the first internationally famous American.

If we accept Warner's characterization of Franklin, then (and it is
hard to refute), we might expect to find no principle of correspondence
between the notorious Stephen Burroughs and the man whose "closest analogue," in Warner's concluding suggestion, "may be the fictive
speaking voice of the written constitution" (*The Letters of the Republic*, 96).
Burroughs, the man whose "deliberate aim," Larzer Ziff writes, seems
to have been "to discomfit authority" (*Writing in the New Nation*, 61), gives
us what appears to be a direct antithesis of Franklin, the exemplary republican. Burroughs, in his paradigmatic childhood scene, succeeds in
making the law into an ass (in the service of an individual appropriation
of sovereign power), while Franklin, time and again, succeeds in tran-
substantiating his words into the forcefully anonymous text of public law.
Burroughs registers an unusual desire to appropriate the law's sovereign
violence for himself; Franklin displays an equally unusual investment in
transferring sovereignty to the anonymous text of the law.

If we are to persist in thinking of Burroughs and Franklin as figures
for the double-aspect of democracy's citizen-subject then perhaps we
need to consider certain structural similarities between their respective
scenes of secret pleasure. For in both Burroughs' watermelon patch and
Franklin's Father Abraham sketch, an economy of secrecy is indissociable

from the drama of power redeployed. The sovereign violence in the watermelon patch and the sovereign force of Poor Richard's maxims are both shadowed by the secret presence (or non-presence) of Burroughs, on the one hand, and Richard (which is to say, ultimately, Franklin) on the other. The revolutionary Burroughs and the lawmaker Franklin share a detour through secrecy at the moment of their realization of power. Franklin's "untempered pursuit of print negativity," as Warner phrases it (*The Letters of the Republic*, 96), represents an engagement with secrecy on the part of republican political practice that does not easily or absolutely distinguish itself from Stephen Burroughs' self-serving concealments. Burroughs' status as representative of an outlaw individuality, consistently confronting structures of impersonal mediation designed to produce a civic order, crosses paths with Franklin's republican personality at the site of a self-dissolution that seems to have everything to do with the citizen-subject's relationship to law and justice. To read these two characters as mutually representative of the subject of American democracy would be to confront their shared relationship to a self-concealment or secrecy that is *undecidably* violent (which is also to say, *undecidably* just). It would also be to find the democratic citizen-subject at the site of a deconstruction of a familiar and resilient opposition between law, convention, or the institution on the one hand, and nature, freedom, and independence (and their political cognates) on the other.[23] Post-monarchophobic political theory recognizes both characters (Burroughs with his appeals to singularity, Franklin with his quasi-erotic fascination with giving the law) as subjects of American democracy. Such a recognition seeks to avoid repeated invocations of one or the other (or of their many descendents) as, in their isolation, quintessentially American or democratic. For while Burroughs' example suggests that we cannot simply stand up for the justice of singularity, it is also easy to see why we might hesitate to embrace the Franklinian subject of the law as the archetypal subject of democracy. Franklin's identification with the forms and instruments of administration can quickly begin to sound like the kind of aestheticization of the disembodied State that we have learned to become wary of, at least since 1939 ("[Mankind's] self-alienation," wrote Walter Benjamin in the 1930s, "has reached such a degree that it can experience its own destruction as an aesthetic pleasure of the first order. This is the situation of politics which Fascism is rendering aesthetic"[24]). Perhaps at this point we need to go behind the scenes and listen to Franklin speaking from behind the closed doors of the law in order to hear again what should never have been "whisper'd abroad."

FRANKLIN'S "SPEECH IN THE CONVENTION"

At the end of his chapter on Franklin, Michael Warner suggests that the persona he has been describing reached a kind of apex in the "Speech in the Convention" that Franklin wrote to be delivered at the end of the Constitutional Convention in Philadelphia in September of 1787:

> It is with the Constitution, therefore, at the climax of Franklin's career, that his lifelong effort to locate himself in the generality of republican letters finds its embodiment. In his well-known speech to the convention, Franklin submerges his own voice to the motion for unanimous passage, authorizing as his own the voice of the document, as publication comes literally to constitute the public in yet another pseudonymous text. (*Letters of the Republic*, 96)

Franklin's speech, in other words, is an instance of that exemplary citizenship which "does not relate to the realization of any foundation or end other than the mere institution of the city."[25] Franklin's speech is an appeal to members of the convention to put aside their petty differences and objections and band together to produce the politically efficacious appearance of unanimity. Franklin (who was apparently prevented by illness from actually delivering the speech in person) wrote:

> If every one of us, in returning to our Constituents, were to report the objections he has had to it, and endeavour to gain Partisans in support of them, we might prevent its being generally received and thereby lose all the salutary effects and great advantages resulting naturally in our favour among foreign nations, as well as among ourselves, from our real or apparent unanimity. (*Writings*, 1140)[26]

The speech is eminently reasonable and explicitly self-deprecating ("the older I grow the more apt I am to doubt my own judgement and to pay more respect to the judgement of others"[27]). What stands out, from a stylistic perspective, is the plethora of words associated with the form and order of government (administration, consideration, information, judgment, Constitution, government, administration [three times], wisdom, production, system, unanimity, efficiency, integrity, instrument). Franklin's short speech represents the work of the convention as the work of selfless and efficient bureaucratic engineering, and he appeals to members' pride in their participation in this eminently civic activity. Franklin, that is to say, appeals to the delegates' public spirit. But Franklin's speech also harbors a word that I think not only contrasts with the dominant register of the piece, but allows us to develop another reading. Franklin writes: "Thus I consent, Sir, to this Constitution, because

I expect no better, and because I am not sure that it is not the best. The opinions I have had of its errors I sacrifice to the public good. I have never whisper'd a syllable of them abroad. Within these walls they were born, and here they shall die" (1140). What is the concept of sacrifice doing here, in the middle of one of Franklin's most important rhetorical efforts? What could be less civic, less reasonable, less efficient, and orderly than sacrifice? Surely, even the commentators who spoke of the secret goings-on within the walls of the constitutional convention (see chapter four) were not imagining that sacrifice was taking place – human sacrifice at that! Here is a ritual violence that seems at odds with the peacemaking rhetoric of compromise that Franklin seems most invested in reproducing in this speech. There is something faintly unnerving about the coincidence of a theologically inflected language of sacrifice and the vocabulary of *technique* in this speech (and it was Franklin, we ought to remember, who attempted to have prayer built into the structure of the convention's proceedings[28]). Franklin's vocabulary, in other words, invites us to think about this scene of the law's construction as a techno-theological scene of efficiency and sacrifice.

What, precisely, has been sacrificed, according to Franklin? It is, to begin with, Franklin's "opinions," the same opinions that, he begins by telling us, he has been obliged to change many times in response to "better information or fuller consideration" over the course of his long life. (Recall, too, his reference to the "little sacrifice of your vanity" that Franklin said was necessary to enjoy the full returns of print anonymity [*Autobiography*, 87].) But Franklin asks that the other men sacrifice their opinions too. He calls for a general sacrifice of opinion, that opinion – or is it? – which he elsewhere refers to in this way: "Much of the strength and efficiency of any government, in procuring and securing happiness to the people, depends on opinion, on the general opinion of the goodness of that government as well as of the wisdom and integrity of its governors" (*Writings*, 1141). Franklin seems to be suggesting that in order to gain the good opinion of the people, the delegates at the convention should sacrifice their own opinions, this despite the fact that, as Franklin observes, the delegates themselves are "part of the people" (1141). The individual opinions of the delegates must be sacrificed in a gesture that acknowledges the sovereign power of popular opinion in order to achieve strong and efficient government.[29] This government, Franklin implies, depends upon a sacrificial subjectivity: one in which the subject's participation in – and benefit from – the general (the people) depends upon the subject's capacity to sacrifice the personal or idiosyncratic. And Franklin presents himself as the exemplary sacrificial subject of this republic. "Most men indeed as well as most sects in religion," writes Franklin, "think them-selves in possession of all truth, and that wherever others differ from them it is so far error" (1139). But this certainty of one's own particular monopoly on the truth is what must be sacrificed, says Franklin, if there is to be a United States of America. In other words, it is the very force of singularity, singularity's claim on justice that must be sacrificed, here at the construction of the nation's defining law. It is an individual resis-tance to the convenience of unanimity (which as Franklin unabashedly points out, gives a nation force in the face of its enemies) that must be sacrificed.[30] It is the subject who is sacrificed here for the sake of citi-zenship. I am using the word "subject" here in its post-feudal sense to refer to that political actor who is usually addressed in the revolution-ary United States as a member of "the people": "Those among us who cannot entirely approve the *new* Constitution," wrote one respondent to Franklin's published speech,

are of opinion, in order that any form may well be administered, and thus be made a blessing to the people, that there ought to be at least, an express reservation of certain inherent unalienable rights, which it would be equally sacrilegious for the people to *give away*, as for the government to *invade*. If the rights of conscience, for instance, are not sacredly reserved to the people, what security will there be, in case the government should have in their heads a predilection for any *one* sect in religion? ("'Z' Replies to Franklin's Speech," in Bailyn, ed., *The Debate on the Constitution*, 1, 6–7)

Franklin asks the delegates to act like citizens and sacrifice their status as subjects in order that they may win the support of – and simultane-ously help bring into being – the subject-citizens of the United States of America, of whom they are, just to complete this dizzying chain, a "part."[31]

Why does Franklin have to proceed so carefully in calling for this sacrifice, if not because he knows that the violence of the sacrifice may offend justice? Such a sacrifice bears all the marks of a revolutionary act, an act about which it will only retrospectively be possible to say that it was or was not violent. This sacrifice that Franklin is calling for, in which it will be hard to say who is the subject and who the object (it demands a self-doubling on the part of every delegate) inscribes a moment of suspense here at the origin of the law. It is Franklin who calls for this act, the self-sacrifice that may or may not succeed in founding the United States. But of course he succeeds very well in making himself out to be listening to this voice too (not merely, as I noted above, by his "fortuitous" inability to deliver the words himself). His speech, its lesson, seems not to proceed from his opinion but from the invisible voice of wisdom. Franklin "*cannot help*" expressing the wish for unanimity; he uses "*we*" constantly; he "confesses" his reservations, but he will ask the listeners to transcend the confessional in their decision; "Information" and "consideration," he admits, have obliged him to change his opinion in the past. The system they have come up with "astonish[es]" him by its proximity to "perfection" (*Writings*, 1140). Franklin's grammatical performance of self-sacrifice (which among other things, succeeds in presenting his own access to the knowledge of perfection in the form of a sentence in which the "I" is merely astonished at the achievement of the whole body of men working together), provides the rhetorical force necessary to encourage the general self-sacrifice of unanimity.[32] Franklin adds to the end of his record of this speech the following remarks: "Then the motion was made for adding the last formula, viz Done in Convention by the unanimous Consent etc. – which was agreed to and added – accordingly" (1141). With these words a sacrifice is completed before the law, at the founding of the Law that will constitute the United States.[33] Oddly enough, the violence exacted upon individual autonomy (opinion) by the requirements of unanimity is paid for not just by the promise of a strong nation (a strength that will reward everyone in the convention as part of the nation) but also by the concept of sacrifice itself. Invoking sacrifice at this moment, Franklin offers the founders a way to inscribe themselves and their founding within the religious or transcendental aneconomy of the gift. If the future returns of this present sacrifice of vanity and opinion are not certain enough to persuade the founders, the shortfall can be more than made up, Franklin hazards, by the aura of sacrifice – the aura of the founding gift.[34] Merely by attending the convention, Benjamin Rush wrote, Franklin exhibited a "spectacle of transcendent benevolence"; a French commentator referred to Franklin as the "soul" of the convention: one could almost be forgiven for thinking that Franklin had returned from the grave for the occasion.[35] But with his invocation and performance of an exemplary self-sacrifice, Franklin made this transcendence available for all the delegates.

That this quasi-theological moment of founding requires a sacrifice should not, perhaps, be surprising. Nor should the fact that it has been forgotten, displaced, and repeated elsewhere. The democratic, post-monarchical political state and its political subjects are indebted to a structure of secrecy and sacrifice that is everywhere repudiated by democracy's insistence on its absolute commitment to transparency and reason. (Nathaniel Gorham, a delegate from Massachusetts, asked Franklin for permission to use his speech to help secure ratification in his home state. However, he first removed the crucial sentence referring to the "sacrifice" of Franklin's opinions for the sake of unanimity. This version was reprinted twenty-six times throughout New England in 1787 [Oberg, "'Plain, insinuating, persuasive,'" 183–4].) Other sacrifices inevitably come to take the place of this founding sacrifice made in secret among these white men, sacrifices that stand in for the rupture in the self that these men discovered was the price of democratic subjecthood and democratic power. The concept of sacrifice, that in one way or another continues to be passed down to us as a way to honor the founders, is the transcendental displacement of an aporetic self-renunciation irreducibly structured into the democratic citizen and his or her state. How, after 1787 or 1789, does this secret and potentially very disorienting, effeminizing, self-sacrifice displace its anxiety onto other sacrificial victims? Franklin's anecdote about the "certain French lady" who claims always to be in the right (at the opening of his speech) serves, it turns out, to prepare the way in advance for a displacement of male anxiety about this sacrifice onto the anonymous woman figured as incapable of such a sacrifice. "*Il n'y a que moi qui a toujours raison*," writes Franklin, in yet another ventriloquization that has everything to do with the self's management of its impossible presence. The French phrase is translated by Franklin (not quite correctly) as "I meet with no body but myself that's *always* in the right" (*Writings*, 1140). In Franklin's version, this scapegoated "French lady" is caught meeting with herself in a scene of self-doubling that displaces the convention's anxiety about its own act of self-authorization onto a "silly" and "effeminate" other.[36] Franklin's "French lady" (voiced, presumably, by James Wilson) is our campy founding "mother": it is the convention, after all, that meets with no body who could be more "in the right" about how to establish the law of the United States.[37] Franklin's anecdote displaces anxiety about the fabulous retroactivity of the founding "coup of force" onto precisely those figures (the feminine, the French, and hence onto all those radical impassioned democrats vaguely collected under the phrase "Jacobin") who are considered to be incapable of the civic self-sacrifice that founds the State in the citizen's self-difference.[38] This complex structure displaces founding anxiety about self-sacrifice by telling a story in which particular others are sacrificed even as a sacred few cash in on the rewards of a patriotic self-sacrifice. The equivocality of sacrifice – sacrifice as annihilation or as transubstantiation – generates narratives (or allegories) which attempt to overcome this equivocality. Sacrifice is one name for the founding gesture of keeping back (secreting) what is yet to come, what can only come if it is kept back or kept secret. And what is kept back here is precisely that privileged subject of independent opinion, the subject of the rights and liberties of the newly independent American citizen, in the name of whom this secrecy takes place. The theological gesture – the sacrifice of a secret that lives and dies "within these walls" – comes in to give a temporal, philosophical, and political structure of undecidability some desperately needed transcendental assurance.

What Franklin is asking these delegates to sacrifice, these delegates who are among the most socially, economically, and legally powerful men in the new nation, is also that in them which corresponds, for our purposes, to the force of Stephen Burroughs' particularity. Recall the words of that "gentleman of high respectability, and an old practitioner of law" (*Memoirs*, 212) whom Burroughs quotes in the *Memoirs* in order to defend his reputation: "When we find a private person injured by a public body, many circumstances are combined to lead the candid mind astray in the investigation of such a subject... Popular clamor will be raised against the injured person; this is like the noise of the waters of Niagara; this swallows up the small voice of the individual" (217). "Popular clamor" versus the "small voice of the individual." These are the terms of a distinction raised, albeit in a more nuanced manner, by Franklin's speech to the convention. But in the speech, Franklin asks that the delegates' individual voices be sacrificed, at the last, in order to help gain the approval of a popular clamor that, he importantly recognizes, the delegates themselves are part of: "I hope therefore for our sakes, as a part of the people, and for the sake of our posterity, we shall act heartily and unanimously in recommending this Constitution, wherever our influence may extend" (*Writings*, 1141). Franklin's speech helps us to recognize the importance of Etienne Balibar's invocation of the two aspects of the citizen-subject of democracy: the constitutive element of the State and the actor of a revolution. What Franklin's speech reminds us is that these two aspects cannot be – or should not be – mapped onto two competing political programs. The State-identified, culturally and politically privileged, legally powerful delegates at the convention are nevertheless addressed by Franklin as the subjects of individual claims on the truth that must be sacrificed before the law. Burroughs, the outlaw, chased from town to town, struggling to support himself and his family, consistently identified with criminal behavior, nevertheless finds himself at odds with the "ordinary" people of New England.[39] Thus, Philp Gura, in his introduction to the most recent edition, tells us what Burroughs kept to himself, namely, that the lawyer who spoke up for Burroughs' "small, individual voice" and against the injustice of "popular clamor" was Robert Treat Paine, Attorney-General of the Commonwealth in 1787, who, among other things, drew up the "black list" against the leaders of Shays' rebellion and led the prosecution in the courts. Not surprisingly, then, Robert Gross, reluctant to embrace Burroughs as a figure for popular freedom, suggests that "Burroughs found his friends in the enemies of the back-country" (Gura, "Foreword," xvi; and Gross, "Confidence Man," 315 n. 28). Stephen Burroughs' "permanent revolution," that is to say, betrays a significant relationship to the State apparatus that helped to limit the spread of excess democracy in western Massachusetts. Burroughs' story suggests that the "small, individual voice" leans on (and supports) a hierarchical and anti-democratic system of political power.[40] At the same time, Burroughs' narrative reminds us that it is only by way of an encounter with sacrifice and self-rupture of the kind that Franklin invoked in the convention (and deployed throughout his career) that the "small, individual voice" can realize political power under democracy. For Stephen Burroughs, however, the power of his voice would be realized in the form of literary infamy. It would be in the form of his popular – and still engaging – memoirs, that Burroughs would inscribe sacrifice and concealment. In a remarkably empirical way, however, this literary sacrifice and secrecy came to be felt by Burroughs proleptically. Stephen Burroughs disappeared into his fictional self.

THE DISAPPEARANCE OF STEPHEN BURROUGHS

Burroughs' revolutionary leanings found their only post-revolutionary outlet in the dispersed charisma of notoriety. Burroughs writes, at first, of the thrill he gets from the excessive reputation that has preceded him to Dartmouth (where he is a student for two years). From his jail cell in Springfield, Burroughs proudly reports that "many people" visit him daily "out of curiosity, to see a character entirely new," and this attention begins to make him think that he was indeed "a man of some consequence" (*Memoirs*, 93–5). As Philip Gura has noted, Burroughs reports "with no small degree of pride," "several greatly inflated, and at times wholly fanciful, accounts of his exploits," for example, that he stole, Robin Hood-like, from the rich and gave to the poor ("Foreword," xiv).

The mythology that surrounds Burroughs, and surrounded him both before and after publication of his *Memoirs*, produces a character whose singular importance coincides with his undecidably referential status in post-revolutionary New England. The man who asserts the singularity of circumstances and the value of an independent self-reliance becomes a peculiarly social, discursive, and reproducible figure. He becomes a fictional character long before his *Memoirs* achieve best-seller status. Late in his narrative Burroughs tells of what would become a familiar kind of experience. Traveling in Massachusetts, he is asked about the wife he has eloped with, and Burroughs, being unmarried, is understandably perplexed. He soon discovers, however, that a man calling himself Stephen Burroughs had recently stolen a young bride from a respectable family who had forbidden the marriage, and taken her off to Hanover. Soon thereafter he is also accused of being "Stephen Burroughs," the horse stealer in Connecticut:

A number of instances, similar to these, have occurred since I came upon the stage of action. You will readily understand what consequences would naturally follow from such events. I found the world ever ready to give credit to such reports. When mankind had once formed an unfavorable opinion, it was hard to eradicate such an idea, even by the most pointed evidence. (*Memoirs*, 223)

(Burroughs then supplys a footnote detailing other such instances of "Stephen Burroughs" getting into trouble in New York in 1808.) Burroughs even takes some pleasure from encounters with individuals who talk to him about the notorious "Stephen Burroughs," including a physician who declares that Burroughs' "countenance" had deceit written all over it, whereas, he tells his unknown companion, "I never saw a more striking contrast, than between the designing, deceitful countenance of Burroughs, and your open, frank, and candid countenance" (224). (He tells at least one more story of enjoying listening to a "gentleman of the law from Boston" complain about the "barefaced and horrid crimes" of Stephen Burroughs as they share a coach together. Upon revealing his true identity, Burroughs "laughed aloud," 263–4).

In addition to these multiple "Stephen Burroughs," of course, we are told of the various personas Burroughs invents to hide his past. Having fled from prison in Worcester, Massachusetts, he is forced to invent a pseudonym in order to take up a teaching position on Shelter Island. Before long, however, his fake identity has become a fully fledged story of important English connection and Burroughs finds himself "in a situation somewhat disagreeable," a condition "in which I was obliged, in some measure, to give countenance to those representations which I found had obtained among the people at large" (251). Sustaining his false identity becomes a burden for Burroughs, and thus it comes as something of a relief when he is recognized and dragged before the Attorney-General. Burroughs continues to try to live down his name, however, and the task takes him to various parts of the country without apparently leading him to any greater success. In one of his last letters he writes, in a tone of dejection: "You will undoubtedly ask why I write at this moment? The only answer I have is, that I am more unhappy in any other situation; it serves to calm the boiling passions of a tumultuated mind" (362). But this same writing is a source of anxiety, since it would seem to have contributed – and may continue to contribute – to his trail of misfortune. Briefly reunited with his family, Burroughs writes to John Griffin, worried that a longer letter might itself contribute to ending his happiness: "I now behold around my fireside, my wife and children, parents and sisters, with pleasure pictured on every countenance. This is a scene at which I tremble when I view it, lest fickle fortune should chance to hear my exultation, *from writing long on this subject*, and again dash the cup of pleasure, with wormwood and gall" (363, my emphases). The *Memoirs* end with an appendix written, apparently, by the publisher, who notes that no one knows for sure where, in 1811, Burroughs resides (although instances of counterfeiters calling themselves Stephen Burroughs have turned up in Boston). A year after writing, in 1798, of his son's new trustworthiness ("As an evidence of my confidence in him, I have committed to his care the whole management of my temporal affairs" [366]), we are told that "a sense of propriety and duty" obliged his "disappointed and dejected father" to notify this same friend, that he had "lost all confidence in his son; and cautioned him against any further recommendation" (367).

Burroughs, the figure for individual resistance, for the specificity of circumstance, and the rebellious presence of the irreducibly singular, suffers an unnerving dispersal in the final section of his narrative. He disappears as a narrative voice even as various "Stephen Burroughs" appear at the site of crimes throughout New England. We are left with an image of him writing as a way merely to live ("I am more unhappy in any other situation; it serves to calm the boiling passions of a tumultuated mind"), as if the story of his life has, as he feared it might, taken on more life than he has left for himself. Burroughs comes to experience – either as nervous pleasure or with increasing dejection – a dispersal of the self in discourse that Franklin had deployed to such significant personal and public effect. Meanwhile, Franklin's individual fame and fortune grew beyond his wildest expectations. In fact, one might be tempted to suggest that Burroughs' disappearance (or dispersal – like Jefferson's "people," he cannot assemble himself) marks him, as I suggested above, as a figure for that which is sacrificed in Franklin's convention (individuality, independence of opinion, etc.). But as we have noted, that founding sacrifice was also made in order to gain the approval of the sovereign "opinion" of the people (the "apparent" unity of the delegates would help to secure the approval of public opinion). That which is sacrificed in the convention returns to the delegates (who are, as Franklin points out, part of the people) in the form of a resolutely multiple or dispersed popular sovereignty. This strange economy turns on a secret: the secret of the convention (the secret of its sacrifice of individual difference of opinion) must be kept not only in order to gain sovereign public approval, but if there is to be a sovereign people of the United States at all. Government, or the law (here exemplified by the Constitutional Convention) keeps a secret from the people and this concealment – for all that it will come to be condemned in the name of justice and in the name of the sovereign people, is nevertheless foundational and irreducible.[41] In Stephen Burroughs and all his outlaw descendents, the people will always recognize themselves, will always recognize the secret sacrifice that was made and kept from them in their founding moment. But they will also (they *do* also) recognize themselves in those figures who stand outside the law by appearing to have produced it and thus to tower above it: those singular founding "fathers," like Benjamin Franklin, whose sanctification can be thought of as a form of social disintegration intimately related to Burroughs' circulation as the name for multiple scoundrels.

CHAPTER 4

An epistemology of the ballot box:
Brockden Brown's secrets

It is an eminent advantage incident to democracy, that . . . its inherent tendency is to annihilate [secrets].
(William Godwin, *An Enquiry Concerning Political Justice*, 531)

It is said, that you are afraid of the very Windows, and have a Man planted under them to prevent Secrets and Doings from flying out.
(William Paterson to William Ellsworth, a delegate at the Constitutional Convention in Philadelphia, August 23, 1787, quoted in *A Rising People*)

INTRODUCTION

William Godwin's antipathy towards secrets could be said to have inaugurated a long tradition of equating democracy with publicity, a tradition that has received further elaboration in recent accounts of the American Revolution. The renewed attention to a Habermasian "public sphere" and to a late-eighteenth-century civic culture of print has focused attention on the relationship between the emergence of modern political forms and a marked proliferation of unfettered political expression. The growth of a discursive space distinct from that of the State yet capable of commenting critically upon the State is said to have facilitated an opening-up of opportunities for political participation and to have contributed to an erosion of the structural secrecies of a pre-modern political world.

But Michael Warner, in his very influential study of the relationship between print culture and the American Revolution, asks an important question about the subject of the public sphere in the preface to *The Letters of the Republic*. "If the discourse of publicity allows individuals to make public use of their reason," Warner asks, "what will individuals be like, and what will count as reason?" (*The Letters of the Republic*, xiii). Publicity, this question suggests, should not simply be seen as offering possibilities for the (pre-existing) individual to bring him- or herself into the light of the political day, but as a mode of production for a new way of being an individual. Rather than offering a transparent link between the individual and the realm of the political, publicity should perhaps be seen as a new way of extending the play of revelation and concealment in the field of political intervention. With this in mind, I want to look at the obsession with secrecy in post-revolutionary American politics and, in particular, at the function of secrecy in the production of the new constitutional citizen. I am interested, in other words, in shifting attention away from the sphere of civic publicity so ably described by Warner and others, and onto the space of democratic citizenship, a space which can also be figured by the enclosure of the ballot box. With its indication of the individual's simultaneous concealment and revelation as citizen and its emphasis on the passage from oral to written voting practices, the ballot box indicates the relationship between secrecy, writing, and the democratic revolution that I would like to trace in the following pages. If the democratic revolution signals a transformation in the economy of political power, I will argue that the citizen's accession to this power cuts a path through an irreducible experience of secrecy. Contrary to Godwin, I want to propose that democracy, rather than simply doing away with monarchy's or aristocracy's secretive political practices, in fact introduced the possibility of a "democratized" secrecy by deploying its constitutive relationship to the democratic subject, the citizen.

No early American novelist was as preoccupied with secrets as Charles Brockden Brown. Taken together, his most compelling pieces of writing comprise a dissertation on secrecy; his novels trace the character of the secret holder and the penetrator of secrets, and they find their narrative propulsion in the labyrinthine endlessness of the quest to uncover secrets. It is not surprising then, that his stories have often been read as literary products of a reactionary post-revolutionary paranoia, expressing a "Federalist" fear that "complicated motives and unknown agents are always threatening to overthrow an apparent order" (Voloshin, "*Edgar Huntly*," 263).[1] Stephen Watts goes even further, and suggests that the obsession with secrets in Brown's work responds to the personal and social incoherence generated by an emerging capitalist order. The "deceptions and fluidities of bourgeois individualism," writes Watts, produced the "fragmented self" that "haunted the roads and waterways, the libraries and parlors, the marketplaces and churches of the early American republic" (Watts, *The Romance of Real Life*, 193).

But what keeps critics returning to Brown's fiction is a familiar uncertainty: Brown's stories cite, or ventriloquize, an obsession with secrets, and we can never be sure whether it is the citation or the obsession that most needs to be read. In this regard, "Memoirs of Carwin, the Biloquist" (1798) is exemplary. Not only does the story pit one secret holder against another in an explicit struggle over the individual and political ends of concealment, but it does so while telling a story about ventriloquism. Carwin, the secret imitator – and the narrator of Brown's unfinished story – is brought face to face with Ludloe, the representative of a zealous and insistently clandestine political sect. And while Ludloe offers Carwin access to the kind of enlightened political philosophy that had once fascinated Brown himself, it is nevertheless Carwin's reluctance to embrace the sect that arrests both our attention and, it would seem, the story's plot. Carwin's hesitation, I contest, provides another example of Brown's continued importance as a source of insight into the transformation of the political subject in the late-eighteenth-century United States. Brown's story, as I hope to show, helps us to think about the modern democratic subject's relationship to secrecy. When Carwin breaks his father's law and enters the uncharted seclusion of the Pennsylvania wilderness, he initiates a movement of independence which will culminate in the obstinate refusal to let go of a fascinating secret. It is this very commitment to secrecy, however, that will distinguish Carwin from the two paternal figures (his unenlightened father and the Godwinian Ludloe) whose mutually determined opposition defines the limits of a static revolutionary antagonism.

Brown's fiction helps us to explore the possibility that the obsession with secret plotting shared by radical democrats (or Jacobins) and Federalists in the post-revolutionary period is the direct result of a democratization of secrecy in the culture of post-monarchism. The late eighteenth century in the United States evidences an expansion of the power and significance of secrecy that coincides with the dissipation and redistribution of monarchic political power. Monarchism institutionalized secrecy in the form of monarchic arbitrariness and monarchic absolutism. But it is power's refusal to subordinate itself to reason that produces a secrecy that democratic citizenship seeks, however ambivalently, to inherit. In the second half of this chapter I will look at how Brown characterizes just such a "perverse" attachment to secrecy in both "Memoirs of Carwin, the Biloquist," and his short story, "A Lesson on Concealment." But first I want to turn to the secrecy of political beginnings.

CONSTITUTIONAL SECRETS

In an 1815 letter to Thomas Jefferson, John Adams reminisced on the American Revolution with characteristic hyperbole. The American innovation in politics, he exclaimed, had replaced the "fictitious miracles" with which priests and kings ruled the world, with the "laws [of] nature." In America, he wrote, "authority is originally in the People" and is no longer "brought down from heaven by the holy ghost in the form of a dove, in a phyal of holy oil" (*The Adams–Jefferson Letters*, 445). In fact, as early as 1765, Adams had insisted upon the demystifying tendencies of the American people, when he contrasted what he called the "two greatest Tyrannies . . . the canon and the feudal law" with the American settlers' "love of universal liberty" (*Works*, III, 454). The colonists, he continued, possessed "an utter contempt of all that dark ribaldry of hereditary, indefeasible right – the Lord's anointed – and the divine, miraculous original of government with which priesthood had enveloped the feudal monarch in clouds and mysteries" (454).[2]

But the revolution against mystery and dark ribaldry ushered in an era that commentators have singled out for its paranoid sense of secret machinations, and its heated and haunted political imagination.[3] Political debate conjured up a covert world of secret aristocrats and Jacobin conspirators as Republicans and Federalists sought to define each other in terms of their post-revolutionary relationship to French radicalism and English reaction. According to one recent history of the period, the most extreme positions in this debate shared something in common: "each indeed was enveloped in ideological nightmares" (Elkins and McKitrick, *The Age of Federalism*, 583). For arch-Federalists, the nightmare was given shape by the publication of Scotsman John Robison's *Proofs of a Conspiracy Against all the Religions and Governments of Europe, Carried on in the Secret Meetings of Free Masons, Illuminati, and Reading Societies*.[4] This tract inspired New England Federalists and Anglophiles, including Jedediah Morse and Timothy Dwight, to publish their own highly influential pamphlets on the conspiratorial Jacobin threat to the stability of the new republic (Hofstadter, *Paranoid Style* 10–14; and Stauffer, *New England*).[5] Their hysteria fueled many a New England sermon and found a ready audience in a period that produced some of the nation's most xenophobic and repressive legislation, the Alien and Sedition Acts of 1797.

At the same time, as François Furet has shown, an obsession with secrecy was central to the ideology of those figures most feared by Federalists, the French radicals and their American sympathizers. Furet

argues that the concept of the secret plot appealed to a "democratic conviction that the general, or national, will could not be publicly opposed
by special interests" (*Interpreting the French Revolution*, 53). The discourse of
the secret plot, explains Furet, was "marvelously suited to the workings
of revolutionary consciousness" (53):

there was no need to name the perpetrators of the crime and to present precise
facts about their plans, since it was impossible to determine the agents of the plot,
who were hidden, and its aims, which were abstract. In short, the plot came
to be seen as the only adversary of sufficient stature to warrant concern, since
it was patterned on the Revolution itself. Like the Revolution, it was abstract,
omnipresent and pregnant with new developments; but it was secret whereas
the Revolution was public, perverse whereas the Revolution was beneficial, ne-
farious whereas the Revolution brought happiness to society. It was its negative,
its reverse, its anti-principle. (53–4)

In post-revolutionary America, however, the most powerful political
voices maintained a careful distance from "French" radicalism and thus
directed their suspicion towards what were frequently called the excesses of democracy. If the "dark ribaldry" of ancient institutions had, in
Adams' words "enveloped the feudal monarch in clouds and mysteries,"
George Washington feared in 1786 that the various excesses of democracy
(figured most significantly by Shays' rebellion) might leave "the great
body of the people . . . so . . . enveloped in darkness, as not to see rays of
a distant sun through all this mist of intoxication and folly" (quoted in
Hart, *American History*, 190). And James Madison added rhetorical force
to his condemnation of majority factions in the *Federalist Papers* by referring to the "*secret* wishes of an unjust and interested majority" (*Federalist
Papers*, no. 10, 128).

But of course it was not only the Shaysites, Jacobins, and anarchists
who seemed to want to keep post-revolutionary Americans in the dark.
In September of 1786 a small gathering of state representatives met in
Annapolis, Maryland, ostensibly to discuss trade on the Potomac. James
Madison, one of the representatives from Virginia, already had his sights
set on a more consequential series of national discussions. The report
that the commissioners finally delivered to their respective state governments contained a carefully worded proposal that would eventually
succeed in precipitating the Constitutional Convention of 1787. "Your
commissioners," the report announced with remarkable management
of the rhetoric of disembodied compulsion, "cannot forbear to indulge
an expression of their earnest and unanimous wish, that speedy measures may be taken to effect a general meeting of the states, in a future
convention, for the same and such other purposes, as the situation of

public affairs may be found to require" (quoted in Elliot, *Debates*, 151). The French Minister, Louis (Guillaume) Otto, reporting back to his country on the document produced by the Annapolis assembly, seems to have been acutely suspicious of what he called the commissioners' "secret motives" and "pretext[s] for introducing innovations." The calculated "infinity of circumlocutions and ambiguous phrases," which the commissioners employed, noted Otto, gave to their report "an obscurity which the people will penetrate with difficulty" (quoted in Hart, *American History*, 185–7).[6]

This practiced obscurity continued to inform the progress of the Constitution's formation. Indeed, three of the five rules agreed upon at the start of the convention pertained to secrecy, forbidding copies to be taken of any entries in the journal and requiring that "nothing spoken in the House be printed, or otherwise published, or communicated without leave" (Farrand, ed., *Records*, I, 15).[7] "The members of the Convention," wrote William Blount in 1787, "observe such inviolable secrecy that it is altogether unknown out of doors what they are doing" (quoted in Burnett, *The Continental Congress*, 691).[8] In his final speech to the convention, Benjamin Franklin spoke of the opinions he had entertained of the proposed constitution's errors. "I have never whispered a syllable of them abroad," he announced proudly, "Within these walls they were born, and here they shall die" (*Writings*, 1140). When the convention finally issued its report in September of 1787, the Deputy Secretary of Congress breathed a sigh of relief and declared that "the important secret is now exposed to public view" (quoted in Burnett, *The Continental Congress*, 694).

Of course, the surreptitious procedures of the Federalists did not go unnoticed by their contemporaries. Massachusetts Congressman Stephen Higginson was among the many who suggested a "plot" originating "in Virginia with Mr. Madison" (Ketcham, *James Madison*, 185), and Madison's caution did not prevent him from suggesting to Thomas Jefferson that "the public is certainly in the dark with regard to [the imminent Constitution]." "I do not learn however," he later added, with more than a hint of apprehension, "that any discontent is expressed at the concealment" (letter to Thomas Jefferson, July 18, 1787, in Madison, *Papers*, X, 105–6). Jefferson was not entirely assuaged. "I am sorry," he wrote John Adams in August of 1787, "[that] they began their deliberations by so abominable a precedent as that of tying up the tongues of their members" (*Political Writings*, 136).

Not surprisingly, the secrecy of the convention figures repeatedly in letters from the delegates to their friends and family outside of Philadelphia. George Mason, for example, explained his support for the convention's silence in a 1787 letter to his son. The secrecy of the debates was "a proper precaution," he suggested, "to prevent mistakes and misrepresentations until the business shall have been completed, when the whole may have a very different complexion from that in which the several crude and indigested parts might in their first shape appear if submitted to the public eye" (Farrand, ed., *Records*, III, Appendix A, 28). This mildly gothic sense of rather unsightly and disturbing goings-on within the convention room recurs in Alexander Martin's letter to Governor Caswell of North Carolina. It is best for the convention to keep its proceedings hidden, wrote Martin, "till their deliberations are moulded for the public Eye . . . lest unfavourable Representations might be made by imprudent printers of the many crude matters and things daily uttered and produced in this Body" (Farrand, ed., *Records*, III, Appendix A, 64).[9] Many years later, Jared Sparks recorded notes from a visit with James Madison in his journal, notes which included references to the secrecy of the convention. It was best for the convention to "sit with closed doors," recorded Sparks, "because opinions were so various and at first so crude that it was necessary they should be long debated before any uniform system of opinion could be formed. Meantime the minds of the members were changing, and much was to be gained by a yielding and accommodating spirit" (Farrand, ed., *Records*, III, Appendix A, 478–9).[10] Sparks continues:

Had the members committed themselves publicly at first, they would have afterwards supposed consistency required them to maintain their ground, whereas by secret discussion no man felt himself obliged to retain his opinions any longer than he was satisfied of their propriety and truth, and was open to the force of argument. Mr. Madison thinks no Constitution would ever have been adopted by the convention if the debates had been public. (479)

Intriguingly, Madison's account, as Sparks records it, suggests that rather than shielding delegates from persuasion and influence, the secrecy of the convention gave full play to the "force" of persuasion.[11] And if this secrecy concealed the "yielding" of delegates, it also concealed what Franklin called the "sacrifice" of opinion that members might have to consider in the name of the new nation (see chapter three, above). Reminding delegates of the "salutary effects and great advantages" that would follow from "our real or apparent unanimity" (*Writings*, 1141), Franklin appealed to delegates to put their names to the proposed constitution and thereby "make *manifest* [their] *unanimity*" (*Writings*, 1141). Above all else, the success of the convention depended on the achievement of a unanimous voice with which to present the constitution to the people. This voice, which, as origin of the law, would eventually succeed by appearing to come from nowhere, was discovered in, produced by, secrecy.[12]

Thus, in the 1790s, secret political maneuvering became an object of acute public apprehension even as it was put to work in the name of law, order, and the consolidation of revolutionary achievement. But for many interpreters this secrecy continues to have a decidedly conservative profile. The post-revolutionary obsession with secrecy was the result, suggests Linda Kerber, of a "common Federalist fear that the Jeffersonians were insufficiently conscious of the precariousness of revolutionary accomplishments, and that this laxity might well prove disastrous" (*Federalists in Dissent*, 174). And Jefferson's dissatisfaction with the secrecy of the convention reverberates in Joshua Miller's attempt to account for the failures of American democracy. The devious Federalist combination of highly secretive political maneuvers with a rhetoric of "popular sovereignty," argues Miller, secured power for an elite class while "transform[ing] the body politic into a specter" (Miller, "Ghostly Body Politic," 115).[13] Conservatives deployed secrecy, these accounts suggest, in order to circumvent some of the democratic consequences of revolutionary success. Such a line of interpretation received one of its most memorable articulations in Richard Hofstadter's 1965 study, "The Paranoid Style in American Politics." Hofstadter identified a tendency to convert feelings of persecution into "grandiose theories of conspiracy" in the history of post-revolutionary American politics. The spokesman of the paranoid style shares many characteristics with the "clinical paranoid," writes Hofstadter, but whereas the latter feels conspiracy to be directed specifically against him, the former "find [hostility and conspiracy] directed against a nation, a culture, a way of life whose fate affects not himself alone but millions of others" (*Paranoid Style*, 4). Despite acknowledging that this "style" has been adopted by activists belonging to a variety of political movements (from anti-Masonic and anti-Catholic movements to certain elements of abolitionism and of course McCarthyism), Hofstadter, whose own political and intellectual allegiances are strongly shaped by the McCarthy experience, maintains that "the term 'paranoid style' is pejorative, and it is meant to be; the paranoid style has a greater affinity for bad causes than good" (5).

Hofstadter's pathologizing paradigm is one that Gordon Wood, perhaps the most widely read contemporary historian of the revolutionary period, finds unsatisfactory. In "Conspiracy and the Paranoid Style: Causality and Deceit in the Eighteenth Century," Wood suggests that the paranoid characterization fails to do justice to late-eighteenth-century Americans. Far from representing a pathology, Wood argues, the obsession with secret political activities marked an enlightened response to "the expansion and increasing complexity of the [eighteenth century] political world" (Wood, "Conspiracy," 410). As the century went on, he explains:

there were more people more distanced from one another and from the apparent centers of political decision making . . . The more people became strangers to one another and *the less they knew of one another's hearts*, the more suspicious and mistrustful they became, ready as never before in Western history to see deceit and deception at work . . . [this] Society was composed not simply of great men and their retainers but of numerous groups, interests, and 'classes' whose actions could not be *easily deciphered*. Human affairs were more complicated, more interdependent, and more impersonal than they had ever been in Western history. (410–11, my emphases)

Where the tradition that he critiques introduces psychologizing, clinical terminology to explain historical behavior, Wood stresses the external pressures of number, distance, and class interest. Complexity is the key term here, and it serves to link a widespread concern with secrets and plots to a historical reality, rather than to an anachronistic diagnosis.

Interestingly, Wood's explanation has some precedent in the period which he addresses. His argument participates in the logic of a theory that argued against the viability of large republics on the grounds that in such republics interests become too diverse, and the homogeneity vital to order disappears. This anti-federalist argument drew heavily upon the writings of Baron de Montesquieu. "In an extensive republic," wrote Montesquieu, "the public good is sacrificed to a thousand private views. In a small one, the interest of the public is more obvious, better understood, and more within the reach of every citizen" (Montesquieu, *The Spirit of the Laws*, 124).[14] Wood's emphasis on the explanatory importance of "the growing number of persons and interests participating in politics" ("Conspiracy," 430) follows Montesquieu, then, in equating the disunity of interests with number. Wood's article does register some discomfort with a neo-Montesquiean account of the demographic sources of a conspiratorially minded populace. Wood refers to the "*widening* gap" (my emphasis) between "events and the presumed designs of particular individuals" in the expanding public sphere of the eighteenth century, a formulation that would seem to suggest the possibility of an originary gap ("Conspiracy," 430). And, indeed, this is something that his essay explicitly suggests. Conspiratorial modes of interpretation, notes Wood, "rested on modes of apprehending reality that went back to classical antiquity" ("Conspiracy," 409). "There was nothing new," he continues, "in seeing intrigue, deceit, and cabals in politics. From Sallust's description of Cataline through Machiavelli's lengthy discussion in his *Discourses*, conspiracy was a common feature of political theory" (409). Nevertheless, Wood returns to his central contention by asserting that the difference between the operation of conspiracy theory in modern as opposed to pre-modern politics is merely a difference of scale: classical and Renaissance conspiracies, he writes, occurred "within the small ruling circles of a few great men – in limited political worlds where everyone knew everyone else" (410). The apparent relationship between modern democratic political organization and a heightened discourse of secrecy, this account suggests, is merely a contingent effect of social and economic expansion.

Wood's theory of the obsession with conspiracy leaves us with an important question about the political philosophy of one of the most careful thinkers of the revolutionary period. Why, if it is true that suspicion and uncertainty expand with an expanding society, would James Madison argue, as he did in the famous *Federalist* no. 10, that an extended republic would be more likely to safeguard liberty and order than a narrow one? Political historians have long recognized the originality of Madison's defense of large-scale federalism against the classical critique exemplified by Montesquieu's *Spirit of the Laws*, a defense he carries out, most notably, in *Federalist* no. 10 and in an October 24, 1787 letter to Thomas Jefferson (reprinted in Banning, 132–43). Defending the constitution proposed by the Philadelphia convention, Madison contests that the proliferation of interests and factions in an extended political State can, contrary to classical political philosophy, form the basis for *preserving* individual rights and protecting against the tyranny of majority. The advantage of the constitutional republic's "extensive sphere," Madison contends, consists (in part) in "the greater security afforded by a greater variety of parties, against the event of any one party being able to outnumber and oppress the rest" (*Federalist Papers*, no. 10, 128). The fact that a large republic produced a proliferation of "strangers" who, to use Wood's phrase, knew less of "one another's hearts," is not denied by Madison so much as it is exploited to demonstrate the obstacles to tyranny in such a diverse society. In his letter to Jefferson, which he wrote to complement Jefferson's receipt of the results of the convention, Madison went into more detail in order to explain some of the key Philadelphia resolutions. In discussing the constitutional negative on the laws of the states, Madison knew he had to take pains to counter his friend's suspicions. "It may be asked," Madison writes, "how private rights will be more secure under the Guardianship of the General Government than under the State Governments, since they are both founded on the republican principle which refers the ultimate decision to the will of the majority, and are distinguished rather by the extent within which they will operate, than by any material difference in their structure" (*Federalist Papers*, no. 10, 212). A full answer to this question, Madison continues, would "unfold the true principles of Republican Government." Those who contend that a democratic government can only operate "within narrow limits," he writes, "assume or suppose a case which is altogether fictitious"; "They found their reasoning on the idea, that the people composing the Society, enjoy not only an equality of political rights; but that they all have precisely the same interests, and the same feelings in every respect... We know however that no Society did or can consist of so homogenous a mass of Citizens" (*Federalist Papers*, no. 10, 212). Here, Madison rejects, as a founding political principle, the idea that any community, no matter how small or homogeneous, can be said to share "the same feelings in every respect." This rejection is thus also a rejection of any account of political development that nostalgically emphasizes a falling away from simpler and more harmonious beginnings.

Listing the kinds of differences that counter such an idea of homogeneity, Madison begins by citing economic differences: between "rich and poor; creditors and debtors; a landed interest, a monied interest, a mercantile interest, a manufacturing interest" (*Federalist Papers*, no. 10, 213), for example. But in his letter to Jefferson, Madison gives as much space to distinctions founded on "accidental differences in political, religious or other opinions, or an attachment to the persons of leading individuals." "However erroneous or ridiculous these grounds of dissention and faction, may appear to the enlightened Statesman, or the benevolent philosopher," Madison continues, "the bulk of mankind, who are neither Statesmen nor Philosophers, will continue to view them in a different light" (Banning, 138–9). What is most intriguing about this catalogue of differences is not just Madison's reluctance to dismiss their importance for political thought, but also the implicit suggestion that some of these differences indicate a more intimate dislocation – a dislocation internal to the citizen.

As Samuel Beer has recently pointed out, Madison's theory of faction (a faction that is "latent," "sown in the nature of man," *Federalist Papers*, no. 10, 124) is intimately connected to what he called "self-love." "As long as the connection subsists between his reason and his self-love," wrote Madison in the *Federalist*, "[the citizen's] opinions and his passions will have a reciprocal influence on each other; and the former will be objects to which the latter will attach themselves" (10, 123–4). If Montesquieu's political theory sought to found government on a renunciation of the self's disruptive self-love ("which is ever arduous and painful," Montesquieu writes, and "requires a constant preference of public to private interest" [*The Spirit of the Laws*, 35–6]). Madison's begins with the impossibility, or the refusal, of that renunciation. Beer explains:

Madison focused his attention on a source of republican disorder inherent in human nature: self-love . . . Even if *ex hypothesi*, a society small enough to be composed only of persons with identical and equal interests could be found or created, self-love would still persist. Conflict would be ruled out only if we also supposed that its members had vanquished self-love and lived wholly according to the dictates of self-sacrificing virtue. (*To Make a Nation*, 259–60)[15]

The crucial aspect of Madison's argument then, is not what seems to be a more pessimistic attitude towards the possibility of civic virtue, but its suggestion that an irreducible resistance to "self-sacrificing virtue" might itself correspond to something politically valuable. The aim of the federalist project as he sees it, after all, is not simply to get rid of faction; it is "To secure the public good and private rights against the danger of such a faction, *and at the same time* to preserve the spirit and the form of popular government" (*Federalist Papers*, no. 10, 125, emphasis added). "Liberty is to faction," Madison continued, "what air is to fire, an aliment without which it instantly expires" (*Federalist Papers*, no. 10, 125). Madison seems here to suggest that just as number and social complexity guard against the destructive aspects of faction, so the tendency to faction bears an integral relationship to the "spirit" of popular government. In Madisonian political philosophy, in other words, the *spirit* of democratic politics is indissociable from an originary non-self-identity of the political subject.[16] It is not the tension between a disruptive "self-love" and virtuous citizenship that defines Madison's political subject; rather, it is the curious tension marked within the concept of "self-love" itself: the splitting that occurs within the unit of the citizen, between, in Madison's formulation, a self that loves and the self that that self loves.[17] Selfhood, indeed, would be produced as the object of a disembodied affection. "Self-love" does not merely name an impulse at odds with love of nation, State, or the common good; it names a constitutive disjunction in the self, a "latent" factionalism. "Self-love" is one way of naming that which ambiguates the singularity of the individual as source of political authority, wisdom, and virtue.[18] If there is a profound sense of the unknowability of "one another's hearts" (to use Wood's phrase) in the post-revolutionary United States, the *Federalist* (and James Madison in particular) suggests that this unknowability may be constitutive of both the republican State and the state of the individual. The constitutional citizen is a secret to himself; he is, first and foremost, "secreted."

But why would one still want to defend this Madisonian theory of republicanism against the kind of argument proposed by Gordon Wood in his 1982 article? In the first place, to guard against a familiar – yet worrying – component of Wood's argument. Wood's albeit somewhat qualified assertion of the relationship between modern social complexity and the rise of conspiratorial modes of thinking shares too much with those theories of political organization that identify harmony with the tendency towards more localized, ultimately more homogeneous, social bodies. The sentimental allusion to the possibility of "knowing one another's hearts" signals (even if Wood would not want to be associated with) a recognizable tendency to invoke figures of bodily union in any portrayal of the harmony of small groups. Theories of the incohesion of complex social organizations, in other words, need to guard against becoming theories of the essential cohesion of the body, of the identity between interest and bodily integrity or bodily relation, theories, in other words, of the political privilege of blood, family, and ethnicity. One of the effects of an attempt to rethink the positive social effects of an extended political space, made up of a multitude of interests (including those that Madison noted might seem to arise out of "accidental," "erroneous or ridiculous" grounds of difference [*Federalist Papers*, no. 10, 213]) is to disable the temptation towards theories of essential identity as the grounds for successful democratic government. And it is as a contribution to the disruption of this temptation that I want to invoke Madison's articulation of the self-different subject of "self-love" (the subject of "artificial" and "accidental" attachments) with the structures of an irreducibly contentious constitutional democracy.

In *Common Sense* Thomas Paine wrote, as I noted above, of "something exceedingly ridiculous in the composition of monarchy":

it first excludes a man from the means of information, yet empowers him to act in cases where the highest judgment is required. The state of a king shuts him from the world, yet the business of a king requires him to know it thoroughly; wherefore the different parts, unnaturally opposing and destroying each other, prove the whole character to be absurd and useless. (*Common Sense*, 69)

Paine here condemns monarchy's institutionalization of a rupture in the conversion of empirical knowledge into executive decision, a rupture that constitutes the absurdity (what was most often called the "arbitrariness") of the English monarch. But what Paine here calls the king's "different" and "unnaturally opposing parts" can also be seen to be at play in Madison's constitutional democracy. Paine's picture of the absurdity of monarchy is simultaneously an analysis of monarchy's power, its highly effective *spell*, and it is that power that the American Revolution, Madison's theory suggests, wants to reconfigure for democracy. Hazarding a daring translation, Madison made precisely this point in his letter to Jefferson: "*Divide et impera*," wrote Madison, "the reprobated axiom of tyranny, is under certain qualifications, the only policy, by which a republic can be administered on just principles" (Banning, 140). Madison's formulation recognizes, quite powerfully, that the divisiveness deployed by the tyrant sovereign is not to be destroyed and buried by democracy; rather, democracy will abrogate this power for the democratic state: it is the sovereign subject of democracy whose experience of power will be simultaneously an experience of self-division.[19]

I want, then, to suggest that the democratic subject promised by the modern (American) revolution has a new and vital relationship to secrecy. Perhaps the revolution can even be said to have democratized secrecy, to have begun to deploy its constitutive relationship to the democratic subject, the citizen. If the "arbitrariness" of monarchical forms of government names a secret relation to reason at the source of political power, democracy, rather than simply abolishing this arbitrariness, this secrecy at the origin of political decision-making, displaces it, reinscribes it across a new topography of political legitimacy. The democratization of secrecy that is ambivalently marked in the political and literary discourse of the post-revolutionary period would consist not in the transfer of any particular property of secrecy – any particular secrets – but in an institutionalization of the definitive obscurity, the definitive non-self-identity, of the democratic subject of power, the obscurity that distances the citizen from him- or herself in the act of political intervention. If the federalist constitution seems to betray the "spirit" of '76 and succeed only in turning the "body politic into a specter," as Miller puts it ("The Ghostly Body Politic," 115), perhaps we need to reassess our understanding of the ontology (what Jacques Derrida might call the "hauntology") of the democratic subject (*Specters of Marx*, 10). Such a reassessment cannot avoid a detour through the ballot box.

THE SECRET BALLOT

One of the more visible ways in which the democratization of secrecy took place in the late-eighteenth-century United States was through transformations in electoral practice. Robert Dinkin explains:

by the end of the Revolutionary era, voting procedures had been substantially reformed. Many arbitrary practices had been eliminated. Elections had become more regular and frequent, representation in the legislature more just and equitable, polling places more numerous and accessible, and balloting more orderly and secret. While a few states still clung to some of their old ways, which limited popular participation and control, the majority of them had moved in a more democratic direction. (Dinkin, *Voting in Revolutionary America*, 106)[20]

These lines contain most of the key words we might associate with democracy: representation, justice, equity, accessibility, and popular participation. But in addition, and as if it were merely one more link in this revolutionary chain, Dinkin makes reference to secrecy. British precedent had determined that most elections in colonial America were held by the method of "viva voce," that is to say, voice vote. One of the democratic revolution's successes, however, was the institutionalization of a certain secrecy at the site of origin of democratic legitimation. The revolution in the name of the "people-out-of-doors" realized itself by giving its citizens an indoors, a ballot box, ultimately a voting booth. Democracy gave the citizen a secret space where he could be alone with him- (later her-) self.[21]

Why was the secret ballot so essential to the progress of democracy? Its advocates pointed to the numerous practices of fraud associated with public voting: the use, for example, of bribes, threats, and rewards. The secret ballot was necessary, it would seem, because voters were in danger of casting a vote that was not (in some way) their "true" vote.[22] The secrecy of the ballot box was necessary, it was suggested, to avoid the citizen's susceptibility to influence, his tendency to fail to voice his true opinion, his tendency to misrepresent himself.[23] The fear generated by public voting was that the purity and singularity of the citizen's desire, the originary and only legitimate desire of democratic politics, would be compromised by scheming individuals or interest groups. The secret ballot would preserve the democratic citizen from that which might cause him to betray his civic responsibility. In 1785, Madison told Caleb Wallace that "as to the mode of suffrage I lean strongly to that of the ballot, notwithstanding the objections which be against it" (Madison, *Papers*, VIII, 354). With a rare flourish of (mixed) metaphor, Madison continued: "It appears to me to be the only radical cure for the Arts of Electioneering which poison the very fountain of Liberty. The States in which the Ballot has been the Standing mode are the only instances in which elections are tolerably chaste and those arts are in disgrace" (354).

But the secrecy of the secret ballot perhaps keeps another secret. The institutionalization of secret voting marks a revolutionary recognition:

the "people," democracy's source of legitimacy, can only be found, democracy discovers, in the inaccessibility of the secret ballot. Which is also to say, in writing, for in this period the term "secret ballot" is used interchangeably with the term "written ballot" in order to emphasize its distinction from the viva voce procedure. What the ballot's hinge also conceals (and thereby reveals) is the citizen's written relationship to himself, to his own political will.[24] The secret ballot restages in miniature, so to speak, every time a vote is cast, the drama of closed-door political origination that was the Philadelphia convention. The insistent secrecy of the Constitutional Convention (and indeed of the procedures leading up to the convention) is remarked in the secret performance of the citizen's elective authority.[25] The ballot box, site of the unseen and of the written offers us an architecture of the democratic citizen's political subjectivity. In this closet, the doubled citizen of democracy (doubled by what Madison in *Federalist* Papers, no. 10 calls his "self-love," or by what Rousseau recognized as the citizen's status as both giver and receiver of the law) sends himself an anonymous letter; with his secret, written vote, he envelops himself into the text of democracy.[26]

CARWIN'S ECHO

How does a Charles Brockden Brown character experience independence? Or, to give this question a more specifically political inflection, how does Brown figure the transfer of power announced by democratic revolution? I want to show how these questions cross paths with a discussion of secrecy by taking a close look at Brown's unfinished supplement to *Wieland*, "Memoirs of Carwin, the Biloquist" (1798). The story is narrated by the second son of a smallholding farmer in pre-revolutionary rural Pennsylvania. Like Edgar Huntly, another of Brown's impetuous protagonists, Carwin stands to inherit little from his family, and his socioeconomic uncertainty adds a degree of practical anxiety to what he himself calls a "restless" and "unconquerable" curiosity (*Wieland*, 247).[27] "My attention," Carwin tells us, "fastened upon everything mysterious or unknown" (247). Carwin is at pains to distinguish himself from his "unenlightened" family. While his brother never progressed beyond learning to sign his name or spell out a chapter in the bible, "my character," he insists, "was the reverse" (247). His brother's ideas "never ranged beyond the sphere of his vision," while Carwin, the writer and lover of books, possesses a "fancy [which] teemed with visions of the future" (247). His father, not unpredictably, determines to restrain Carwin's thirst for knowledge, and thus "the most vigilant and jealous scrutiny was exerted" in an attempt to "keep me within . . . limits" (247). Carwin's rebellious tendencies, then, take the form of intellectual indulgences, indulgences that are often marked by a tendency to exceed "the period assigned" for any of his father's tasks. His story begins with just such an act of filial disobedience.

Carwin has been assigned to bring his father's cattle home from a far pasture. Discovering that the cattle are gone, Carwin exercises his curiosity in an attempt to determine the cause of the broken fence through which the cows escaped. Recognizing that his first duty should have been to return with the news, an anxious Carwin gathers his thoughts. "I was terrified at the consequences of my delay," he recalls, "and sought with eagerness how they might be obviated. I asked myself if there were not a way back shorter than that by which I had come" (249). Thus, Carwin attempts to follow a short-cut home through uncharted territory. Carwin's strange career begins with this detour, this decision to follow a passage whose "practicability was to be known only by experiment" (249–50).[28]

Brown's famous preface to *Edgar Huntly* stressed the significance of the wilderness to his literary project, and "Memoirs of Carwin, the Biloquist" provides another opportunity to test this significance. Brown's wilderness marks the site of the unwritten, the uncharted, the mazy, and impassable. But as the site of new spatial and temporal possibilities, the wilderness also offers Carwin the possibility of both exceeding the period assigned for his task *and* arriving home in time; breaking his father's law yet remaining within the law. Carwin's short-cut, in other words, represents another of Charles Brockden Brown's attempts to theorize the paradoxical movement of revolution. To traverse the "abrupt points" and "gloomy hollows" of this "unbeaten" terrain (249) is to chart a supplement to the legal landscape, and thereby return to the father.

Following a familiar logic of the supplement, however, Carwin's detour through the wilderness generates further displacements. The unfamiliar landscape begins to unnerve him, and he falls prey to anachronistic trepidation. "By a defect common in everyone's education," he tells us, "goblins and specters were to me the objects of the most violent apprehensions" (250). Hence, Carwin feels the necessity to find another detour, a detour around his apprehension.[29] The "terrors," that the wilderness brings on, Carwin notes, can be "lessened by calling the attention away to some indifferent object," and thus he begins to "amuse" himself by "hallowing as loud as organs of unusual compass and vigour would enable me" (250). Carwin utters "the words which chanced to occur to me," and thus repeats "in the shrill tones of a Mohock savage . . . 'Cow! cow! come home! home!' " (250). Carwin imitates an Indian voice and thereby calls his attention away. His anxiety, itself the result of inhabiting a space that is paradoxically outside and within the law, a space associated with the undoing of a temporal delay, is placated by a practice of self-distraction (a determined splitting of the self's presence) that requires an accomplished artifice and an "indifferent object" (250).

No sooner is he calmed, however, than Carwin is re-frightened, this time by the echo that reverberates from the rocks "which on either side towered aloft": "I was startled by this incident, and cast a fearful glance behind, to discover by whom it was uttered. The spot where I stood was buried in dusk, but the eminences were still invested with a luminous and vivid twilight. The speaker, however, was concealed from my view" (250). Boxed in by the towering rocks, Carwin hears himself again and for the first time, and the experience is both disturbing and thrilling.[30] Hearing his *own* voice "at a distance . . . not uttered by another . . . but by myself," Carwin imagines a further possibility. "The idea of a distant voice, like my own," he recalls, "was intimately present to my fancy" (252); "To talk from a distance, and at the same time, in the accents of another, was the object of my endeavours, and this object . . . I finally obtained" (253).[31] With this achievement, Carwin begins a new stage of his life. From this point on he will begin to plot his break from his father, a break that will finally take him to Europe and introduce him into the world of radical international politics.[32]

But, Carwin's discovery of his secret voice cannot be read simply as the culmination of an act of (revolutionary) resistance to authority. Certainly, Carwin discovers his voice when he is both temporally and spatially (geographically) outside the law: he has entered the Pennsylvania wilderness that *Edgar Huntly* and indeed Carwin's "chance" imitation marks as Indian territory, while under the threat of punishment for having exceeded the designated time for his task.[33] But it is equally true to say that Carwin discovers his voice in the course of an attempt to return to legitimacy and retrospectively nullify his disobedience. If, as I am suggesting, Carwin's narrative recounts an origin story for his independence, it does so by suggesting that independent subjectivity coincides with an apparently impossible temporal and spatial position (it takes place under, or within the spell of democracy). This subject founds itself in the supplement of legitimacy, in an outside that is also an inside, both too late and in time. And, of course, in secret.

Michael Warner has notably written of the new republic's need to find a "hinge" between "a delegitimizing revolutionary politics and a nonrevolutionary, already legal signification of the people" (*The Letters of the Republic*, 104). For Warner, this "hinge" was to be found in the unique efficacy of print: its structural anonymity "masked the contradiction" (104). For this reason, Benjamin Franklin becomes for Warner (as for others) an exemplary figure in any account of the American Revolution. Franklin's recognition of the efficaciousness of print's anonymity marked his biography as proto-revolutionary: "Franklin's career," writes Warner, "is preeminently that of the republican man of letters, the citizen of print" (77). Franklin succeeded in performing the role of republican statesman; he was able to "embody representational legitimacy," Warner suggests, by making a career out of the "involution of republicanism and print" (73). Given this paradigm, Brown's pastoral narrative would seem to be almost perversely archaic. What could be further from the cultural context of the modern American revolutionary than Carwin's gloomy wilderness? What could be more anathema to the theory of the revolution's indebtedness to print anonymity, than a tale of vocal (theatrical?) prowess? Carwin's story might seem, albeit in a uniquely distorted manner, to be a version of the kind of story that identifies the achievement of independence with the discovery of one's own voice. This latter position has been given renewed attention in recent years, in part as a way of countering the attention neo-Habermasians have given to late-eighteenth-century print culture.[34] Christopher Looby, for example, writes of a "distinct countercurrent in the literature of the period that valorizes the grain of the voice in addition to, or instead of, the silence of print" (*Voicing America*, 3). He continues: "Precisely because the new nation's self-image was characterized by its difference from a traditional (quasi-natural) conception of the nation, indeed by the conscious recognition of its historical contingency that was produced by the abrupt performativity of its inception, vocal utterance has served, in telling instances, as a privileged figure for the making of the United States" (3–4). Carwin's "biloquism," however, fails to fall comfortably into either an oratorical theory of revolutionary assertion or a print-based civic interpretation. Rather, his othered voice, the voice of disembodiment and imitative repetition, effectively challenges the opposition between print anonymity and vocal utterance that would seem to dominate these recent discussions. Carwin discovers that the individualizing properties of voice are indissociable from the masking, self-distancing properties of what Michael Warner calls "writing's unrestricted dissemination" (*The Letters of the Republic*, 40). Carwin's secret is not just that his voice comes to him as an originary appropriation of the Native American's voice (the Mohock's cry), but that it is this homeless voice that simultaneously produces him as an independent subject.

Biloquism's oddity ought to remind us that an investment in the anonymity of print discourse and in the individualizing dimensions of oratory are mutually determining investments. It should not be surprising that the revolutionary period can be read as the site of both an expanded print sphere and a vital oratorical culture. The effective importance of an anonymous intervention can only be measured against the figure of the public speaker and vice versa. What Brown's Carwin and the discourse of the revolutionary period give us to consider is the possibility that democratic transformation crucially extended the field of political intervention, which is to say the field of interventions in the name of interests or positions that can only ever be represented. To participate in democracy's expansion is to find one's voice as a voice of representation. Following the logic of the ballot box, the democratic citizen, the member of the "people out of doors," necessarily and inevitably conceals himself into political power. The impossible or aporetic space and time of Carwin's revolution gives Carwin both a voice and a secret and the two are mutually dependent on one another. The wilderness, in other words, the dusky space in which Carwin finds himself surrounded, the place where he tries to placate anachronistic and superstitious fears, the place where as he disobeys he nevertheless seeks relegitimation, this wilderness that Brown chose to replace the castles of the tired European gothic novel, is also a defamiliarizing figuration of that most banal of democratic constructions: the ballot box.

The second part of "Carwin the Biloquist" follows the young man's precarious independence as it is put to the test in the form of an encounter with a radical, international political organization. After a series of botched attempts to use his biloquism to advantage, Carwin is taken under the wing of a wealthy Irishman named Ludloe, who takes him along when he returns to the Old World.[35] Carwin's encounter with Ludloe brings the singularly secretive Carwin up against an insistently clandestine political movement. While the story refuses to be explicit about the exact nature of Ludloe's or his sect's politics, we are encouraged to hear echoes of Rousseau and particularly Godwin in Ludloe's pronunciations.[36] The sect holds, for example, that "the absurd and unequal distribution of power and property gave birth to poverty and riches, and these were the source of luxury and crimes" (*Wieland*, 276). "Man," Ludloe tells Carwin, "is the creature of circumstances... his progress has been stopped by the artificial impediment of government" (276). In the utopian community that the sect hopes to found, "justice should be universally understood and practised... the interest of the whole and of the individual should be seen by all to be the same" (277).[37] Ludloe's organization calls to mind the movements that attracted the period's most profound political anxieties (the Jacobins, Illuminati, and freemasons), but all the sect's political conviction seems to pale in comparison to what appears to be its primary preoccupation: its preoccupation with secrecy.[38] Ludloe, who wants to induct Carwin into the sect, begins by passing on a series of solemn injunctions. He tells Carwin: "A number of persons are leagued together for an end of some moment... Among the conditions of their alliance are mutual fidelity and secrecy... Their existence depends on this: their existence is known only to themselves. This secrecy must be obtained by all the means which are possible" (281). "Compared with this task," Ludloe warns Carwin, "the task of inviolable secrecy, all others are easy" (282). Well, all others except one: the prospective member must also "disclose every fact in his history, and every secret of his heart" (284). And "if secrecy were difficult to practise," remarks Carwin, "sincerity, in that degree in which it was here demanded, was a task infinitely more arduous... Any particle of reserve or duplicity would cost me my life" (284). Ludloe explains that a member may decide to leave the fraternity, but if he chooses to do so he must maintain his commitment to its absolute secrecy: "Admit not even a doubt as to the propriety of hiding [the secret of the society] from all the world," he warns, "There are eyes who will discern this doubt amidst the closest folds of your heart, and your life will instantly be sacrificed" (282).[39]

The double imperative of Ludloe's sect, to remain secret yet hold no secrets from one another, underlines the extent to which a certain commitment to secrecy corresponds to a profound unease about secrets.[40] The need to keep its existence secret from the outside world that the sect will defend to the death, is protected in the name of a society that will have banished secrets forever: "the interest of the whole and of the individual should be seen by all to be the same" (277).[41]

But Carwin resists. He holds onto the secret of his biloquism in the face of the sect's demands. Moreover, his resistance to Ludloe's sect is made not in the name of an alternative philosophy, but under the sway of what he calls a "perverse" attachment to his own secret, his defining secrecy. "My character had been, in some degree, modelled by the faculty which I possessed," he remarks, and "by some fatal obstinacy" he resolves to conceal it from Ludloe (297). This attachment, he suggests, follows "no conceivable reason" (304). It is as if in holding onto his secret, and to the secrecy of his "inconceivable reason" (what Madison might have called his "accidental attachment") Carwin holds onto himself, or to the possibility of a self. His secret (which is the secret of his self-differing voice) produces him as an independent subject. Refusing the sect's claim on his secrecy, Carwin simultaneously acknowledges that his very subjectivity is in some way in debt to the echo of his ventriloquism.[42] He is also in debt to something that is *not* reasonable – "perverse." By demonstrating his investment in this character, Brown betrays an attachment to a model of free subjectivity that resists a State (or State-like) monoploy on secrets (Ludloe's sect) but does so *not* in the name of a liberating or individuating end to secrecy, but in the name of an irreducible secrecy at work in any political voice. Where Ludloe's sect attempts to turn the secrecy of self-difference into a border that preserves political unanimity, Carwin's biloquism locates the subject's independent voice at the site of an internal division figured by the thrown and echoed imitations of Carwin's biloquism. In Carwin and Ludloe, then, Brown brings together two different relationships to secrecy, two different ways of conceiving secrecy. Ludloe's resistance to secrecy, his sect's ethics of disclosure, participates in what I would call a revolutionary sentimentality. Secrecy, in this scheme of things, marks the line of a border that protects the sanctity of an enlightened community, a community in which the particular and the general are no longer distinguishable. But Brown's unsympathetic portrayal of Ludloe's sect would lead us to suspect that the assertion of this reconciliation coincides with the invocation of a border, a border whose secret policing finally shares too much in common with the invisible borders of ethnic separation. Ludloe's politics rejects secrecy as a constitutive component of its individual members by asserting that they are all one, as if they are all of one blood (and the familial model is referenced in the sect's fraternal and patriarchal invocations of brotherhood and inheritance). To share a secret is to belong, to be outside is not to share the secret, and the maintenance of this distinction would appear to demand all the sect's attention. In his typically too quick, yet nevertheless unique portrait of Ludloe's political philosophy, Brown gives us a late-eighteenth-century critique of Godwinian democratic theory's troubled relationship to secrecy.

Carwin, on the other hand, remains the subject of the border he crossed at the start of his story. I want to claim Carwin as an insistently democratic subject because of his attachment both to his Enlightenment faith in the "empire of reason" *and* to his own inscrutability, his "own" surprising voice. Brown's young American approaches independence by participating in the democratic displacement of monarchic arbitrariness. The king's defining unreasonableness becomes the citizen's inscrutability, his own difference from reason in the exercise of power as secrecy, power as non-knowledge. Carwin refuses the discourse that fears the secrecy – the internal self-differing – that is constitutive of political subjectivity. In *Wieland*, Carwin will be repeatedly invoked as an author figure, a dramatist, and plotter, an inventor of characters and of other people's lives, he who casts (characters, voices, spells), and it is also this relation to the literary, to fiction with all its attendant investments in authorial obfuscation, that I would contend marks a post-revolutionary, democratic subjectivity. Distancing himself from himself in the moment of revolution, Carwin tricks himself into independence. The secret that Carwin, like the ballot box, conceals for us is the secret of the citizen's enveloped self.

THE LESSONS OF CONCEALMENT

"A Lesson on Concealment" could have been the subtitle of all Brown's major works of fiction. But it was in fact the title of a long short story that appeared in Brown's *Monthly Magazine, and American Review* (2.3), in March of 1800.[43] The story deserves to be taught with Rowson's *Charlotte Temple* or Foster's *The Coquette* because at its center is a sentimental story of a woman's fall from the virtue offered by an acceptable marriage. The heroine of this story, Mary Selwyn, was raised by her brother and father and at the age of eighteen she bows to their demand that she marry a man of their choice (a young cousin of her father's). Once married, Mary meets and falls in love with Haywood, a man with whom she feels she can exercise complete sincerity. Their adultery leads, with familiar novelistic efficiency, to a pregnancy that ensures her disgrace and her excommunication from the world of her father, brother, and husband. Having assumed a new name and begun a new life, Mary is confronted by a Dr. Molesworth, who finally succeeds in persuading her to marry him. This temporary respite from tragedy comes to an end when the possibility that her secret past will be revealed precipitates a fatal sickness.

If the conventionality of this story were not already clear to readers, Brown helps to make the point by referring within the story to the kind of story Mary herself reads after her fall. We are told that she is moved to sighs and pensive musings by accounts of "the hardships to which the loss of reputation and honor subject her sex" ("A Lesson on Concealment," 67). The narrator suggests that in these moments, "the comparison was secretly made between her own experience and the reasonings or relations of the book" (67). Brown's version of this sentimental story is, not surprisingly, a little more Godwinian than most; the explicitly political dimension of the marriage question is addressed by Mary when she protests (with more vehemence and clarity than one usually finds in the genre): "O! How blest are they whose conduct is exempt from parental or fraternal dominion; who are suffered to consult the dictates of their reason, and are not driven, by imperious duties, to the sacrifice of independence, the abjuration of liberty, and the death of honour!" (86).[44] But despite this ostensibly sympathetic relation of Mary's tragedy, the story of her fall is unexceptional. What characterizes "A Lesson On Concealment" as a Brockden Brown story and thus as a unique piece of early American fiction is not the story of Mary Selwyn's adultery but the explicit registration of the power exerted by its concealment. Mary's story comes to us carefully framed, as if Brown had decided to pull the camera back, so to speak, and turn our attention towards the complex politics of concealment and revelation that is at work around the border of the sentimental tale. Even before we know the contents of Mary's secret we are aware that the very act of concealment has initiated a crisis in power and it is with this crisis that Brown's tale begins.

This opening crisis takes the form of a letter, a desperate, pleading letter from one man to another. The man's wife has died and he writes from what he calls "an house of sorrow" (53). But we soon begin to suspect that this man is not suffering from the loss of his wife so much as from the effects of a concealment. His wife went to her grave concealing a secret from her husband, and he spent the last days of her life trying to discover it. Upon realizing the seriousness of her illness, he writes, "I opened my eyes as if I had awakened in the grave. My fears for her life swallowed up every other fear, and I sought, with a vehemence that bordered upon frenzy, to extort from her the secret of her woe" (54). The letter is addressed to Henry Kirvan and it claims that Kirvan knows the secret. "Part of this misery," the writer tells Kirvan, "I believe it to be in your power to remove. You held secret conferences with her . . . You shared with her her tears" (54). And thus we are prepared for the long revelatory letter that will make up the bulk of Brown's story.

The full extent of this crisis only emerges, however, after we have discovered that the addressee and the one who has it "in [his] power" to reveal the secret is in many ways the letter writer's social inferior. It is bad enough that one man is writing to another man pleading for the secrets of his late wife's heart; but in this instance the writer is Dr. Molesworth and the addressee, Henry Kirvan, is the doctor's apprentice, and the beneficiary of the doctor's good will. Kirvan came to the doctor with no training and no means of financial support (Kirvan refers to himself as a "green youth"). Certainly Molesworth must be aware of the incongruity. He has been suffering in great part from a sense of the injustice of his wife's concealment. Among other things, Mrs. Molesworth's secrecy is a violation of the marriage contract. She has not only kept something from him, but she has concealed in violation of the law. The law frowns on this behavior and Dr. Molesworth cannot help but acknowledge this fact. "This terror, this concealment, this duplicity, is not due to an husband such as I have been" (54), writes Molesworth. Or rather, and this is important, it is not Molesworth, strictly speaking who says this. It is, well, who? Here is the full sentence: "I could not be deaf to that secret voice which said – This terror, this concealment, this duplicity, is not due to an husband such as I have been" (54). Somebody is whispering in Dr. Molesworth's ear. Dr. Molesworth, perhaps, is whispering in Dr. Molesworth's ear. But is it also the voice of justice? Of law? Of authority? This concealment is not "due," the voice says. But why is it a secret voice that tells Molesworth how unjust this concealment is? Who is this secret keeper of accounts who knows what concealment is due to whom? Apparently, this accountant must himself (?) be kept secret – a secret voice, heard within but nowhere seen. Striving to balance the books, this secret accounting must not be seen to proceed from any particular individual. This absolute sense of what is due, of what concealment is due, has to be secret. Its authority is indebted to this secrecy. Its absoluteness and its secrecy are coextensive.[45]

We might say of secrecy what Walter Benjamin said of violence, that it is not the ends to which secrecy is employed that the law resists, but secrecy's "mere existence outside the law" ("Critique of Violence," 281). It might even be true to say that no system of law can exist without this explicit or implicit commandment: thou shalt not keep secrets from the law. But at the same time no modern system of law can exist without the invocation of a secret voice, the anonymous, constitutional voice of democratic law. Dr. Molesworth's secret voice says: "there is an undue secret out there. Somebody is keeping a secret from us, from you, Dr. Molesworth, and from the secret voice of what is due, from the accountant of secrets." The secret voice says "there shall be no secrets."

This is an entirely familiar scenario to the reader of Charles Brockden Brown.

The framing letter of "A Lesson on Concealment" is vital, then, insofar as it introduces the story as proceeding from the urgings of a secret voice. It is the voice that whispers to Dr. Molesworth of what is not due to a husband that initiates his frenzied attempt to unravel the secret and, as we shall see, initiates Henry's tell-all epistle.

It is important, too, to take note of the force of Dr. Molesworth's secret voice. His use of the phrase "I could not be deaf" to this secret voice suggests a certain helplessness in the face of an authoritative voice. It is as if the authority of the law, the authority of the marriage vow, has forced this husband to feel injustice, even against some part of his will. His anger, his frenzy is given to him, forced upon him. In other words, Dr. Molesworth experiences injustice in something like the same way that his wife experiences her illicit desire. In a quite typical fashion, Mary Selwyn constitutes herself as a subject of the sentimental narrative by listening to her heart rather than to the voice of convention, authority, even a certain "justice." Moreover (and here we are reminded of Carwin's "perverse" attachment to his secret ventriloquism), it is her "perverse heart" that she blames (Mary claims that her failure to accept the husband her brother favored proceeded from the "perverseness of [her] heart" ["A Lesson on Concealment," 78], and again she wishes she had always listened to the "dictates of her heart" [86]; her faith in the idea of a marriage founded in love rather than in propriety or convenience was evidence, she says, of an "intractable soul" [79]), and this perversity constitutes a very particular kind of secrecy, the heart's secret logic, secret from Enlightenment rationalism, secret from patriarchal authority, secret from convention etc. And indeed it is out of a sense that she is secreted from every other person in the world that Mary is drawn towards Haywood in the first place. The man with whom she commits adultery is immediately attractive to her in part because of his "pensive reserve, a musefulness that studied to screen itself from observation, and bespoke some latent sorrow" (79). Her love for him develops out of a sense that he might be the one person in the world with whom she could share her secrets, the one person with whom she might be able to form "an entire union of affections" (81). In other words, and Brown's repetitions reinforce this idea, it is not just that Mary Selwyn hides her crime: her crime is intimately bound up with the performance of secrecy, the enjoyment of secrecy, the erotics of secrecy. Her secret, we could say, is that she indulges in secrecy. She attempts to draw on secrecy and arouses the resistance of patriarchy, the same patriarchy that in the form of Dr. Molesworth, the tormented subject of the marriage contract, now inhabits a house of sorrow and seeks with a frenzy to master a secret that seems to have escaped him.

What we are given then is a crisis figured as a confrontation between two secret voices: the secret perverse voice of Mary Selwyn's heart and the secret voice of patriarchal justice whispering in Dr. Molesworth's ear. The implications of this way of framing the confrontation are many. Not the least is the tale's implicit recognition of the erotics of power, a recognition made by the face-off between Mary's secret desire and Molesworth's secret voice of authority. The story suggests that the obscure agency or disembodied voice of post-feudal political authority (that is to say modern, constitutional, democratic political authority) has its own particular kind of erotic charge. Every gesture whereby the law or justice is invoked as an anonymous voice forcing its authority upon us – and this includes all those gestures of inevitability, natural progression, the sway of reason, even the spontaneous impulse of justice with which Brown was so familiar, gestures that were crucial to the success of the American Revolution and the development of our political modernity – all these gestures need to be thought alongside the sentimental novel's discourse of love as an undeniable force, love as the urging of the heart's secret voice, love as the experience of the subject's absolute seclusion from every other member of society, every law, every convention, even from their own most enlightened and rational selves. Illicit love would seem to produce literary subjects as the subjects of secret desires even as the law was producing political subjects as the subjects of bodiless, anonymous legal pronouncement. This is another way of saying that the Declaration of Independence, for example, is a sentimental text in so far as it presents us with a subject (the American "we") giving in to the pleasures of an independence that has been "impelled" upon them, an independence that "necessity ... Constrains them to." The impetuous and fascinating woman who gives in to a desire that she cannot resist and thereby ensures her fall *and* her literary immortality mirrors the willing subject of a law that forces its deputies to honor its perversely secret authority. Dr. Molesworth, we should recall, opens this story in the sway of a justice he is mad about.[46]

The structure of Brown's tale helps us to think about the curious political possibilities of the standard seduction novel. If we take *Charlotte Temple* for a moment as our example of the genre, it is clear that the narrative's omniscience provides readers with all their voyeuristic pleasure even as it mimics the law's insistence that nothing be kept secret. This is perhaps the source of some of the confusion over this novel's (and this genre's) relevance for feminist critical study. No matter how much sympathy it displays for its central female characters, the seduction novel finds itself in the structural position of police informer, telling all, and thus depriving the female characters of anything like an interior life. It has been suggested that the epistolary form of Hanna Foster's *The Coquette* lends, at least initially, more agency to its protagonist precisely to the extent that it allows her voice to determine what is known and when. The reader's lack of omniscience corresponds to Eliza Wharton's secrecy and the result is a character whose agency is in direct proportion to her obscurity. (The subject's own "real" voice preserves the subject's secrecy.) Here we should recall Brown's Carwin as a more perverse example (as befits Brown's gothicism) of an individual whose independence is bound up with an insistent secrecy; he finds his own voice in the form of a dissimulation. In "A Lesson on Concealment" the threat to a certain position of power occasioned by the mere existence of a gap in its knowledge is explicitly written into the structure of the story. Moreover, the telling of the story is presented to us as an exchange of power between two men. Dr. Molesworth, oddly but significantly appealing to Henry Kirvan as "my brother" tells Kirvan that it is in *his* power to reveal all. The seduction story then comes to us in the form of an informer's report, the intelligence of a spy, the patriarchy's undercover agent.

One of the most effective aspects of this tale is its portrayal of Henry Kirvan, the nobody who arrives in America with nothing and proceeds to make a life for himself by carrying secrets, keeping accounts, and secreting himself. Brown carefully establishes a sense of Kirvan's dependency on his own anonymity and on other people's secrets. Indeed, his very life, as Warner Berthoff pointed out in his excellent 1958 article on this story, depends on the exchange of secrets (" 'A Lesson,' " 45–57).[47] The first thing that happens to Kirvan is that the captain of the ship he arrives on promises to introduce him to a wealthy merchant to whom he must deliver some confidential letters (imagine Franklin with his loaves of bread arriving in Philadelphia and replace the image with that of Henry Kirvan carrying the much more Brockden Brownian and post-revolutionary bundle of confidential letters). Kirvan delivers himself and the confidential letters into the hands of this man and thus his American nativity coincides with the arrival of some secret letters. The merchant (who turns out to by Haywood, Mary Selwyn's adulterous lover) offers Henry employment as his personal secretary and accountant.

"I lived with him four months," Kirvan tells us, and "During this period I was a near spectator of his manners and habits" ("A Lesson on
Concealment," 57). As secretary, accountant, and near spectator, Henry
soon reveals a gift for secret observation. Brown's portrait of Henry gathers fascination from the accumulation of references to what can only be
called his invisibility. He describes his first employer's fits of melancholy
thus: "A cloud would sometimes gather on his brow at moments of loneli-
ness, or when my occupation, though in the same apartment, left him, in
some sense, alone" (58). On another occasion, arriving home before his
employer, Henry goes to the drawing-room, where a visitor is waiting:
"the stranger was walking to and fro, with an air of much impatience and
anxiety," he writes. "He looked up eagerly at my entrance; but seeing
who it was, withdrew his eyes in seeming disappointment, and resumed
his pace" (58). Henry then proceeds to sit at his writing desk, entering
the day's transactions in his accounting book while "steal[ing] glances at
the visitant" (58). Observing the visitor's perturbed demeanour, Henry
explains, "My fingers trembled, the pen lost its regularity, and I merely
scribbled at random, as affording opportunity of viewing this scene without being noticed by him" (58). Again and again he plays the role of what
he calls "a neglected and unthought-of witness" (60).

The result of Henry's invisibility seems to be that he becomes the
repository of everybody's secrets. Most importantly, he turns up in Mary
Selwyn's house like the spectral presence of her secret. He is the secretary
par excellence. But as such he is also self-emptied, maybe dangerous,
maybe pathetic. Like the invisible author of the omniscient sentimental
story, his knowledge of everyone else's secrets produces him as a ghost
and a suspect ghost at that. We want to say "get a life" but he keeps getting other people's. In Dr. Molesworth's house he starts to watch Mary
Selwyn (now Mrs. Molesworth) very closely. He becomes possessed by his
possession of her secret. He adores her and watches her. Once again he
is able to watch with a peculiar intimacy because when he is in the room
with her she, like others before her, is "forgetful that there was any to
observe her" (67). The revelation of her full story to Kirvan occurs when
this intense watching finally produces a spectre watching over Mary's
shoulders, a spectre who is surely Kirvan himself.

Thus Henry Kirvan finally accounts for all the details of Mary
Selwyn's tragic life and thereby produces himself as the ideal subject
of Dr. Molesworth's desire. And what is the price of Kirvan's betrayal?
He had told Mary that he would "sew up [his] lips" (71) rather than tell

her secret, and from a mundanely meta-textual perspective it is true that as soon as he gives up this secret Kirvan shuts up, for ever. But of course he does not need to tell all. In doing so he honors one request (that of a man, his elder, his benefactor, the man who can help him to make it in the world) at the expense of a promise made to Mary Selwyn herself. The seduction story is presented to us as the betrayal of a woman by a man on the make, and it is a betrayal that will restore patriarchy to its position of full knowledge, a position originally threatened by Mary Selwyn's refusal (her perverse refusal) to acquiesce completely in her brother's and father's orders concerning marriage. What is the lesson on concealment here?

If American subjectivity after 1789 was theoretically guaranteed by the Constitution and by the new nation's legal (as opposed to monarchic) structure of legitimation, then it is fair to say that all American citizens were indebted to the anonymity of the law, the secret voice and obscure agency of the law. But in their role as the sovereign people, those who according to the prevailing political philosophy constituted the original source of the law's legitimacy, the people, also retained a crucial sovereign obscurity of their own, their own secrecy from the law. The republic of law retains an irreducible relationship to a sovereign people who stand outside the law as its originators. No one is above the law, and yet this state can only come about because the people have given themselves the law. One could imagine the democratic subject as caught between two secrecies: the secret anonymous voice of a disembodied constitutional law and the secret (because nowhere ontologically realized) sovereignty of popular political authority (the people can nowhere be seen as such; they cannot, to quote Jefferson's words again "be assembled"). Certainly this image of the citizen corresponds to the imaginative life of Brockden Brown's fiction. The tension set in place between the law's monopoly on secrecy and the people's claim to a sovereign secrecy from the law could be said to be peculiar to the kind of legal political structure established for the first time by the American Revolution. Brown's "A Lesson on Concealment" (and it is not alone among Brown pieces in this respect) addresses precisely this tension (a tension Brown himself experienced when he struggled with his philosophical objections to the practice of the law). Insofar as Henry Kirvan emerges as the central character of this story, he gives us the example of an individual faced with a demand from the law: tell all to the law, because it is just. In this position, Kirvan calls to mind Carwin in his encounter with Ludloe's secret sect. But where Brown's investment in Carwin has everything to do with Carwin's perverse refusal to tell all to the sect, Brown's depiction of Kirvan presents us with a character who has sacrificed some of his sovereignty (his own sovereign secrecy) to the law when he gives up Mary Selwyn's secret. Hence this character's unnerving emptiness, his spectral hollowness – as a secretary he bears too close a resemblance to a piece of office equipment, a bureau(crat). Kirvan is Brown's disturbing version of the Franklinian state-identified subject I discussed in chapter three. Brown's story tells a complex lesson on concealment: a concealed voice may be the voice of the law that gives us a just political being (a voice Franklin was unusually at home with) or it may be the occulted voice of a particular interest within the polity. Anonymity seems to be the password of force and justice. Political life involves a calculation concerning when we are going to give ourselves up to a voice we are content to let remain secret and when we are going to demand that all secrecy be relinquished. "A Lesson on Concealment" succeeds, in other words, as an intriguing lesson in political philosophy. One of the political questions it helps us to formulate is this one: how does the legal subject, the citizen-subject of democracy, resist the deification of the secret voice that conjured him or her into political being? Via Brown's stories I have tried to suggest that such a resistance can only take the form of a radicalization of secrecy, a radicalization that recognizes the constitutive secrecy of the voice of any political subject, be it the citizen or the State. Democracy, in the radical form that we have been pursuing it in this book, proceeds by re-sisting attempts to delimit secrecy, attempts which thereby seek to create commuinites – or identities – bound by a phantasmatic insistence on their own lack of secrecy. This insistence, as my discussion of "Memoirs of Carwin, the Biloquist" tried to show, belongs with an ethnocentric (or quasi-ethnocentric) insistence on an outside of others who do not and must not share in the secret-less fraternity. Democracy, as Brown's work often seems to acknowledge, albeit with a great deal of hesitation, consists in the multiplication of secrets, the democratization of secrecy, a process that includes the institutionalization of the citizen's own secret relationship to his or her subjected self: the ballot box (like the rooms in Philadelphia that walled in the Constitutional Convention in 1787) is one of the more visible theatres of this democratic secrecy. Democracy's translation of the arbitrariness, the madness, and the unreasonableness of monarchic absolutism takes the form of a structural and individual inheritance of power as secrecy, and the task of any reading of just such a democracy is to identify – without reducing – all the modes of this political secrecy. To give up all secrets, Brown knew this, is to become the spectral, hollow secretary of the law (be it the law of the State, the patriarchy, or the radical political sect). But to hold onto a secret is not to hold onto a fullness that guarantees identity: it is, as Brown's figure of the biloquist suggests, to insist on claiming the self's irreducible relationship to appropriation, echo, and imitation. It is to claim as one's own a subjectivity that, like Carwin's voice, never quite coincides with its speaker.

CHAPTER 5

Luxury, effeminacy, corruption: Irving and the gender of democracy

> In a democracy the people are, in certain respects, the monarch; in other respects, they are the subjects.
>
> They can be the monarch only through their votes which are their wills. The sovereign's will is the sovereign himself. Therefore, the laws establishing the right to vote are fundamental in this government. Indeed, it is as important in this case to regulate how, by whom, for whom, and on what issues votes should be cast, as it is in monarchy to know the monarch and how he should govern.
>
> (Baron de Montesquieu, *The Spirit of the Laws*, 10–11)

> There is no reality in any power that cannot be coined into votes.
>
> (Petition from woman's rights advocates to the Wisconsin State Constitutional Convention, 1848)[1]

THE "CARNIVAL OF FRAUD"

Why did the American Revolution not extend the franchise to women? Because, explained John Adams in his famous reply to Abigail, "We [men] have only the name of masters, and rather than give up this, which would completely subject us to the despotism of the petticoat, I hope General Washington, and all our brave heroes would fight" (*Book of Abigail and John*, 123).[2] Adams was less playful in his response to James Sullivan on May 26, 1776. Responding to Sullivan's proposal that "every person out of wardship" should have a say in the passing of legislation, Adams wrote: "Depend upon it, sir . . . it is dangerous to open so fruitful a source of controversy and altercation, as would be opened by attempting to alter the qualifications of voters. There will be no end of it. New claims will arise. Women will demand a vote" (*Papers of John Adams*, IV, 212–13, 24).[3] "There will be no end of it," writes Adams. His remark and his reference to franchise extension as a dangerous Pandora-like opening-up suggests a sublime terror of bottomless or endless political ground. To extend the franchise is to knock down the fences that mark the borders of the legitimate "people out of doors." This new political order, it would seem, needs "ends" of one sort or another, and the specter of the woman voter somehow introduces the end of ends just as the new republic is trying to get started. And in the late 1790s and early 1800s, Adams might have found proof of his worst fears in New Jersey.

In 1776 the Second Continental Congress had urged the people of the colonies to form new state governments and draft new constitutions. One of the purposes of these constitutions was to outline the criteria of eligibility for voting in state and local elections.[4] In colonial times, the New Jersey franchise had been restricted to freeholders, but the revolution issued a call for a wider franchise in all the states of the union.[5] New Jersey's constitution, drawn up hastily and in secret in 1776, declared that

All inhabitants of this colony of full age, who are worth fifty pounds proclamation money, clear estate in the same, and have resided within the county in which they claim a vote for twelve months immediately preceding the election, shall be entitled to vote for representatives in council and assembly; and also for all other public officers that shall be elected by the people of the county at large.[6]

This wording dramatically expanded the number of New Jersey householders who were eligible to vote. Indeed, it expanded the franchise beyond many people's wildest dreams.[7] The absence of any reference to gender in the 1776 constitution ("all persons" are referred to; there is no use of "he" or "she" in the text), however, does not seem to have been noticed until 1790 when Joseph Cooper, a Quaker representative from West Jersey, pointed out the implicit enfranchisement of qualified women and urged that the revised election law then under consideration in the legislature be rewritten to explicitly recognize women's right to vote, by using "he or she" in the phrases describing eligible voters (Turner, "Women's Suffrage," 168).[8] The revised Bill became law on November 18, 1790 and the same phrasing was used when the law was once again revised in 1797. "I congratulate the ladies of New Jersey," wrote Susan Bradford (née Boudinot), "that they are in some thing put on a footing with the gentlemen and the most extraordinary part is, that it has been done by the gentlemen themselves but these are a few who have been more enlightened than the rest."[9]

It was not until October of 1797, however, that the practical implications of these issues were felt in New Jersey. A significant number of women turned out to vote in a closely fought county election between

John Condict, Republican, of Newark and William Crane, Federalist, of Elizabeth. Newspaper accounts of this election voiced the suspicion that women voters, attracted by something other than political principle, had been persuaded to vote for the Federalist candidate (who nevertheless lost by a narrow margin): "The husbands and sweethearts of these heroines," ran one newspaper report, "began to suspect that some motive other than a love of the Federal cause excited the enterprize" (quoted in Turner, "Women's Suffrage," 170).[10] Writers in the *Newark Centinel* and *New Jersey Journal* took up both sides of the question of women's right to vote, one referring readers to Mary Wollstonecraft's influence and another supporting "women's rights" by way of a song, "The Freedom of Election" (Turner, "Women's Suffrage," 171–2).[11] Edward Turner finds evidence to suggest that women voted in statewide elections in 1800 and 1802 and probably again in 1806. But from 1796 on, there was also an ongoing public discussion about the desirability of voting privileges for women. A series of articles examining the Constitution of New Jersey appeared in the *Trenton State Gazette* between March 1796 and 1798, and the question of women's voting rights drew a number of responses. Some wrote to demand that the rights of "the electors and the elected" be placed upon "safer and more rational principles," the implication being that the right of women to vote should be reconsidered. Another writer referred to the Elizabeth election as having been corrupted by Federalists, who brought out "widows and maids" to vote for their candidate. Even as writers acknowledged that the "letter of the charter" appeared to guarantee voting rights to "persons" regardless of gender, they insisted that "political right and the nature of things" – or what another writer referred to as "the spirit and intention of the law" – surely barred women from voting.[12] One writer, granting an authority to text unusual in this kind of dispute, suggested that while the framers of the original state constitution probably did not intend their gender-neutral language to imply that women had the right to vote, nevertheless "such is the phraseology of the constitution, that it seems a violation of it, not to admit their votes" (quoted in Turner, "Women's Suffrage," 174 n. 39). Certainly, evidence suggests that Republicans and Federalists in New Jersey actively campaigned for women's votes in the presidential election of 1800, and Republicans even went so far as to propose an amendment to the election law specifically designed to insure that inspectors "shall not refuse the vote of any widow or unmarried woman of full age." The proposal was turned down on the basis that "this section would be clearly within the meaning of the constitution . . . [that] gives this right to maids or widows, black or white" (quoted in Klinghoffer and Elkin, "The Petticoat Electors," 181). The strength of opinion on the side of women's right to vote (or is it on the side of a sacralization of the original "phraseology" of the law?) can also be gathered from the failure of a proposed amendment to New Jersey's 1802 state election law that would have excluded "all persons from voting, excepting free white males" (Turner, "Women's Suffrage," 174).

This proposed revision reminds us, as a writer in the *Centinel* for November 11, 1800 had reminded his readers, that the state's 1776 constitution not only gave the right to vote to women ("maids or widows"); it also failed to exclude the vote on the basis of color. As Marion Wright noted in a 1948 study titled "Negro Suffrage in New Jersey, 1776–1875," "the loose construction of some of [the first state constitutions] resulted in Negroes exercising the privilege in several states, including New Jersey" (Wright, "Negro Suffrage," 171–2). Wright reports that single and married women, black as well as white, voted in New Jersey during the presidential election of 1800, and she cites one history of the state that records the decisive influence of votes by colored females in a legislative election in Hunterdon County (173).[13] "In 1802," Wright continues, "a petition to the Legislature to set aside an election in Trenton included among its charges that Negroes and actual slaves, aliens, persons not worth fifty pounds, and married women voted." The election, however, was not set aside. In another instance, in which charges of illegal voting were laid, complainants referred to the votes of "negresses supported by charity," a charge in which the financial rather than the racial circumstances of the voters was most at issue (174).[14]

It was not until 1807 that an amended election law finally addressed what many had come to regard as a flaw in the original state constitution. A large majority of both houses of the New Jersey legislature passed an amendment to the 1797 election law that explicitly restricted the franchise to the "*free, white male citizen* of this state, of the age of twenty-one years, worth fifty pounds proclamation money, for at least twelve months immediately preceding the election." The amendment was supported by speakers who claimed that it was

highly necessary to the safety, quiet, good order and dignity of the state, to clean up the said doubts ["in regard to the admission of *aliens, females,* and *persons of color,* or *negroes* to vote in elections"] by an act of the representatives of the people, declaratory of the true sense and meaning of the constitution, and to ensure its just execution in these particulars, according to the intent of the framers thereof. (quoted in Turner, "Women's Suffrage," 184–5)

I want to look at the specific events that led up to this odd political announcement and amendment. In February of 1807 there was a hotly contested Essex county vote over the location of the new court house (Newark or Elizabethtown). Feelings ran high on either side and charges and evidence of voting fraud escalated. Men and boys voted and voted often. Outsiders were transported in, spies went over to check the numbers voting in either town and the polls threatened, for some, to descend into chaos. A sense of the anxiety occasioned by this vote spills over into the newspaper accounts that Turner draws on in his description of what took place: "Women and girls, black and white, married and single, with and without qualifications, voted again and again. And finally men and boys disguised as women voted once more, and the farce was complete...Men usually honest seemed lost to all sense of honor, so completely were they carried away by the heat of the strife."[15] Up until 1807 the largest recorded turn-out for any vote in Essex County was 4,500. For this vote, 14,000 votes were recorded. The township of Acquacknon, said to have a population of 350 eligible voters, polled almost 1,900. "A more wicked and corrupt scene was never exhibited in this state, or in the United States" wrote the *New Jersey Journal* on February 17, 1807; "It affords a melancholy picture of the morals of the people of Essex," said the *Federalist*, February 23, 1807, "and excites the most unpleasant sensations in the breast of every person favorably disposed to free, elective government." In November of 1807, an act of the legislature declared the election void, and the whole incident helped animate a legislative drive to rewrite the franchise law.

One of those who pushed through the amendment in 1807 was John Condict, the Republican who had almost been beaten by the votes of women in Elizabeth ten years earlier. Condict made an impassioned speech in support of a franchise limited to free, white males.[16] The incidents in Essex county only served to confirm Condict's sense that an enlarged franchise threatened to subvert the liberty of the people, and with no substantial opposition, he and his supporters won the day. There was little or no public response to the amended law and no petitioning or even letter writing on the part of New Jersey women or non-whites in response to their newly enshrined exclusion. The amended election law was reaffirmed by the state legislature in 1820, 1839, and 1844, although by the 1830s the Convention Movement was bringing together African Americans from various parts of the country to discuss, among other things, how best to petition for inclusion in state electorates.[17] In 1875 an amendment to the Constitution admitted, in principle, negro men into the electorate, but in 1912 the state Supreme Court decided against a suit brought by a New Jersey woman who claimed voting rights under the original 1776 constitution.

What emerges from this crisis is a sense on one side of the question (the prevailing side) that any extension of voting rights beyond the free, white male (with property and habitation) constitutes precisely John Adams' dangerous opening-up, an opening-up wonderfully figured by Turner's reference to a "carnival of fraud" in the Essex election. The widened franchise, according to the panicked reading of events, turns democratic election into theatre or fiction, and the woman voter comes to figure, synecdochally, all those who "held the privilege doubtfully."[18] Woman becomes the name for an endless difference that threatened to subvert the sovereign democratic individual. With the free, white male there is an "end" to the beginning of democratic legitimacy; with woman comes endlessness.[19]

From a rhetorical point of view, then, what is most striking about anxiety over the franchise is the regularity with which it deploys a gesture of *accumulatio ad infinitum* to arouse antipathy towards any extension of the franchise. The opposition thereby established is between some notion of the singular proper voting subject, on the one hand, and an endless string of voting types on the other (the white married woman and the white single woman and the black single woman and the alien etc). When, in 1844, the New Jersey legislature established a committee to draft a new version of the franchise law, suggestions that the right of suffrage be considered "universal and inalienable" were greeted with outright contempt. As Wright puts it, "The report [of the committee] contended that if there was to be no examination of the fitness or qualifications, then women, children, Negroes, mulattoes, paupers, slaves, and convicts had a right to vote, and no one had a right to exclude them, because 'if it was their right, society had no right to prevent the execution of that right'" ("Negro Suffrage," 183). This same anxiety crops up in Charles Brockden Brown's *Alcuin* (1798), when the male participant in a conversation about women's political opportunities responds to his female host's frustration with women's exclusion from the franchise with this by now familiar question: "Shall the young, the poor, the stranger, and the females, be admitted, indiscriminately, to political privileges? Shall we annex no condition to a voter but that he be a thing in human shape, not lunatic, and capable of locomotion; and no qualifications to a candidate but the choice of a majority?" (68)[20]

The woman voter and the black voter bring with them the grammar of conjunction (not only men *and* women, black *and* white, married *and* single, but also the "he *or* she" of Joseph Cooper's 1790 amendment). The complex tensions at work in such terms as "the people," "man," "persons," and other nouns that fail to make distinctions within the species are brought into crisis by the sight of women and black voters. Perhaps, these conjunctions suggest, there is no end to "man." Man will be this and this and this... And of course, this "there will be no end of it" also expresses a fear of the absence of teleology, the absence of a horizon, and is thus also a specifically Christian fear. Woman is charged with introducing (with bearing in her very person) an atheistic and revolutionary grammar of conjunction ("and" and "or") that refuses the desperate closure sought by sovereign and indivisible "man."[21]

The New Jersey example demonstrates, then, that the patriarchal exclusion of women from politics in the post-revolutionary period must also be thought of as a resistance to *all* the distinctions that in their otherness helped to define, even as they threatened, the "free, white male." Under these circumstances it is difficult to separate misogyny from a more general panic about the integrity of the category of "the people" and its correlative individual "citizen." In chapter three, I drew attention to the delegates at the Constitutional Convention engaging in a secret act of self-sacrifice which, I argued, threatened to compromise their (masculinized) self-presence. This gesture had to be performed in secret and thereafter repudiated in the form of displacement onto other bodies ever after marked by the sign of a lack or bodily rupture in self-presence that a political elite could only acknowledge at the cost of a loss of power. It is precisely this displacement and repudiation that is on display in the case of the New Jersey franchise in the post-revolutionary period.[22]

The visual correlative of the grammatical discomfort produced by the woman's conjunction is the kind of spectacle witnessed in Essex county in 1807. In this "carnival of fraud," the singular "voter" became a plethora of voters, and the non-singularity of the citizen exposed itself to an outraged elite. Descriptions of the voters in contemporary accounts move from a catalogue of types (all of whom would eventually become legitimate voters) to individuals voting more than once, and finally (in Turner's version) to men and boys dressed as women. These lists rehearse (for the white, male, political imagination) a correlation between women and blacks voting at all and *any* individual voting twice or in disguise. There is a kind of willed slippage here between the metaphoric and metonymic registers. The endless proliferation of kinds of voter initiated by the law's "or she" represents a metonymic corruption of the election's purity; but this corruption causes, or is identified with, a metaphorical corruption, a transformation or substitution affecting the very person of the hegemonic citizen: white men vote more than once as if they "contained multitudes," as Whitman would say, and they cross-dress to facilitate (or celebrate – hence the carnival, or farce) a constitutive substitutability or re-presentability of the self. (Of course one could also say that what the fraudulent male voters of Essex county here illustrated was the capacity, indeed the desire, for an internal metonymic relation: they were beside themselves in their desire for electoral power: "So completely were they carried away," writes Turner, "by the heat of the strife.")

The image of the woman voter and her train of other others thus conjures up the specter of the corruptibility of the lynchpin of revolutionary republicanism: the citizen-voter, the individual political will, the singular sovereign force of democratic legitimacy figured by the very homogeneity of the white propertied man of standing. It is the idea of the individual self-present political will, purified from all external contamination, that a certain revolutionary idealism needs to preserve at the center of its political system.[23] From this perspective, the extension of the franchise could be read as a kind of *extra-vagance* of the real (in Thoreau's sense of the word[24]), a luxury that threatened democratic idealism with an excess of political identity that could always be confused with the material excesses of pre-democratic forms of luxury. Hence "'Luxury, effeminacy, and corruption,'" writes Linda Kerber, "was as much a revolutionary-era refrain as 'life, liberty and the pursuit of happiness'" (*No Constitutional Right*, 10). There is an echo between John Adams' list of the corrupt luxurious items he saw too much of in Europe ("Gold, silver, precious stones, Alabaster, Marble, Silk, Velvet and Lace" [*Book of Abigail and John*, 217]) and his fear of those who would enter the franchise in the wake of women's political empowerment ("There will be no end of it" [*Papers of John Adams*, IV, 212–13]). Similarly, attention to the monarchophobic limitations of republican ideology helps to explain why the married woman is regularly distinguished from the widow or single woman in debates over the franchise at this time. Democratic idealism is invested in the independence of the individual political will, and the married woman presented an unavoidable image of the compromise or subordination of will. As Kerber has recently shown, the question of a married woman's political responsibility was decided in the post-revolutionary years in terms that reasserted her husband's all-consuming authority: "Recognizing that husbands could easily pressure the electoral choices of married women, legislators concluded not that husbands should be controlled, but that women – unmarried as well as married – should not vote" (*No Constitutional Right*, 15).[25] Another way of putting this is to note the revolutionary investment in the sovereignty of the citizen, that is to say, the revolution's anti-monarchism was also, following a familiar logic, invested in the democratic inheritance of monarchical absolutism.[26] The married woman, however, absorbs some of the post-revolutionary anxiety about the inevitable failure of this idealized translation. Marriage shares with slavery the distinction of being a sanctioned institution whose very existence seems to undermine the logic of democratic idealism. The prevailing philosophy of the married woman marked her as the image of everything the idealized revolutionary citizen should not be. She was ontologically obscure at the borders of her personhood, and she was so in accordance with law or custom. Her proper place was at the site of a constitutive displacement; she was the citizen supplemented by and thus compromised by law.[27] Furthermore, the married woman's compromised individuality threatened hegemonic republicanism by appearing to inherit the monarch's "absurdity," his incapacity to think and act like a self-contained, self-identical individual (Paine's "ridiculous" monarch, discussed in my introduction, excluded from information, shut off from the world, and yet being expected to know the world and act decisively in it any way). In this respect she shared something with a slave like Olaudah Equiano, whose freedom, paid for by himself and represented by a signed manumission form, could be patronized by white males resting assured that their freedom and individuality was free of the ambiguous prosthesis of law.[28] The slave, and even the freed slave, thus provided post-revolutionary Americans with a terrifying image of compromised individual sovereignty. It was the American Constitution, after all, that invented the "three-fifths" of a person that helped to displace the self-sacrifice that Franklin called upon the delegates to perform in secret. In this respect, the slave, like the married woman and like the tyrant King George, was not, in the gothic imaginary of democratic idealism, all there.[29]

There is nothing, in other words, to suggest that Robert Ferguson is wrong when he says in his recent survey of the American Enlightenment, that "All of the major patterns of exclusion from citizenship grow stronger within the presumed benefits of increasingly democratic culture." Indeed, he continues, "it is worth reexamining the conventional premise that these patterns represent 'paradoxes' in the republican experiment. Black Americans, Native Americans, and women all lose ground in the first decades of the Republic even as the rights of citizenship are spreading to a broader population base: the workings of political interest and economic advantage only begin to explain these discrepancies" (Ferguson, "The Limits of Enlightenment," 497–8).[30] One of the aspects of the "republican experiment" that we have to recognize, I would suggest, if we are to stop seeing these "paradoxes" as odd aberrations, is the coincidence of an accession to political power with a threat to the singular self-containment of the subject so empowered. Political power can always be read as gain or loss at the level of the subject's independent self-identity, and the management of this ambivalent inheritance produces the violence of franchise restriction as well as the fascination of literary works like the one I wish to turn to in the second half of this chapter.[31]

RIP VAN WINKLE'S REVOLUTION

What are the politics of Washington Irving's deceptively simple story, "Rip Van Winkle"? How does the story theorize – by figuring – the relationship between the pre-and post-revolutionary United States? What is its theory of the relationship between gender and the democratic revolution? "Rip Van Winkle," published in *The Sketch Book* in 1819, is the first notable – and at the same time the most comically dismissive – literary account of the American Revolution. Irving's story seems to mock any attempt to take the revolution too seriously as a significant event of socio-political transformation. That this story's hero (the "simple, honest" Rip) should sleep through the momentous event is an immediate slap in the face to any one inclined to spend too many waking hours evaluating the revolution's achievements. For some readers, the story is a fine example of Irving's pervasive wit, while for others the story merely demonstrates Irving's well-known antipathy towards the democratic revolution. Hence, Larzer Ziff writes:

[Irving's] conservative political outlook was entirely in keeping with a literary instinct that sought out antiquated settings and old-fashioned mannerisms for its effects . . . So far is the American Revolution from making a distinctive difference in everyday life that it is rendered as an event that, so to speak, did not happen. Rip Van Winkle sleeps through it to awake to changes that fail to disguise the basic similarity between present and past. (*Writing in the New Nation*, 146)[32]

That change has not really taken place where it might ordinarily have been thought to have occurred is a recognizable satirical charge: the satirist sees through the illusion of change and his wit alerts him to the endless repetition of man's folly and self-delusion. Irving's enjoyment of this mode is palpable, not least in the framing of the story: it has been found among the papers of Diedrich Knickerbocker, an unsigned preface assures us; Rip was a real person with whom Knickerbocker actually spoke, we are told in a note signed by D.K. Even the epigraph taken from William Cartwright's "The Ordinary" announces, with relish, that "Truth is a thing that ever I will keep." Irving, in other words, multiplies opportunities to assert his lack of authorial anxiety about the possibility of speaking in a sincere voice: there is a very deliberate and delighted performance of fictionality and (Franklinian) pseudonymity in Irving's work that serves, among other things, to ward off any charge of responsibility for the story itself.[33] The authorial presence that controls all of this irony and allows for its enjoyment is announced in its very invisibility by the layers of mock authenticity. To believe any one of the various authoritative voices, or, conversely, to try to determine what "Irving" sincerely wanted to say, is to come up short as a reader of this text. Full narrative authority only returns to Irving, then, insofar as his "voice" can be said to be indistinguishable from the entire performance of the story.

But the relationship between voice and bodily presence or between voice and authority is, of course, one of the major preoccupations of Irving's story. One of the most immediately striking features of "Rip Van Winkle" is the figural effort that goes into describing the "voice" that might seem to be most important in Rip's pre-revolutionary life: the insistently objectified "mouth" of Dame Van Winkle. "Morning, noon, and night," the narrator tells us, "her tongue was incessantly going, and everything [Rip] said or did was sure to produce a torrent of household eloquence" ("Rip Van Winkle," 771). We are never directly informed of the substance of this eloquence, because it is clear that it is the force of her speech that Irving wants us to remember. Her speech is a "torrent," or a "fresh volley" (772), her tongue is repeatedly invoked as a weapon or as "the only edged tool that grows keener with constant use" (772). For Dame Van Winkle, this excess results in what is supposed to be a comical self-destruction. In what is undoubtedly one of the more explicitly misogynist versions of the anxiety about the self-disrupting consequences of the claiming of an authoritative voice, Irving's Dame Van Winkle is blown apart by her own speech: "she broke a bloodvessel in a fit of passion at a New-England pedler" (782).[34]

If Dame Van Winkle's character suggests a link between femininity and the embodied force of language as noise, Rip's circle of male friends give us what appears to be a directly antithetical semiotic imaginary:

For a long while [Rip] used to console himself, when driven from home, by frequenting a kind of perpetual club of the sages, philosophers, and other idle personages of the village, which held its sessions on a bench before a small inn, designated by a rubicund portrait of His Majesty George the Third. Here they used to sit in the shade through a long, lazy summer's day, talking listlessly over village gossip, or telling endless sleepy stories about nothing. (772)

We know right away that these "listless" talkers are the counterparts of Dame Van Winkle. Not only does their speech demand as little physical exertion as possible, but it is also empty and harmless where Rip's wife's is always threatening to drown him or draw blood. Anticipating Rip's sojourn in the mountains, the men's speech is already somnolent (they tell "sleepy" stories about "nothing"). We are told that the only newspapers they read are old ones that occasionally fall into their hands "by chance," and that they deliberate "sagely" upon "public events some months after they had taken place" (772). Rip's sleep and his missing of the revolution are, it is quite clear, on a continuum with the experience of his male associates in the pre-revolutionary village.

The man at the center of these marginal figures is Nicholas Vedder, landlord of the inn, who "took his seat" at the door of the inn "from morning till night, just moving sufficiently to avoid the sun and keep in the shade of a large tree; so that the neighbors could tell the hour by his movements as accurately as by a sun-dial" (772). Vedder is the "great man" of this junto, even though, as we might by now have come to expect, "he was rarely heard to speak." Instead, he smokes.

His adherents, however . . . perfectly understood him, and knew how to gather his opinions. When anything that was read or related displeased him, he was observed to smoke his pipe vehemently, and to send forth short, frequent, and angry puffs; but when pleased, he would inhale the smoke slowly and tranquilly, and emit it in light and placid clouds; and sometimes, taking the pipe from his mouth, and letting the fragrant vapor curl about his nose, would gravely nod his head in token of perfect approbation. (773)

The most authoritative and unequivocal expression, according to Rip and his friends, is silent; it is not contaminated by the materiality of the tongue. Nicholas Vedder's smoke performs a marvelously effective transubstantiation of the messy and antagonistic breath of the body into the "perfectly understood" clouds of smoke, clouds that recall the opening of Irving's story:

Whoever has made a voyage up the Hudson must remember the Kaatskill Mountains. They are a dismembered branch of the great Appalachian family, and are seen away to the west of the river, swelling up to a noble height, and lording it over the surrounding country. Every change of season, every change of weather, indeed, every hour of the day, produces some change in the magical hues and shapes of these mountains, and they are regarded by all the good wives, far and near, as perfect barometers. When the weather is fair and settled, they are clothed in blue and purple, and print their bold outlines on the clear evening sky; but sometimes, when the rest of the landscape is cloudless, they will gather a hood of gray vapors about their summits, which, in the last rays of the setting sun, will glow and light up like a crown of glory. (769)

In retrospect, this opening description not only serves to remind us that Nicholas Vedder's "perfectly understood" speech shares a great deal with the "perfect barometers" of the natural world, but also that both Nicholas and the Kaatskill mountains share a relationship to monarchism.[35] The mountains swell up to a "noble" height and can be seen "lording it over the surrounding country." They are sometimes clothed in "blue and purple" but at other times, the gray clouds around their summit will catch the sun and "glow and light up like a crown of glory." Vedder is not only the proprietor of the George the Third Inn; he is also a "great man," a "patriarch" and an "august personage," who "completely controlled" (773) the opinions of his council of men. Hence, revolutionary antagonism, in this story, occurs on those occasions when Dame Van Winkle confronts Nicholas Vedder: "From even this stronghold Rip was at length routed by his termagant wife, who would suddenly break upon the tranquility of the assemblage and call the members all to naught; nor was that august personage, Nicholas Vedder himself, sacred from the daring tongue of this terrible virago, who charged him outright with encouraging her husband in habits of idleness" (773). If Vedder is "Rip Van Winkle"'s rather sorry version of a monarch, then Dame Van Winkle is (oddly, perhaps) the story's revolutionary, a fact brought home by the comprehensive redistribution of Dame Van Winkle's principal characteristics in the world Rip returns to after his sleep.[36] Rip returns to a post-revolutionary village in which "the very character of the people seemed changed." In place of the town's "accustomed phlegm and drowsy tranquility," Rip encounters everywhere "a busy, bustling, disputatious tone" (779). "He looked in vain for the sage Nicholas Vedder, with his broad face, double chin, and fair long pipe, uttering clouds of tobacco-smoke instead of idle speeches" but what he sees instead is "a lean billious-looking fellow, with his pockets full of hand-bills . . . haranguing vehemently about rights of citizens – elections – members of congress – liberty – Bunker's Hill – heroes of seventy-six – and other words, which were a perfect Babylonish jargon to the bewildered Van Winkle" (779).

Revolution, it would seem, has simply allowed democratic politicians to take over the tyrannical position vacated by Dame Van Winkle.[37] Power, figured as the force of speech (speech as sound, as air, as biliousness, as the whip of a tongue) simply proceeds from a new despotic source. Crucial to this perspective is the absolute irrelevance, once again, of what the speakers have to say. Instead, the narrator emphasizes the semiologically empty "noise" of speech and the simple substitution of a new source for this noise. From Rip's perspective, the tongue-wagging populace has simply taken over the role played by his now deceased wife. To speak the language of democratic empowerment is, according to "Rip Van Winkle," to be compromised as a man, to be feminized or "termagant." But it is also to become "bilious," nauseated by a speech that the body experiences as an unwelcome excess.[38] Democracy has feminized men and raised the noise level.[39]

One way of reading Irving's story then, would be to emphasize the allegorical opposition which it sets up between an ideology of natural speech, speech without words, speech without the interference of the human body, speech that is noble and unforceful, and speech that is nothing but human bodily interference (the tongue, the bad air, the noise of human speech). This opposition is insistently gendered, of course, leaving us with a strong sense of male nostalgia for pre-democratic silence, the silence of mountains, monarchs and proud subjects, the silence that is simultaneously "perfect" speech, uncontaminated by rhetorical force or semiological equivocality.[40] It is certainly hard not to ignore the fact that while Dame Van Winkle's self-destruction is coded as an end to despotism in this story, Rip's peaceful retirement from unemployment is rendered as a happy ending. Indeed, the story, somewhat bewilderingly, tells us that what we are reading is Rip's story above all:

He used to tell his story to every stranger that arrived at Mr. Doolittle's hotel. He was observed, at first, to vary on some points every time he told it, which was, doubtless, owing to his having so recently awaked. It at last settled down precisely to the tale I have related, and not a man, woman, or child in the neighborhood but knew it by heart. (783–4)

The story, in other words, is overwhelmingly invested in the nostalgic appeal of Rip's pre-revolutionary, monarchic imaginary. Moreover, this imaginary is insistently and defensively masculine. The last sentence of the story tells us of the lasting impact of Rip's story on the community and that, "It is a common wish of all hen-pecked husbands in the neighborhood, when life hangs heavy on their hands, that they might have a quieting draught out of Rip Van Winkle's flagon" (784). As such, the story could be said to give popular, aesthetic support to the ideological work being done by post-revolutionary legislatures bent on limiting political power to a select group of white, male citizens. Irving's story, with its outrageous depiction of Dame Van Winkle, fits perfectly alongside of the hysterical descriptions of an expansive franchise. Replying to his wife's call for women's political rights to be remembered in the independent nation's new "Code of Laws," John Adams, it is important to remember, begins by writing, "As to your extraordinary Code of Laws, I cannot but laugh" (*The Book of Abigail and John*, 123). Laughing at the female political voice is a joke that Irving shared with the founding fathers. In New Jersey, the extended franchise came to be thought of as a "farce," as not only women and girls but also boys and men disguised as women voted over and over. "Rip Van Winkle"'s investment in the ludicrousness and the eventual death of Dame Van Winkle seems fully attuned to the political climate that insisted on women's exclusion from the political sphere.

In the same year that the New Jersey legislature was trying to explicitly write women out of the franchise, Washington Irving, who was already anticipating "Rip Van Winkle,"[41] was at work with his brother William and with James Kirke Paulding on a periodical entitled *Salmagundi; or, the Whim-Whams and Opinions of Launcelot Langstaff, Esq. and Others*. This mixed bag of prose and verse appeared in twenty duodecimo numbers separately issued between January 24, 1807 and January 25, 1808. A two-volume edition appeared in 1808. The periodical was, among other things, a platform from which to launch satirical Federalist attacks on Jefferson and his administration.[42] Writing as "Mustapha Rub-a-Dub-Keli Khan," a Tripolitan prisoner writing home on the customs and institutions of America, Irving indulged in extended mockery of what he called the "blustering windy assembly (congress)" where "everything is carried by noise, tumult and debate" (*Salmagundi*, 147). Often, he says, all the endless talking is about "an affair of no importance" and ends "intirely in smoke" (148). The representatives frequently do nothing, in Mustapha's opinion, but "exhibit the length of their tongues and the emptiness of their heads." Finally, Mustapha lets his reader into a "secret":

I have been told in confidence, that there have been absolutely several old women smuggled into congress from different parts of the empire, who having once got on the breeches, as thou mayst well imagine, have taken the lead in debate, and overwhelmed the whole assembly with their garrulity; for my part, as times go, I do not see why old women should not be as eligible to public councils as old men, who possess their dispositions – they certainly are eminently possessed of the qualifications requisite to govern in a logocracy. (148)[43]

It seems undeniable, to repeat the point, that Irving is preoccupied with the effeminizing potential of democratic politics, so much so that we can begin to see how the explicit extension of the franchise to women might have been resisted precisely insofar as it served to highlight the extent to which democratic transformation had already compromised the masculine subject (and, of course, the subject of an imaginary lack of ethnicity). Hence, the panic and preoccupation generated by the "final" disgrace of the 1807 election in New Jersey: the image of the male voter disguised as a woman.[44] An election, as Irving's Mustapha described it in *Salmagundi* (June 2, 1807) precipitated a "courtship" between the candidates and *"mother mob"* (*Salmagundi*, 208). Mother mob preferred the company of "the rabble, or of fellows of her own stamp," and she was not to be fooled with: "for she was the most pestilent, cross, crabbed, scolding, thieving, scratching, toping, wrong-headed, rebellious, and abominable termagant that ever was let loose in the world" (208). American elections, the fictional observer concludes, "are the orgies of liberty" and they only convince him that American democracy will end in dictatorial tyranny ("some ambitious leader, having at first condescended to be their slave, will at length become their master; and in proportion to the vileness of his former servitude, will be the severity of his subsequent tyranny," 209).

But if Irving's work can be read as proceeding from a familiar misogynist anxiety about democracy, we might also expect to find his texts complicating their own fantasies of the relationship between gender, speech, and power. Glancing again at the excerpt from *Salmagundi*, it is curious to note that the effeminized congressmen intent on exhibiting the "length of their tongues" are not only versions of Dame Van Winkle and her post-revolutionary descendents in Irving's story. The speech of these representatives, we are told, often concerns "an affair of no importance" and ends "intirely in smoke" (148). Speech that ends in smoke? Where have we heard that before? In fact, prompted by this connection, we discover upon turning again to "Rip Van Winkle's" economy of gendered speakers that things will not stay in their place. Just as smoke, for Irving, seems to be capable of signifying the empty speech of effeminized democratic politicians *and* the wise judgments of the reticent but lordly Nicholas Vedder, so the male circle's reverence for "perfect" wordless pronouncements from their patriarch aligns them with the "good wives" of the village who read the "noble" Kaatskills as "perfect barometers." In fact, I would argue, it is more accurate to say that while a tendency to draw absolute distinctions between a sympathetic, male economy of honest, disembodied, noble speech on the one hand, and noisy, aggressive,

excessively embodied, female, democratic speech on the other undoubtedly drives this story and Irving's work elsewhere, it is nevertheless the
case that the distinction will not hold.[45]

To say that the revolutionary antagonism at the heart of "Rip Van
Winkle" is that between Nicholas Vedder and Dame Van Winkle is also
to say that these two figures represent a mutually defining opposition. As
such, they inhabit what we should call the same discursive field. When
Rip returns to his post-revolutionary village the two people whose absence he most explicitly registers are Vedder and his wife. But where
previously Dame Van Winkle had been figured as the disruptive revolutionary force impinging upon Nicholas Vedder's monarchic male circle,
now she is herself aligned with the monarchic order displaced by the
revolution. Thus, Rip is gradually informed of what he has missed:

> How that there had been a revolutionary war, – that the country had thrown
> off the yoke of old England, – and that, instead of being a subject of his Majesty
> George the Third, he was now a free citizen of the United States. Rip, in fact, was
> no politician; the changes of states and empires made but little impression upon
> him; but there was one species of despotism under which he had long groaned,
> and that was – petticoat government. Happily that was at an end; he had got his
> neck out of the yoke of matrimony, and could go in and out whenever he pleased,
> without dreading the tyranny of Dame Van Winkle. ("Rip Van Winkle," 783)[46]

That the opposition between Nicholas Vedder and Dame Van Winkle
might in fact disguise something they share can be seen most clearly, however, when we consider their respective relationships to the materiality
of language. Dame Van Winkle, who is all noise, actually says nothing.
As far as the story is concerned, it is the physical force of her speech
that predominates over any content, a fact brought home by the form
of her death. Language achieves an irrepressible materiality in Dame
Van Winkle's presentation. Nicholas Vedder, as we have already noted,
materializes his language by issuing it as smoke. That smoke should be as
impoverished in its materiality as Dame Van Winkle's "dinning in [Rip's]
ears" (148) is brought home to us by Irving's reference (in *Salmagundi*)
to the semiotic impoverishment of democratic congressmen whose
speech ends "intirely in smoke." Both Dame Van Winkle, the mother
of all democratic politicians, and Nicholas Vedder, the last patriarch, are
associated with distinctive materializations of language. Both, also, find
correlatives in the natural world (Dame Van Winkle with her "torrent
of household eloquence," Vedder with his metaphorical relationship to
the lordly and authoritative Kaatskill mountains). What we find is that

any attempt to figure the unadulterated wisdom or grandeur of any kind of authoritative pronouncement (be it the Kaatskill's barometer or Vedder's pipe) suffers from an irreducible association with various representations of speech (feminine and/or democratic) at its most violent, meaningless, and degraded.[47] The lordly Kaatskills are read as perfect barometers, certainly, but by the "good wives" of the region, which is to say by those whose relationship to reading and understanding is already regarded with a mild degree of condescension by the anthropological "Diedrich Knickerbocker." The men of Vedder's junto participate in a perfect circle of unanimity and unequivocality, but they are out of the circle of history, reading only old newspapers and deliberating on "public events some months after they had taken place." Indeed, one could convincingly argue that "Rip Van Winkle," far from merely participating in the exclusionary ideology of a white, male democratic idealism, in fact carries out a devastating parody of just that fantasy. The homogeneous male assembly in Irving's story demonstrates a fantasy of perfect understanding and "perfect approbation" binding together a group who are nevertheless stuck outside of time as history (they have no relationship to the historical: they *are* history, as we might say). Their disembodied fantasy of the civic republican voice of wisdom is simultaneously a fantasy of historical irrelevance that is finally and most memorably figured in Rip's complete absence from the revolution. Irving's representation of Rip's circle of male friends demonstrates lines of continuity between a monarchic imaginary (Vedder is the "great man"; his pronouncements are equivalent to those of the "noble" Kaatskills) and a male republican fantasy of the disembodied citizen, the transcendent voice of civic authority. Moreover, it aligns both of these political fantasies with an exit from history that can only be figured as a form of sleep or death.[48]

"Rip Van Winkle" can thus be shown to highlight a correspondence between the authority of speech that – like smoke or mountains – transcends any particular body (thus the speech of law; the speech of anonymous print proclamation; the speech of republican unanimity) and the emptiness of speech as noise, speech as smoke, or speech as dead air. This correspondence is, finally, made most tangible in the figure of Rip himself, who is at once the central character of the story (it is named for him, he draws our sympathy, he begins and ends the story) and the embodiment of emptiness, sleep, and indeed death itself. Rip's characteristic gesture (it had "grown into a habit," 772) is described twice in the story: "He shrugged his shoulders, shook his head, cast up his eyes, but said nothing" (772, 783). When he does speak, as he does in his role as storyteller at the end of the tale, it is merely to tell his own story over and over again with what eventually becomes a mechanical lack of variation. There is something of a *mise-en-abîme* structure at play here, whereby we are told that the story we have been reading is the very one that Rip repeatedly told to anyone who would listen (so exactly that townspeople "knew it by heart" [784]). Rip's "voice," that is to say, becomes indistinguishable from the automatic repetition of the story, a repetition that has everything to do with the hypostasization of authorial voice produced by a literary text such as "Rip Van Winkle." Rip, the archetypal emblem of vacuousness and sleep-filled subjectivity, is not only at the centre of this story; in his role as generator of the text of his story he is also implicitly identified with the authorial voice (we would standardly call it "Irving's") that ostensibly commands and controls all the irony at play in this overflowingly empty story.[49] The witty command of irony that serves to contain irony's dissemination (and which points us not only towards the personality of Washington Irving himself but towards the authority of all those republican voices that claimed to have transcended difference), is finally indistinguishable from the depthless, mechanical voice of Rip Van Winkle, R.I.P.[50]

There is an animating tension built into Irving's story, then, between its satiric, jovial investment in Rip's "simple" but honest perspective on the revolution's grandiose self-deception, and its simultaneous registration of the morbidity of Rip's eternal repetitions, his alienation from history, his mechanicity.[51] Rip is one of America's enduring figures of externality: his detour in the mountains figures a fantasy of an outside of politics, civility, law, and order that is simultaneously distanced from the forces of feminization.[52] Leslie Fiedler put it most forcefully:

> The figure of Rip Van Winkle presides over the birth of the American imagination; and it is fitting that our first successful homegrown legend should memorialize, however playfully, the flight of the dreamer from the shrew – into the mountains and out of time, away from the drab duties of home and town toward the good companions and the magic keg of beer. Ever since, the typical male protagonist of our fiction has been a man on the run, harried into the forest and out to sea, down the river or into combat – anywhere to avoid "civilization," [and revolution?] which is to say, the confrontation of a man and woman which leads to the fall to sex, marriage, and responsibility. (quoted in Fetterley, *The Resisting Reader*, 1)

Rip's escape is figured as a general fantasy of all "hen-pecked husbands" who "when life hangs heavy on their hands, [wish] that they might have a quieting draught out of Rip Van Winkle's flagon" (784). Rip can always be reappropriated for an American tradition that could include Henry Thoreau and Huckleberry Finn, individuals who flee to the mountains (or the woods, or the river) whenever the noise of democratic or feminized speech threatens their masculine taciturnity.[53] And it would be wrong to forget that this Rip is indeed part of the inheritance of the American Revolution.[54] Rip bears a relation to a revolutionary machismo that rejects monarchism's effeminacy along with its excessive trappings and turns to a nature that is repeatedly figured as the source of unequivocal wisdom (it is the site of that "economy," in Thoreau's sense, that is the antithesis of monarchic extravagance). From this perspective, democracy – that which the revolution ushered in – can always be experienced as a loss for the subject of uncompromised individuality.[55] Democracy does not speak like the idealized nature of the revolutionary imagination; it demands that the political voice confront its irreducible relationship to embodied speech – speech that is historical, material, and political, speech that comes with bad air, with noise, with translation difficulties, and speech constructed around a mutual contamination of referential clarity and rhetorical force. But as the story of "Rip Van Winkle" and Fiedler's commentary reminds us, in fleeing democracy this version of the American subject also misses the revolution. To be nostalgic for Rip Van Winkle is to participate in the curious double logic of a revolutionary monarchophobia that misses the revolution in the very act of revolting; it is also to participate in an American literary imagination that is more at home with outlaws of "majestic" nature than with the revolutionary founders of the structures and institutions of an emasculating democracy.[56]

Dame Van Winkle's death calls to mind late-eighteenth-century associations of democracy with the violence and destruction of the passions, and it is this death that allows for Rip's comfortable assimilation into post-revolutionary village life. Insofar as Irving's story (and its ideal reader) registers pleasure in Dame Van Winkle's death and Rip's return, it constitutes a nostalgic and reactionary story that itself misses the revolution precisely insofar as it fails to move beyond the revolutionary antithesis it so memorably figures.[57] The transformative violence that such a missing fails to record (the revolution *is* a violence) is replaced in this story by the misogynist violence directed at Dame Van Winkle. Her death is the story's registration of the explicit exclusion of women (and by implication all those other others) from the franchise in the post-revolutionary United States. That exclusion allowed for (and is coterminous with) the post-revolutionary affection for Rip Van Winkle and his descendents.[58]

In "Rip Van Winkle," to be inside of the political is to be feminized; to be outside of the political is to be a subject of one or another version of monarchism (the monarchistic idealization of nature, God, or great men). Democractic outlaws are always figures for both revolutionary founding and monarchic subjectivity, and the irreducible simultaneity of monarchic and revolutionary political subjectivity at the founding moment of democracy needs to be recognized and thought through as part of the structure of democracy. Nature is most often the space associated with this doubled founding subjectivity, but nature is also the rhetorical figure for an absence – the absence of divine wisdom, the absence of a totalitarian command of the political – that founds politics as the tumultuous and windy discourse of competing claims to legitimacy, justice, and right.

Afterword: the revolution's last word

> Thus, not only does democracy make every man forget his ancestors, but it hides his descendants and separates his contemporaries from him; it throws him back forever upon himself alone, and threatens in the end to confine him entirely within the solitude of his own heart.
>
> (Alexis de Tocqueville, *Democracy in America*, 194)

In recent years, the novels of James Fenimore Cooper have provided literary critics with useful examples of how an ideologically motivated refusal to think through the complexities of white, male subjectivity ends up contributing to a racist and proto-fascist aesthetic. This is an aesthetic, moreover, that is deemed to be entirely consistent with some of the ways in which Americans were trying to reimagine their national past and future in the wake of the war of 1812. "Cooper's fictions operate as strategies of containment," writes Jonathan Arac, "imaginary techniques for negotiating the complexities of the life that both he and his readers were living" ("Establishing National Narrative," 614). "*Last of the Mohicans*," claims Dana Nelson, became a "culturally iconic text" because it "sidesteps the neurotic vantage of the son and assumes the more symbolically stable (if sterile) position of the father." This move, she suggests, "complements the novel's misogynist obsession with racial purity" (*National Manhood*, 269–70). Finally, Nancy Ruttenburg suggests that Cooper's Natty Bumpo, with his "anomalous presence in the Indian landscape," "permits the work of genocide to be figured as the companionable transfer of democratic personality from the noble savage to his white comrade as the latter's rightful legacy and the unpolluted source of his representative Americanness" (*Democratic Personality*, 324). Enshrined as the official novelist of a patriotic and historically reverential national literature, Cooper has become our favorite (because most flagrant) American propagandist: what would we do without him?

I want to close this study of the opening-up of American democracy by exploring the "strategies of containment" that agitate and propel Cooper's attempt to record the revolution of 1776 in *The Spy* (1821). This novel of the founding founders on an intriguing structure of impossibility that I believe provides us with a surprisingly nuanced attempt to think through the demands of democracy. Put simply, Cooper found in his figure of the spy an ideal revolutionary American whose exemplarity paradoxically demanded that his commitment to the revolution remain a secret. Cooper's spy is a figure, that is to say, for the impossibility of the "pure" revolutionary and by extension of the "pure" democratic subject. The implications of that discovery and the ways in which Cooper's novel attempts to "contain" it will be the focus of attention in the pages that follow.

With *The Spy* the United States finally had a national novelist and a national novel. And it had written the revolution into its literary history in a monumental fashion. "We have to thank our author," wrote W.H. Gardiner in the *North American Review* (July 1822), "for having demonstrated so entirely to our satisfaction, that an admirable topic for the romantic historian has grown out of the American Revolution" (in Dekker and McWilliams, *Fenimore Cooper*, 65). He continues: "[the author] has the high praise, and will have, we may add, the future glory, of having struck into a new path – of having opened a mine of exhaustless wealth – in a word, he has laid the foundations of American romance, and is really the first who has deserved the appellation of a distinguished American novel writer" (65–6). Gardiner's remarks were echoed one hundred and fifty years later, when, in the midst of bicentennial celebrations, James Beard referred to *The Spy* as "crucial in the history of our national literature" (Beard, "Cooper and the Revolutionary Mythos," 84).[1] More recently, Michael Kammen has claimed that "For better or for worse, Cooper's imaginative perception of that pivotal period in our history has become the reference point for hundreds of authors ever since" (*A Season of Youth*, 24). Cooper's novel sits easily at the opening of a burst of American literature emerging out of the War of 1812 with a new thirst for literary and artistic celebrations of the nation's past. *The Spy* exemplifies the investment in the country's dead or aging revolutionary heroes that Michael Kammen has so usefully identified with the 1820s, and it is often read alongside Cooper's ebullient article on the nostalgia-fest surrounding Lafayette's tour of the United States in 1825.[2] Cooper himself, however, referred to his second novel as immoral and whatever he may have meant by this, it ought to be at least somewhat disconcerting to find that a revolution (and hence a nation) founded on the repudiation of monkish and monarchical obfuscation and mystique should be celebrated in literature via the figure of the spy.[3] Maria Edgeworth, who declared that despite its flaws, *The Spy* was "a work of genius," nevertheless thought the centrality of the peddler spy "injudicious": "No sympathy can be excited with meanness, and there must be a degree of meanness ever associated with the idea of a spy," she wrote;

Neither poetry nor prose can ever make a spy an heroic character. From Dolon in the Iliad to Major André, and from Major André to this instrument of Washington, it has been found impracticable to raise a spy into a hero. Even the punishment of hanging goes against all heroic stomachs – the scaffold is a glorious thing, and may be brought on the stage with safety – but would even Shakespeare venture the gibbet?[4]

Edgeworth's sentiment echoes one which appears in the novel itself, when one of the American judges presiding over young Henry Wharton's trial for espionage explains, "A soldier, Captain Wharton, should never meet his enemy but openly, and with arms in his hands. I have served two kings of England, as I now serve my native land; but never did I approach a foe, unless under the light of the sun, and with honest notice that an enemy was nigh" (*The Spy*, 302).

Cooper's hero is thus, in this regard, an unorthodox or perhaps we should say revolutionary, kind of hero. By choosing to idealize an out-cast type, Cooper, we could say, makes a democratic gesture, one which helps to counter the over-emphasis on the historical importance of the revolution's political elite. One way of accounting for the popularity of *The Spy*, then, is by noting the efficaciousness of a figure, Harvey Birch, who manages to combine an investment in the simple, honest citizen of democratic ideology with an increasing idealization of in-dividual character. Birch belongs (retrospectively) to the pantheon of revolutionary heroes, and yet his role demands that he maintain the anonymity of humble citizenship. The requirements of a nineteenth-century American society uneasy with excessive displays of venera-tion directed at elite individuals were uniquely addressed by a figure whose patriotism coincided with his invisibility.[5] With its choice of hero, moreover, *The Spy* demonstrates its generic identity: "The historical ro-mance," notes Jonathan Arac, "asserted that in the past even apparently commonplace individuals had been involved in a process of great signifi-cance, the making of world history" ("Establishing National Narrative," 617).[6] Cooper's Harvey Birch simultaneously seems to participate in what Ruttenburg has recently called "an American aesthetic of innocence," through which "democratic personality would be recognized and eventually rehabilitated (domesticated) as the essence of genuine American character and thus the exemplary subject – both representing and represented – of the national literature" (*Democratic Personality*, 291). Ruttenburg's aesthetic values a "withdrawal from the economic and political life of the nation" (294) and a characteristic tendency towards speechlessness that can be found, almost too perfectly, in the figure of the spy. At the same time, Cooper's peddler spy is intimately tied throughout the novel to none other than George Washington, the individual who more than any other was identified – in his person – with the revolution, the founding, and the American people themselves. ("Americans!" exclaimed Governor Morris in one of the many orations on the death of Washington, "he had no child – *but you* – and *he was all your own*."[7]) Indeed, the novel opens with a description of a "solitary traveller . . . pursuing his way through one of the numerous little valleys of West-Chester" (*The Spy*, 9), and readers would be forgiven for presuming that the spy of the novel's title is *this* figure – the figure who will turn out to have been Washington. If it participates in the idealization of an American personality that is most at home outside of the economy of language, politics, and commerce, *The Spy* suggests that this space belongs to its founders as much as to its outlaws.

To suggest that the American Revolution found its heroes outside of the visible circles of economic and political exchange is to suggest, of course, that secrecy was necessary to, and thus belongs to the formation of, the democratic United States. In fact, *The Spy* begins by suggesting, oddly enough, that the revolution produced "great numbers" who "wore masks," which "even to this day have not been thrown aside" (10). Some apparent patriots, in other words, could their "hidden repositories" be "opened to the light of day," would turn out to have enjoyed "royal protections . . . concealed under piles of British gold"; and on the other hand, "many an individual . . . stigmatised as a foe to the rights of his countrymen," would turn out to have been, "in secret . . . the useful agent of the leaders of the revolution" (10). Cooper's novel, initially at least, claims that the revolution opened up an economy of secrecy and duplicity, and that this was not by way of a fall, an accident, or an unhappy side-effect. Rather, *The Spy*'s revolution is most admirably and unequivocally embodied in the persons of those characters (Washington and the peddler) who recognize the singular importance of duplicity for the success of the revolution. But what makes Harvey Birch's story so compelling is that his deception appears to demand no compensatory revelation: like the actual figure who apparently inspired the story, a spy who came to the attention of John Jay (chair of New York's Committee to Detect Conspiracy), the radical secrecy of Birch's patriotism was crucial to his operation. In his 1831 introduction to a revised edition of *The Spy*, Cooper recalled the origins of the novel in a conversation with Jay (thirty-four years after the end of the war) on "the effects which great political excitement produced on character, and the purifying consequences of love of country, when that sentiment is powerfully awakened in a people" (*The Spy*, 3). What struck Cooper in Jay's account of one particular agent was not just the extent of the spy's concealment ("all but a few highly placed Patriots such as Jay thought he was 'a bold and inveterate Tory' " [Franklin, "Introduction," xviii]) but the idea that his relentless commitment to secrecy was driven not by hope of financial gain (according to Jay, the man in question had turned down offers of payment from Jay himself) but by "Patriotism," which was "uppermost in the heart of this remarkable individual" (Cooper, *The Spy*, 5).[8] It was in the figure of the unremunerated, secret patriot that Cooper found his representation of what he called the "purity" of "real Patriotism" (quoted in Franklin, "Introduction," xviii).[9] In seeking out the purist example of patriotism for his novel, in other words, Cooper lighted on a character who would receive no payment either in the form of money or of public recognition. This, of course, did not reflect actual practice during the war. As historians of American espionage have pointed out, Washington recognized the need for an organized network of spies as early as 1777 when he turned to Philadelphia merchant and congressman Robert Morris (later to be known as the Financier of the Revolution) for "'hard money to pay a certain set of people.' "[10] John Jay's story of the spy who would take no money circulated, one has to presume, precisely because of its oddity: in this respect, there was nothing representative about Harvey Birch. What lay behind Cooper's (and later his readers') fascination with this particular spy was perhaps the immediate economic atmosphere of the United States in the post-war (of 1812) period. Cooper was writing *The Spy* in the midst of a dramatic expansion of the capitalist economy that would force even older revolutionaries, like James Madison, to acknowledge the intimate relationship between financial appetite and republican vigor. Recognizing that, as Steven Watts puts it, "self-interest had become the dominant social and economic fact of postwar America," Madison came to approve what he called "the policy of leaving to the sagacity of individuals, and to the impulse of private interest, the application of industry and capital . . . profit being the object of each, as the profit of each is the wealth of the whole" (Watts, *The Republic Reborn*, 318).

Birch's rejection of any kind of economic remuneration, we might cynically imagine, allows an expanding capitalist society to celebrate in literature what it cannot afford to encourage in practice. Both the facts of the revolution and of contemporary economic life in the United States, in other words, were registered in *The Spy* only in the form of a determined disavowal that has long been associated with the form of the historical romance.[11] Cooper, wrote Donald Ringe in a 1977 article, "viewed the matter-of-fact realities of American life as unsuitable for fiction [and] even the events of American history were sometimes seen as too well known to serve as the basis for fiction: they could become useful to the romancer only after a lapse of time had veiled them in obscurity" ("The American Revolution," 356). What was more important than historical accuracy for Cooper the romancer, Ringe notes, was "the essential truth of the whole experience of the Revolutionary War" (357). The essential truth of patriotism, according to *The Spy*, was that it stood outside of any demeaning economy: patriotism would, in the figure of the spy, be its own reward – it would not be caught up in an economy of exchange that would threaten its purity. And thus the figure castigated by Maria Edgeworth and the novel's juridical representatives as despicable, dishonest, and unmanly turns out to be the very soul of patriotism, the "spirit of '76."

This spirit is, not surprisingly, a go-between. As John McWilliams notes, Harvey Birch, the undercover American spy, spends most of the novel trying to rescue a British soldier from American prosecution, a fact which, McWiliams suggests, undermines the sacredness of the American Revolution even as it increases the reader's admiration for the integrity of the spy (*Political Justice*, 51). In fact, what Birch is engaged in here is the work of reconciliation that this novel, for all its patriotic ardour, cannot wait to announce. " 'I wish, from the bottom of my heart,' " declares the loyalist Mr. Wharton in the novel's opening chapter, " 'this unnatural struggle was over, that we might again meet our friends and relatives in peace and love' " (*The Spy*, 15). This desire, suggesting as it does that the revolutionary war was, as Cooper himself put it, a "domestic" affair ("At the time of our tale," he writes, " we were a divided people" [150]), finds its resolution in the appearance in the novel's closing chapter of a young man – Wharton Dunwoodie – who represents in his person (as off-spring of a union between the revolutionary and the loyalist's daughter) the coming together of two opposing families. Michael Gilmore has suggested that in choosing *The Spy* as a literary model over *Precaution* and the collection of stories about marriage that Cooper considered at the same time, Cooper shifted "toward masculine subjects and preoccupations."

"Gravitating toward Scott and military-historical adventure," Gilmore continues, "was a means of fending off the derogation of novelists as unmanly" ("James Fenimore Cooper," 679). But it is also clear that what some have recognized as a tension in Cooper's literary aspirations between his penchant for the domestic novel of marriage on the one hand and the masculine novel of struggle and violence on the other, finds itself resolved in the figure of the spy as military hero and successful matchmaker. For it is the marriage of Frances Wharton and Major Dunwoodie as much as the independence of the United States that Harvey Birch appears to risk his life for. His reward, then, is to gaze at the beatific head of young Wharton Dunwoodie in his last moments: " 'Tis like our native land!' exclaimed the old man with vehemence, 'improving with time; – God has blessed both' " (*The Spy*, 403).

The Spy is, then, the story of a figure who facilitates independence and union but only at the price of his own peculiar exclusion from the circle of those who will come to benefit from both. Harvey Birch, like Washington, will not leave any progeny: his name will die with him. Indeed, he is marked for death throughout *The Spy* according to a logic – or should we say an aesthetic? – that Cooper will come to perfect in *The Last of the Mohicans* (1826). The "spirit of '76" is insistently spectral:

The trooper turned from gazing at the edifice, to the speaker, and to his astonishment, instead of one of his own men, he beheld the pedler.
"Ha! The spy," he exclaimed: "by heavens, you cross me like a spectre." (*The Spy*, 267)

"Well to say the truth [whispers Katy], Harvey was a mystified body, and he was like the winds in the good book; no one could tell whence he came, or whither he went." (295)

Escaping execution at the last minute, Birch appears before a number of characters who are sure he is a spirit or a devil: "I see a Johnny Birch come out of the grave," says the black servant Caesar, "Johnny walk afore he buried" (251). This spectrality which is repeatedly commented upon in the novel, even seems to mark an inheritance from Birch's father, who rose from his death bed with "the appearance of being from another world," in order to deliver a last "benediction" to his son, words which, we are led to believe, enjoined Birch to the cause of independence in the very moment of his "parting breath" (132). True patriotism is indistinguishable from death, then, and the spy's post-mortem presence throughout the novel is linked explicitly, by Birch himself, to the role he plays as spy. Passing by a gallows intended for young Henry Wharton, Birch tells his companion what it really is to die:

It is hard to die at the best, Captain Wharton; but to spend your last moments alone and unpitied, to know that none near you so much as think of the fate that is to you the closing of all that is earthly; to think, that in a few hours, you are to be led from the gloom . . . to the face of day, and there to meet all eyes fixed upon you, as if you were a wild beast; and to lose sight of everything amidst the jeers and scoffs of your fellow-creatures – that, Captain Wharton, that indeed is to die! (343)

Twice, Birch explains, he has faced this experience. It is as if to say that only a spy such as he is, one whose secrecy isolates him from all his fellow patriots, can know what it is to die. Death, real death, is linked here to an experience of absolute singularity. There is an intimate encounter with death, the novel suggests, structured into the experience of the spy (" 'To hear him,' laughs one character, " 'one would think there was not a rope around his neck already' " [130–1]), which is also to say, structured into the experience of the pure patriot. One way in which Cooper presents – and perhaps contains – his portrait of the exemplary revolutionary, in other words, is by marking him with a relationship to death that is both sacrificial and highly aestheticized. In this respect, we might want to read *The Spy* in terms suggested by Dana Nelson, who writes, in *National Manhood*, of white American men who repeatedly "seem able to achieve the equalitarian reassurance of unmediated brotherhood only with dead or imagined men" (x). To be a revolutionary, to be a pure American, says Harvey Birch, "that, Captain Wharton, that indeed is to die!"

But of course Harvey Birch is not *entirely* alone: " 'Have you comrades, who have assisted you to escape?' [asks Major Dunwoodie] 'No – no,' replies Birch, 'I am alone truly – none know me but my God and *Him*.' 'And who?' Asked the Major, with an interest he could not control. 'None,' continued the pedler, recovering his composure" (217). Cooper's language (not to say typography) is odd here. "Him" so used would usually alert us to a reference to God, but in this novel God appears to be more easily named than George Washington (Birch's secret *"Him"*). For Harvey Birch and for *The Spy*, Washington is God. He is the one figure who knows all and whose omniscience holds out the possibility of Harvey Birch's redemption. Anyone who has seen the remarkable pictures of Washington ascending to heaven that were produced in large numbers on the occasion of his death in 1799 knows that this deification of Washington was a familiar motif even before Cooper took it up. Cooper himself never hid his worshipful attitude towards Washington. In *Notions of the Americans: Picked up by a Travelling Bachelor*, Cooper's observer visits Washington's grave and reflects at length on the founding father:

"If there be a name in the records of history that can afford to stand before the eyes of criticism devoid of artificial aid, it is that of the man who now sleeps beneath a few stunted cedars, and within mouldering walls of brick, on the banks of the Potomac" (*Notions of the Americans*, 420). "His private deeds," the praise continues, "were alike founded on the immutable principles of justice and truth. Men already regard him with the admiration with which they gaze at a severe statue of Antiquity" (415). In Cooper's version of events, Washington is not just one of the high-ranking officials who knows about Harvey Birch: he is the only one who knows, and as such, he provides Birch and the novel with what would seem to be the only way out of the aporia of patriotic anonymity. The only acceptable return for Birch's dedication, the only reward that magically escapes the corruption of economy or exchange, is Washington's recognition. But that recognition becomes, in the crucial final pages of the novel, curiously if inevitably textualized.

The Spy ends with a scene that takes place many years after the main events of the story. The next generation of Americans are again at war (the War of 1812) and two young men come across the old and unrecognized Harvey Birch still operating on a hostile frontier. Moments later, Birch lies on the battlefield with a bullet in his heart, but he is clutching a tin box that contains a note designed to close the novel and dispel the charm of secrecy that had bound Birch to Washington:

Circumstances of political importance, which involve the lives and fortunes of many, have hitherto kept secret what this paper now reveals. Harvey Birch has for years been a faithful and unrequited servant of his country. Though man does not, may God reward him for his conduct!
GEO. WASHINGTON. (407)

Washington's note, and in particular his signature, appears here as the revolution's last word. His signature brings the last (and first) patriot back into the fold of national recognition. The man who unfolds the note is Wharton Dunwoodie, the next generation American whose name registers the reconciliation of patriot and loyalist revolutionary factions and whose very countenance, as we have seen, inspires Birch with hope for the future of America. Dunwoodie's discovery of Washington's note revealing Birch's secret patriotism inscribes the end of the revolution (a kind of Cooperian "end of history") and the beginning of America's blessed future. The secrecy necessary for the success of the revolution can now be dismissed. Washington's signature is what Harvey holds onto in his dying moment and it is what returns him to America. It is all he is given in exchange for his patriotic self-sacrifice. Washington's signature, in other words, has an exchange value equal to Harvey's pure patriotism: Washington's signature is equal to the essence of the revolution. And it is, in an important way, the signature of the good people of America (Washington signs here as the representative of the American people). Harvey's patriotism finds its only possibility of exchange, that is to say, in the signature of the people of the United States, and this is how Cooper's novel closes the circle and writes the last word of the revolution. The people of the United States find their absolute corollary in the selfless purity of the spy who dies holding onto the text of their approval, their signature in representation. The United States identifies itself, through an act of fantastic exchange that simultaneously negates its own economy, with the purity and dedication of one who asked for no recognition, no reward. Here then, is another version of the founding sleight of hand whereby a people not only becomes the subject of its own annunciation but is its own reward too. This final scene surely reinscribes, in a most melodramatic way, the American relationship to its founding documents, particularly the Declaration of Independence. Harvey Birch grips Washington's signature as the subjects of the American Revolution grip the Declaration, in an economy of legitimation whose reciprocity can only, apparently, be guaranteed by death. "Only in the generation after 1815," Michael Kammen explains, "would the Declaration achieve unequivocal standing as a sacred text to which the entire society should subscribe its fealty" (*The Origins of the American Constitution*, 46). Kammen supports this claim by documenting the publication of a series of letters between John Adams and Thomas McKean on the genesis of the Declaration (in the *Niles' Weekly Register* during the summer of 1817); popular engravings of the Declaration in 1818 by two competing firms that enjoyed very wide sales; and, of course, John Trumball's tableau of Jefferson's committee presenting its draft to the Continental Congress, a picture completed in 1818 and exhibited in cities around the country before being permanently installed at the Rotunda of the US Capitol. "Finally," writes Kammen, "John Quincy Adams caused an exact facsimile of the Declaration to be made in 1823, and Congress directed a thorough distribution of numerous copies in 1824" (46). Given this climate, it is even harder not to read Cooper's closing scene as a portrait of a contemporary infatuation with the sacred words and documents of the founding generation. And yet, if, in Cooper's version, young America inherits the founders' text at the dawn of a bright new era (in a move that is replicated elsewhere in his fiction – notably at the end of *Last of the Mohicans*), why does this moment require the death of the go-between?

How should we read the spectral presence of the man who passes the note (like the benediction on the dying breath of his father) from George Washington to Wharton Dunwoodie?

The spy does not live to witness the end of revolutionary secrecy. Indeed, his death seems to be a prerequisite since only death can ensure the patriot's absolute externality with regard to any economy of reward and exchange, and thus only death can retroactively guarantee that Birch will always have been the perfect spy and the pure patriot. Birch's sacrificial death coincides with the revolution's fulfillment, and hence we can see how his persistent spectrality, his post-mortem existence throughout the war for independence, figured the revolution's success as the future anterior of an always already dead. And if the spy is, as we have suggested, the spirit of the United States, that which is equal to the United States in a founding economy, then his demise suggests that they too are purified by a death that has all the features of an aestheticization – an aestheticization that repudiates the nation's relationship to political history and, indeed, to secrecy.[12] For the death and revelation that ends *The Spy* also registers an exorcism of sorts: secrecy and its role in the forming of the nation is exorcised with Birch's death and the discovery of (the also dead) Washington's writing. Cooper's novel, and here it might be contrasted with Charles Brockden Brown's narratives of secrecy, works relentlessly towards a revelation of secrets that will coincide with the moment of what was sometimes called the second war of independence, the War of 1812. Brockden Brown, Cooper's most important predecessor in the early history of the American novel, produced novels and stories that failed for critics, in part because they seemed incapable of resolving their secret spirals. Brown, perversely some would say, followed his character Carwin (in the "Memoirs of Carwin, the Biloquist") in refusing to give up on a secrecy that was nevertheless always in danger of disrupting his and other people's lives (hence, *Wieland*).[13] *The Spy*, however, will not end before the spy's secret has been opened up for all to see, until the secrecy that was necessary to the revolution's success has been dispersed. It is hard to decide, finally, whether in ending Harvey Birch's secret, *The Spy* inscribes the successful end of the American beginning or the ominous end of a revolutionary subjectivity. If Harvey Birch's revolutionary exemplarity coincides with his secrecy, what does it mean to identify the beginning of a new era with that figure's death and with the dissolution of his defining obscurity? The public revelation of Birch's service to his country announces closure as an achievement of justice that is indistinguishable from an aestheticization of death. Writing recently of

The Spy, Charles Hansford Adams claims that "the effort to shape a law that is just creates a moral stage on which the central drama of Cooper's moral imagination is enacted: the tension between the claims of personal identity, and need to find a context for personal identity in an external authority structure" ("*The Guardian of the Law*," 41). For Adams, who emphasizes Birch's "enduring alienation" rather than his posthumous redemption, "Harvey's selfless devotion to the abstract principles of the revolution raises him above the artificial distinction between public and private justice" (41). But it is precisely this aesthetic "raising up" that, as a form of patriotic death, reinscribes the discourse of political justice within a tradition of Christian sacrifice at its most powerfully banal. Indeed, it is with the sacralization of Washington and, finally, with the discovery of the crucial letter from beyond Washington's grave, that *The Spy*, itself participating in Washington's god-like power, seeks to reappropriate the aporia of Harvey Birch's patriotic subjectivity, reinscribing sacrifice "within an economy by means of what thenceforth comes to resemble a reward" (Derrida, *The Gift of Death*, 96). What we ought to consider in refusing the easy sentimentality of Cooper's ending is the question of what it was about Birch's "enduring alienation" that, given its association with secrecy, had to be celebrated in its passing in much the same way as Cooper celebrated the birth of the United States in the passing of the Native American.

"Not only does Democracy," wrote Alexis de Tocqueville ten years after *The Spy*, "make every man forget his ancestors, but it hides his descendants and separates his contemporaries from him; it throws him back forever upon himself alone, and threatens in the end to confine him entirely within the solitude of his own heart" (*Democracy in America*, 194). This threat, with its irreducible relationship to democracy, agitates Cooper's novel even as it gives it continued relevance as a text of political propaganda. De Tocqueville, as is his wont, reaches his conclusion by way of a comparison of forms of association under aristocracy and under American democracy. It is the very importance of equality in a democracy, he notes, that, surprisingly perhaps, weakens even as it extends the "bond of human affection" between individuals:

As, in aristocratic communities, all the citizens occupy fixed positions, one above the other, the result is, that each of them always sees a man above himself whose patronage is necessary to him, and, below himself, another man whose co-operation he may claim. Men living in aristocratic ages are therefore almost always closely attached to something placed out of their own sphere, and they are often disposed to forget themselves. It is true that, in these ages, the notion of human fellowship is faint, and that men seldom think of sacrificing themselves for mankind; but they often sacrifice themselves for other men. In democratic times, on the contrary, when the duties of each individual to the race are much more clear, devoted service to any one man becomes more rare; the bond of human affection is extended, but it is relaxed. (193)

The unstated further conclusion, here, is that if aristocratic men are more likely to sacrifice themselves for particular individual others, democratic men are more likely to sacrifice themselves for "mankind," or at least for *their* people. There is a direct link in de Tocqueville's brilliant analysis between the notion of equality, the idea of sacrifice for "mankind," and the threat of a democratic confinement to "the solitude" of one's own heart. The very political philosophy that produces the kind of patriotism the spy exemplifies, threatens its subjects with the kind of solitude from which Cooper's novel desperately wishes to rescue its central character. Cooper's novel, that is to say, while it reassured contemporary critics that the revolution could indeed furnish "romantic historians" with an "admirable topic," nevertheless narrates a very immediate and persistent anxiety about the relationship between democracy, community, and individualism.

The novel seeks, then, to dispel secrecy (with its unnerving association with the darkness and mystery of pre-democratic politico-religious corruption), for those who live in Birch's wake and in the wake of the War of 1812. In Cooper's novel, secrecy is finally repudiated according to a political ideology that refuses to acknowledge democracy's inheritance of the persistent and irreducible relationship between political freedom and political force. This democracy, that is to say, repudiates – even as it depends upon – the secrecy not just of patriot spies like Harvey Birch, but of that ideal figure he also represented: the sovereign subject of democratic election. The spy's secrecy (his patriotism must remain unknown to everyone) troubles Cooper's novel precisely insofar as it registers the constitutive secrecy of the democratic citizen. It is the radicalism of his alienation, in other words, that allows Harvey Birch to represent the spirit of '76, the American cause, in his person. Cooper's unredeemed spy is a figure for the isolated subject of individual political sovereignty, and as such he figures the democratic subject's inalienable rights of birth as necessarily alienating. Like his childless familiar, George Washington, Birch's singularity is simultaneously the condition for his representative stature: *"he was all your own,"* as Morris extolled. This coincidence of isolated singularity and representative transparency marks the spy's inheritance of the monarch's charismatic and impossible presence in the pre-democratic state. Thus it is that Birch comes to be identified with a spectrality that translates the monarch's two bodies (the monarch's political immortality) for democracy. Cooper's novel, often despite its own more explicit anxieties and investments, registers political power as an experience of ruptured presence that can be thought of in language and imagery that is more or less gothic, mystical, or paranoid. Harvey Birch belongs at one and the same time to Cooper's insistently feudal imaginary and to what we could call his novel's reluctantly democratic unconscious. The ideology of democracy resists the citizen's inheritance of monarchic subjectivity (even as it activates the language of "popular sovereignty") and instead seeks new ways to replicate the feudal subject's spacialization of the relationship between political founding and political obeisance. The spy's spectrality is given to us as an indication (and effect) of his complete subservience to an external figure (call it the revolution, the United States, or his country) whose authority stands outside of any economy of exchange (obedience is its own reward). But a post-monarchic reading of the peddler's spectrality insists that it figures the democratic citizen's deconstruction of the spacialized opposition between political authority and political obedience (a deconstruction previously contained at the site of the monarch). The collapse of a distinction between lawmaking, sovereign power, and the subjectivity produced by subservience to that law, will form the paradoxical and apparently impossible ontology of the citizen-subject. This impossibility, however, also names this citizen-subject's temporal or historical identity. The democratic citizen has no architecture (or only an impossible architecture): but he has a (political) life (which is also to say a mortality). The spacialized distance between the monarch and his people (or, for that matter, between a Puritan God and his people) becomes, under democracy, the internal distance of a subjectivity that experiences political power as a perpetual failure to distinguish founding from preserving, authorizing from obeying. Feudalism aestheticizes the death of the obedient subject as an event; democracy politicizes mortality as the temporal or historical ground of decision. Read against its grain, Cooper's *The Spy* inscribes this translation from monarchism to democracy in its depiction of the (fair) exchange between a morbid patriotism and a political signature. Harvey Birch's life is exchanged for a text – the textual life of a body that can only appear in representation: the United States (here spelled "GEO. WASHINGTON").

In an introduction to *The Spy* written for an 1831 edition, Cooper suggested that "Both Washington and Sir Henry Clinton had an unusual number of secret emissaries; in a war that partook so much of a domestic character, and in which the contending parties were people of the same blood and language, it could scarcely be otherwise" (*The Spy*, 6). What does Cooper mean here? He seems to suggest that the necessity for spies (or is it simply the possibility of using spies) is directly related to the absence of blood- or language-based distinctions between antagonists. Which is also to say that spying is the corollary of ideological or strictly political difference. One of the disturbing implications of this canny observation is that the end of spying might correspond to a kind of reintroduction of a politics of racial or ethnic difference (there is no spy where the only difference is that based on "blood" or "language"). To dispel the spy's secret, as Cooper's novel does in its final lines, is not only to give a kind of ending to the American Revolution, it is also to bring an end to politics (ideological antagonism), in the name of national (and thus inevitably racial, or what we might call pseudo-racial) identity. The end of secrecy would here correspond to the end of a difference internal to people of the same "blood" or "language." By the same token, the failure to end the economy of the spy would leave open the possibility that ideological rather than racialized difference constitutes the dominant political mode. As long as the spy remains at large, unrehabilitated, racially exclusive identity cannot contain itself; the revolutionary democratic subject gives up his relationship to espionage only in the name of a political ideology whose violence we have come to know too well.

That Cooper's novel might be made nervous by the correlation between the spy's world and a deracialized world is brought out in what is supposed to be one of its more entertaining scenes. Cooper's novel, for all that he claims it concerns antagonists of the same "blood," nevertheless contains a character who, under the terms of this distinction, would constitute a racial other: Caesar, the Whartons' predictably if still embarrassingly caricatured black "servant." Caesar functions on the margins of this American family, and this marginality proves crucial. He is the only non-family member permitted access to Henry Wharton when he is placed under house arrest on suspicion of espionage. Following a plan concocted by Harvey Birch, Caesar then switches place with Henry (Henry puts on a black "parchment mask" [*The Spy*, 332]) and allows Henry to escape. Putting on Caesar's clothes, Henry is "unable ... to repress a few signs of loathing" (333) and he is told by Birch (who is supervising the whole business) not to speak or he will be discovered. "'I s'pose Harvey tink a color'd man an't got a tongue like oder folk,' grumbled the black," (334). If the end of the spy's secrecy can be said to correspond with the investment in a homogeneous ethno-nationalist identity, spying and its attendant economy of disguise, deception, and obscurity belong to a world in which the hegemony of politico-ideological antagonism threatens the racist subject with a collapse of racial difference (hence Wharton's "loathing").[14]

The Spy thus harbors a radical reflection on the revolution and on post-monarchic political subjectivity even as it resists its own insights at every move. George Washington stays with the spy and with Cooper's readers from beginning to end; he is always close at hand to limit, with his idealized, patriarchal presence, the play of secrecy and deception. And yet, in the end, all that is left of Washington is all that there ever was – his confirming signature (the authenticity and fraudulent reproducibility of which has already been raised and somewhat desperately passed over in the pages of the novel). Harvey Birch – the spy, the pure patriot, the spirit of '76 – clings to Washington's signature in his dying moments. Only the signature will put an end to secrecy and purify the revolution of a founding obscurity, a founding injustice that is represented in the sacrificial character of Harvey Birch.[15] Without the signature, *The Spy* says, only an endless and irreducible negotiation with a founding obscurity.[16] But what kind of a last word is a signature? "Is there such a thing? Does the absolute singularity of signature as event ever occur? Are there signatures?" These questions are Jacques Derrida's and they precipitate this answer:

Yes, of course, every day. Effects of signature are the most common thing in the world. But the condition of possibility of those effects is simultaneously, once again, the condition of their impossibility, of the impossibility of their rigorous purity. In order to function, that is, to be readable, a signature must have a repeatable, iterable, imitable form; it must be able to be detached from the present and singular intention of its production. It is its sameness which, by corrupting its identity and its singularity, divides its seal. (*Limited Inc.*, 20)

The Spy ends with what looks like a desperate investment in the singular, undivided sovereignty, of Washington's seal. Only a complete faith in the sincerity and authenticity of this signature allows the novel to end (and indeed to begin, that is to say, to have ever been known as a story). And yet even here, as if the novel cannot resist some of its more revolutionary implications, *The Spy* figures what Derrida calls the division of the signature's seal, a constitutive detachability that can always be reinscribed as the violence of an injustice. When Birch is discovered on the battlefield "his hands were pressed upon his breast": "Dunwoodie stooped, and removing the limbs, perceived the place where the bullet had found a passage to his heart. The subject of his last care was a tin box, through which the fatal lead had gone; and the dying moments of the old man must have passed in drawing it from his bosom" (406–7). Is it Washington's signature or the rupture figured by the force of a bullet that we should read as the revolution's last word? And given the constitutive self-division of the signature's seal, how would we finally be able to make this distinction? Washington's signature – the seal of the revolutionary American people – is found at the site of a violence that brings death *and* revelation. Ending the spy's secrecy, this coincidence of the sword and the pen, of writing and death, is concealed by way of an aestheticization of death as purification. This founding secrecy cannot be dispelled, however, because it is constitutive for the subject of democracy: to come into political power, to "find" a political voice, is to become the divided, doubled subject-citizen of representability. "*The Spy*," concludes Michael Gilmore in a recent discussion of the novel, "reflected the era's growing confidence in the power of the sovereign agent" ("James Fenimore Cooper," 681); but Cooper's exemplary American figures the accession to democratic subjectivity as the inheritance of an irreducible secrecy: "the nature of man," wrote de Tocqueville as he contemplated the individual subject of democratic literature, "is sufficiently disclosed for him to apprehend something of himself, and sufficiently obscure for all the rest to be plunged in thick darkness, in which he gropes forever, – and forever in vain, – to lay hold on some completer notion of his being" (*Democracy in America*, 183). Cooper's unreclaimed spy, that is to say, gives us an allegory of the subject of democratic power even as the novel works towards a revelation that will dispel that subject's defining secrecy. In so far as *The Spy* identifies Harvey Birch's rehabilitation with his death, it substitutes a morbid aestheticization for the difficult but persistent correspondence between secrecy and political existence that defines the subject of democracy.

Notes

1 Haiti, of course, could be said to have been the site of the eighteenth century's most radically democratic revolution, one from which the United States and Europe had – and have – much to learn. See C. L. R. James' *The Black Jacobins*.

2 Jonathan Mayhew was ordained in 1747 at the West Church in Boston. *A Discourse Concerning Unlimited Submission and Non-Resistance to the Higher Powers* "created a furor in Boston" after it was delivered and then published in early 1750. The sermon was circulated and read throughout the colonies in the years preceding the revolution. See Warner, ed., *American Sermons*, 901–2.

3 Letter to Roger C. Weightman, June 24, 1826 in Jefferson, *Collected Works*, XII, 477.

4 It would not be out of place here to recall Marx's reference to the "mystical" commodity of capitalism, an object "full of 'theological niceties.'" See Balibar, *Philosophy of Marx*, 59–60: "Contrary to what Max Weber would later assert, the modern world is not 'disenchanted,' but *enchanted*, precisely insofar as it is the world of objects of value and objectified values."

5 Letter to David Humphreys, August 14, 1787 in Dumbauld, ed., *The Political Writings of Thomas Jefferson*, 70.

6 Letter to the elder Mirabeau (July 26, 1767) quoted in Furet, *Interpreting the French Revolution*, 31.

7 See Freneau's "To A Republican With Mr. Paine's Rights of Man," in *The Poems of Philip Freneau*, III, 91.

8 The phrase comes from Wood, *Radicalism*, 8.

9 "Spell," *Oxford English Dictionary*, 2nd edition, 1989. All subsequent definitions of "Spell" used in this chapter come from the same source.

10 As an allegory for the revolution this scene calls to mind Paul De Man's lines in his chapter on Rousseau's *Social Contract* in *Allegories of Reading*: "The metaphorical substitution of one's own for the divine voice is blasphemous, although the necessity for this deceit is as implacable as its eventual denunciation, in the future undoing of any State or any political institution" (274–5).

11 In "Declarations of Independence," Derrida dwells on the "are and ought to be" of Jefferson's founding document:

the "and" articulates and conjoins here the two discursive modalities, the to be and the ought to be, the constation and the prescription, the fact and the right. *And* is God: at once creator of nature and judge, supreme judge of what is (the state of the world) and of what relates to what ought to be (the rectitude of our intentions). The instance of judgement, at the level of the supreme judge, is the last instance for saying the fact *and* the law. (11–12)

12 "Neither God nor nature, having given any man a right of domination over any society, independently of that society's approbation, and consent to be governed by him" (Mayhew, "Discourse," 409n.).

13 "We hold this truth to be self-evident," Forten wrote, "that God created all men equal, is one of the most prominent features in the Declaration of Independence . . . This idea embraces the Indian and the European, the savage and the Saint, the Peruvian and the Laplander, the white man and the African" (Forten, *Letters*, 190).

14 Arendt continues: "it is interesting to note that the Latin word *homo*, the equivalent of 'man,' signified originally somebody who was nothing but a man, a rightless person, therefore, and a slave" (*On Revolution*, 45–6). This tension between the "Man" of rights and the slave "he" would like to disown is a persistent feature of democratic political anxiety. See James, *The Black Jacobins*, and Morgan, *American Slavery*.

15 Was this what Marx had in mind when he referred impatiently to "the pompous catalogue of the 'inalienable rights of man'" (*Capital*, 330)?

16 Letter to James Madison, December 20, 1787 (in Banning, *Jefferson and Madison*, 145).

17 Malcom X was referring to the inadequacy of a rhetoric of American birth-right in "The Ballot or the Bullet" when he wrote:

Well, I am one who doesn't believe in deluding myself. I'm not going to sit at your table and watch you eat, with nothing on my plate, and call myself a diner. Sitting at the table doesn't make you a diner, unless you eat some of what's on that plate. Being here in America doesn't make you an American. Being born here in America doesn't make you an American. Why, if birth made you an American, you wouldn't need any legislation, you wouldn't need any amendments to the Constitution, you wouldn't be faced with civil-rights filibustering in Washington, D.C., right now. (2543)

18 The ongoing discomfort generated by the centrality of the secret ballot to democracy is registered in remarks made by Dana Nelson in her recent account of this period: Nelson wants to challenge the version of America produced by a constitution that puts "a fundamental restraint on democratic energy and possibility." "As it develops in practice," she continues, "federal democratic order cleans up the messiness of radical democratic practice by virtualizing it, abstracting its face-to-face negotiations through the managed competition of private voting booths and the symbolically distancing and organizing mechanisms of party politics." As a result, "'the people' would come to surrender the idea of locally negotiated, face-to-face democracy for the routine expression of their opinion on ballots, and the embodiment of

that 'opinion' in the person of various elected officials" (*National Manhood*, 245 n. 14). All the watchwords of a familiar revolutionary idealism are on display here (the fetishization of the face, the voice, the immediate and self-present) while all that threatens democracy is lined up with the mechanical, the symbolic, the distancing and deferral of representation and, of course, the isolation and secrecy of the voting booth. My hope would be that one could sympathize with Nelson's (and all her revolutionary predecessors') dissatisfactions with the inequalities of the American political and economic system without having to surrender to a predictable and often dangerous idealism.

19 This anxiety is comically brought to the surface in the original Dunlap printing of the Declaration, which, as Fliegelman explains it, takes Jefferson's pause marks as quotation marks and thus gives us a first edition that is virtually a string of quotations (*Declaring Independence*, 8–9).

20 One of the key moves made by the Constitutional framers was to use the language "We the People of the United States" rather than the Declaration's "we" the "Representatives of the United States of America, in Congress Assembled." The elision of the word "representation" testified, in the Constitution, to the Federalists' success in disarming precisely by radicalizing the troubling concept of representation.

21 It might be argued that the "it" here is in fact an expletive and hence that its function is simply to anticipate the "true" subject of the sentence, or to postpone a subject coming after the verb. But this uncertainty is irreducible in the Declaration: it is impossible to decide if the "it" postpones or renders indefinite the subject of the revolution.

22 See too Wills, *Inventing America*.

23 "[Jefferson] does not offer the American revolution as something permissible, merely. It is *necessary* in nature; and the recognition and co-operation with nature is the essence of human virtue. Seeing the impulse to happiness, and co-operating with it, is man's highest calling" (*Ibid.*, 317–18).

24 For Wills, Jefferson's recognition of men's rights participates in an eighteenth-century recognition of man's subservience to the law of his nature: "Men in the eighteenth century felt they could become conscious of their freedom only by discovering how they were bound: When they found what they *must* pursue, they knew they had a *right* to pursue it" (247). Where Wills (brilliantly) emphasizes the laws of nature and their importance for the founders, however, I want to direct attention to the rhetoric of compulsion that accompanies these references and thus to the various ways in which language aids in the equivocation of responsibility. The laws of nature can be read as comforting displacements of the forceful and productive interventions of precisely that which equivocates the opposition between the natural and the non-natural: language.

25 "'FOURTH OF JULY.' Well – I don't feel patriotic. Perhaps I might if they would stop that deafening racket. Washington was very well, if he *couldn't* spell, and I'm glad we are all free; but as a woman – I shouldn't know it, didn't some orator tell me" (Fanny Fern, "Independence," 314–15).

26 See Wills' discussion of the word "course" in this sentence. Jefferson's "when" can also be read to invoke a kind of natural temporality, the temporality of a river that courses, or of the wind: Jefferson records the "course" of the wind and wrote of the "regular course of my husbandry" (Wills, *Inventing America*, 93). This natural temporality would be the same one that gives us a "spell of good weather."

27 Benjamin, "Theses," 261. The phrase comes up again at the end of the theses:

> Historicism contents itself with establishing a causal connection between various moments in history. But no fact that is a cause is for that very reason historical. It became historical posthumously, as it were, through events that may be separated from it by thousands of years. A historian who takes this as his point of departure stops telling the sequence of events like the beads of a rosary. Instead, he grasps the constellation which his own era has formed with a definite earlier one. Thus he establishes a conception of the present as the "time of the now" which is shot through with chips of Messianic time. (263)

28 There are many ways in which *Common Sense* has a particular relationship to speed and immediacy. Newspapers of the day were a major source of Paine's information; it was sold cheaply (though not as cheaply as Paine wanted) in order to assure wide distribution; and it came out in pamphlet form, the form that Bailyn calls "the distinctive literature of the Revolution . . . always aimed at immediate and rapidly shifting targets: at suddenly developing problems, unanticipated arguments, and swiftly rising, controversial figures" (*Ideological Origins*, 8, 4). See too Ferguson, "The Commonalities," on Paine's popular style.

29 Martin Luther King and Malcolm X were adept at invoking the revolutionary now: "We have also come to this hallowed spot," King told marchers in Washington in 1963, "to remind America of the fierce urgency of now . . . Now is the time to make real the promises of democracy. Now is the time to rise from the dark, the desolate valley of segregation to the sunlit path of racial justice . . . It would be fatal for the nation to overlook the urgency of the moment" ("I Have A Dream," 1424). Malcolm X told supporters in Cleveland in 1964:

> If we don't do something real soon, I think you'll have to agree that we're going to be forced either to use the ballot or the bullet. It's one or the other in 1964. It isn't that time is running out – time has run out! . . . Civil rights, for those of us whose philosophy is black nationalism, means: "Give it to us now. Don't wait for next year. Give it to us yesterday, and that's not fast enough." ("The Ballot," 2543, 2548)

> "[Paine] saw that all of history had to be refigured and collapsed into a fresh sense of the present" (Ferguson, "The Commonalities," 480). It is important to remember that Paine can also be dismissive of any position that seems to be *time-bound*. He refers to the uselessness of last year's almanacks and he relishes the disgrace of a "fatal and unmanly thought," attributed to Henry Pelham, to the effect that the measures he had put in place as Chancellor of

the Exchequer "will last my time" (*Common Sense*, 82). In *Crisis no. 1*, Paine condemns parents who sacrifice their children's welfare by thinking only of "'peace in my day'" (*Thomas Paine Reader*, 120), even as he is elsewhere at pains to criticize "those who dare to legislate for the future." (*Common Sense*, 76). These apparent contradictions only alert us to the fact that for Paine the encounter with the present was simultaneously an encounter with a divine time that puts an end to degraded historical time. "The inhabitants of heaven long to see the ark finished, in which all the liberty and true religion of the world are to be deposited" ("A Dialogue," 93).

30 Furthermore, "The reformation was preceded by the discovery of America, as if the Almighty graciously meant to open a sanctuary to the persecuted in future years, when home should afford neither friendship nor safety" (*Common Sense*, 87).

31 The experience of transcendence that can accompany the revolutionary encounter with the now and the new is, as Derrida has suggested, the result of an encounter with something, oddly enough, too close to home:

> The inaccessible transcendence of the law before which and prior to which "man" stands fast only appears infinitely transcendent and thus theological to the extent that, so near to him, it depends only on him, on the performative act by which he institutes it: the law is transcendent, violent and non-violent, because it depends only on who is before it – and so prior to it –, on who produces it, founds it, authorizes it in an absolute performative whose presence always escapes him. The law is transcendent and theological, and so always to come, always promised, because it is immanent, finite and so already past. ("Force of Law," 993)

32 Douglass has just finished a long section praising "your" founders to his white audience while all the time speaking, entirely implicitly, never explicitly, about the present politics of slavery. Only when this powerful section finishes does he turn, with what can only then be a very pointed tongue in cheek, to "the present."

33 We could say that "God" or the "divine" is a displaced name for the revolutionary encounter with political force, with the awful responsibility for (and inevitability of) changing political structures and establishing new laws. The phrases "are and of right ought to be" and "is and ought to be" in the Declaration are also, quite subtly of course, attempts to glance away from the immediacy of the revolutionary break at the moment at which that break is announced. See Derrida, "Declarations of Independence."

34 Crèvecoeur's *Letters From An American Farmer* (1782), as we shall see in chapter two, is one of the few texts to address the revolution as an unknowable event. Writing in the present tense during the War of Independence he laments: "I am divided between the respect I feel for the ancient connexion and the fear of innovations with the consequence of which I am not well acquainted, as they are embraced by my own countrymen" (204).

35 Adams goes on to refer to such thinkers as praying to either "eternal nature" or "almighty chance" ("Discourses on Davila," *Political Writings*, 194).

36 Cf. Marx on the economists' exit from history:

> There are only two kinds of institutions for them, the artificial and the natural. The institutions of feudalism are artificial institutions, those of the bourgeoisie natural. In this they resemble the theologians, who likewise establish two kinds of religion. Every religion which is not theirs is an invention of men, while their own is an emanation from God. When the economists say that present-day relations – the relations of bourgeois production – are natural, they imply that these are the relations in which wealth is created and productive forces developed in conformity with the laws of nature. These relations therefore are themselves natural laws independent of the influence of time. They are eternal laws which must always govern society. Thus there has been history, but there is no longer any. ("Poverty of Philosophy," quoted in Balibar, *Philosophy of Marx*, 81)

37 This claim might be further considered with respect to the cult of the live in contemporary internet/television culture. See Esch, *In the Event*.

38 "The tradition of all the dead generations weighs like a nightmare on the brain of the living," wrote Karl Marx in 1841:

> And just when they seem engaged in revolutionizing themselves and things, in creating something entirely new, precisely in such epochs of revolutionary crisis they anxiously conjure up the spirits of the past to their service and borrow from them names, battle slogans and costumes in order to present the new scene of world history in this time-honored disguise and this borrowed language. ("The Eighteenth Brumaire," in Tucker, ed., *The Marx–Engels Reader*, 595).

Benjamin, commenting on the French Revolution's appropriation of the garb of ancient Rome, takes a slightly different approach: "The French Revolution viewed itself as Rome reincarnate. It cited ancient Rome the way fashion cites costumes of the past." For Benjamin, this structure was not simply to be dismissed as false: it helped to reveal the extent to which the past was "charged with the time of the now" which could be "blasted out of the continuum of history," in, for example, the revolutionary moment ("Theses," 261).

39 "Let America be America Again" (1936) in *Collected Poems*, 191.

40 C. L. R. James' reference to Bonaparte's "revolutionary" soldiers, disconcerted by hearing their black combatants singing the *Marseillaise*, the *Ça Ira*, and other revolutionary songs, gives us a compelling dramatization of this temporal and political fissure in the subject of the democratic revolutions: the soldiers were, in some sense, hearing their own revolutionary identity singing to them from the other side of a racially defined battlefield (see James, *The Black Jacobins*, 317). See too Martin Luther King's most famous speech, in which he told marchers in Washington D.C.:

> In a sense we've come to our Nation's Capital to cash a check. When the architects of our republic wrote the magnificent words of the Constitution and the Declaration of Independence, they were signing a promissory note to which every American was to fall heir. This note was a promise that all men, yes, black men as well as white men, should be guaranteed the unalienable rights of life, liberty and the pursuit of happiness. ("I Have A Dream," 1423)

41 Remarks like Jenyns' were enough to lead some American democrats to suggest, as one Virginian quoted by Gordon Wood does, that representation "is at best, but a species of aristocracy" (*Creation*, 387, quoting from "Loose Thoughts on Government" [1776]).

42 From Richard Gadsden's newspaper essays of the 1780's in South Carolina, quoted in Wood, *Creation*, 193–4.

43 Samuel Peters, "History of Connecticut," quoted in Wood, *Creation*, 195.

44 From the *Pennsylvania Gazette*, March 24, 1779, quoted in Wood, *Creation*, 445.

45 Thoreau, "Civil Disobedience," 18. And what more glaring instance of such black magic is there in the history of American political representation than the Continental Congress' occult production of a "three-fifths" person. The *Journals of the Continental Congress* for March 28, 1783 relate how the three-fifths designation emerged out of a shameless wrangling over numbers: "Mr. Madison said that in order to give a proof of the sincerity of his professions of liberality, he would propose that Slaves should be rated as 5 to 3" (quoted in Kaminski, *A Necessary Evil?* 22)!

46 For a telling example of another kind of "almost invisible" body in which "incarnation" took place, consider the slaves who were sent as substitutes for their masters to serve in the revolutionary army, only to be returned to slave status upon their discharge. See Quarles, *The Negro in the American Revolution*, 183–4.

47 Adams showed us one way of attempting this and he paid the price for it: he was called a "secret monarchist," a charge that was never forgotten. Another way of thinking through this question might begin with Madison's repeated suggestion that "Where the power, as with us, is in the many not in the few, the danger can not be very great that the few will be thus favored. It is much more to be dreaded that the few will be unnecessarily sacrificed to the many . . . " Letter to Jefferson, October 17, 1788, in Kammen, *Origins*, 371.

48 Wood's vocabulary here resonates with that of the French political philosopher, Claude Lefort when Lefort writes (primarily thinking of the French Revolution, but with an eye trained on contemporary democratic societies): "the democratic revolution . . . burst out when the body of the king was destroyed, when the body politic was decapitated and when, at the same time, the corporeality of the social was dissolved. There then occurred what I would call a 'disincorporation' of individuals" (*Political Forms*, 303).

49 The phrase comes from Laclau, "Deconstruction," 47–8.

50 Letter to James Madison, September 6, 1789, in Banning, *Jefferson and Madison*, 170.

1   MONARCHOPHOBIA: READING THE MOCK EXECUTIONS OF 1776

1 In 1936 (in "Let America Be America Again") Langston Hughes makes what is not simply a tongue-in-cheek reference to Freneau: "Let America be the dream the dreamers dreamed – / Let it be that great strong land of

love / Where never kings connive nor tyrants scheme / That any man be crushed by one above" (*Collected Poems*, 189).

2 Revolutionary fervor must dwell upon that from which it celebrates a departure. Timothy Dwight in "Columbia" (1777) wrote "Let the crimes of the east ne'er encrimson thy name. / Be freedom, and science, and virtue, thy fame" (in Jehlen and Warner, eds., *English Literatures*, 1085) and Joel Barlow opens "The Prospect of Peace" (1778) by announcing "The closing scenes of Tyrants' fruitless rage / The opening prospects of a golden age" (in Lauter, ed., *Heath Anthology*, 1073). In Book 1 of "The Vision of Columbus" (1787) Barlow would write of the "blood-stained steps [that] lead upwards to a throne" (in Jehlen and Warner, eds., *English Literatures*, 1097). Lemuel Haynes' "The Battle of Lexington" (1775) reads thus: "Then Tyrants fill'd with horrid Rage / A Fatal Journey went / & Unmolested to engage / And slay the innocent." It continues, "One Son of Freedom could annoy / A Thousand Tyrant Fiends / And their despotick Tribe destroy / And chace them to their Dens," and concludes: "Thus did the Sons of Brittain's King / Receive a sore Disgrace / Whilst Sons of Freedom join to sing / The Vict'ry they Imbrace . . . Oh Brittain how art thou become / Infamous in our Eye / Nearly allied to antient Rome / That Scat of Popery" (quoted in Bogin, "The Battle of Lexington," 499–509). This rhetorical excess can be thought of as working to compensate for the very loss that the revolutionary victory would achieve.

3 As petitions to King George showed no success, newspapers in the colonies began to abandon residual attachments to the crown. The *New London Gazette*, for example, dared to suggest as early as 1772 that the old maxim that the king can do no wrong is "a grand absurdity" ("A Dialogue" [April 10, 1772] quoted in Maier, *From Resistance to Revolution*, 209).

4 See Silverman, who adds: "As the statue was being overthrown, one man in the crowd sensed that the order of things was tumbling too. He expressively quoted Milton's angel addressing Lucifer: 'If thou be'st he! But ah, how fallen! How changed!'" (*A Cultural History*, 324).

5 For further accounts of the use of effigies in the revolutionary era see St. George, *Conversing by Signs*.

6 See too the work of Louis Marin, who writes of the portrait of the king (in this case that of Louis XIV) which "in its sacramentary mystery makes one conceive of the union of subjects in a same collective body whose head is the king, the body of the kingdom whose subjugated members find an identity in the king's name that the portrait inscribes." He continues: "The king's portrait in its mystery would be this sacramental body that would at once operate the political body of the kingdom in the historical body of the prince and lift the historical body up into the political body" (*Portrait of the King*, 209).

7 See too Anderson, *Lineages* and Hill, *The Century of Revolution*.

8 Peter Heylyn, *Aerius redivivus; or, The History of the Presbyterians* (Oxford: 1670), quoted in Weston and Greenberg, *Subjects and Sovereigns*, 47. McKeon adds (in an intriguing attempt to think outside of monarchophobia) that "from this broad vantage point" it is possible to see the emergence of notions of

absolutist sovereignty as signaling "not the culminating triumph of absolute princely authority but the beginning of a process whereby the confident exercise of royal power becomes a more general model for the way in which diverse human exertions aim to reform society to alternative ideals. The movement therefore also provides an initial perspective on the development of progressive ideology" (*The Origins of the English Novel*, 178).

9 The most famous defender of the Parliamentarians, John Milton, took much the same line in his later attempt to deny that treason had taken place. See *The Defence of the English People*.

10 Žižek is talking about money under capitalism, but before long he is quoting Marx's footnote on the feudal "fetishistic misrecognition" that anticipates that of the capitalist marketplace: "'one man is king only because other men stand in the relation of subjects to him. They, on the contrary, imagine that they are subjects because he is king'" (quoted in Žižek, *Sublime Objects*, 25; see Marx, *Capital* 66).

11 "What marks republican writings in the years of the Commonwealth," writes Miwa Saito in a study of the execution elegies written for Charles I, "is a desperate attempt to desecrate the divine image of Charles I." The royal iconography nevertheless proved to be resilient, and thus death on the scaffold provided Charles

> not only with immortal fame, but also a new political life…His body as an embodiment of absolute monarchy may have been destroyed for ever, but the cause of his party has been rendered "sublime," or even sacred. In his lifetime Charles was never a good orator because of a speech defect, but he had scarcely been beheaded before he started to talk eloquently. ("Tears of Blood," 14–15)

12 Again, see Marin for an elaborate analysis of the relationship between the absolute monarch and his representation: "to make the king's portrait, that is, to make a copy of the king's portrait, is not only to reproduce and multiply the links of the mimetic chain but also to celebrate, as officiating priest chosen by Heaven, the ritual of the royal mystery of the transubstantiation of the prince's body" (*Portrait of the King*, 211).

13 Derrida here describes Rousseau's "epoch of natural languages…Between prelanguage and the linguistic catastrophe instituting the division of discourse…a happy pause, the instantaneity of a full language" (*of Grammatology*, 279).

14 Emerson's metaphor aligns the democratic revolution with an effacement of the signifier, an effacement registered by the classical understanding of the progression from hieroglyphs to demotics to alphabetical writing. The pictograph registers a fantasy of one signifier standing for one signified, while the more economical demotic or alphabetic sign allows the same mark to serve multiple significatory purposes and in the process draws less attention to its own material presence: the alphabetic fantasy is that of a transparent signifier. See Derrida, *Of Grammatology*, 284–5.

15 Marin, acknowledging the work of Kantorowicz, proposes the following hypothesis for "'classical' absolutism": "the king has only one body left, but this

sole body, in truth, unifies three, a physical historical body, a juridico-political body, and a semiotic sacramental body, the sacramental body, the 'portrait,' operating the exchange *without remainder* (or attempting to eliminate all remainder) between the historical and political bodies" (*Portrait of the King*, 14). Representations of the (living) king play a privileged role, according to Marin, in resolving the tensions between the king's two bodies, and thus killing an effigy of a living king would, as I am suggesting, at once confirm the effective power of monarchical representation ("The king is only truly king, that is monarch, in images. They are his *real presence*," 8) and more conclusively undo the absolutist fantasy of the monarch than would any mere attack on his body. Whether they knew it or not, the American revolutionaries were engaging in an empirical confirmation and exemplification of the intimate relationship that Marin describes between power and representation.

16 See too this quotation in Maier, *From Resistance to Revolution*, from a writer in the *New London Gazette*, June 7, 1776: "that worst of plagues, the KING'S EVIL; which disorder...Will soon be [extir]pated from this otherwise happy land, and nevermore be suffered to infect it again" (295).

17 St. George continues: "The use of effigies also derived from traditional English harvest festivals, during which two figures – one a god-like spirit... and the other its human embodiment... appeared alongside each other in a ritual doubling of opposed yet interdependent forces" (*Conversing by Signs*, 251).

18 A thirteen-stringed harp with the motto *Majora Minoribus Consonant* ("the greater and the lesser ones sound together") was one of the devices that appeared on state-issued paper money during the revolutionary period (see Silverman, *A Cultural History*, 321).

19 The real Bertram's son, William Bertram (note Crèvecoeur's slight alteration of the spelling) was an early proponent of the Indian as divinely inspired, natural model for Euro-Americans. Among the Cherokee he finds "a sylvan scene of primitive innocence" and a "gay assembly of hamadryades." The Eolian harp, in fact, is entirely at home in the Native American world William Bartram imagined. (See Bertram's *Travels* [1792] quoted in Pearce, *Savagism and Civilization*, 142–3).

20 This harp hanging in the woods resonates eerily with the caged slave that James comes across in the woods outside Charleston, South Carolina. James first feels "the air strongly agitated" and then hears "a few inarticulate monosyllables" that draw his eyes towards a mass of large birds of prey surrounding the suspended cage (Crèvecoeur, *Letters*, 177–8). If the Eolian harp figures the fantasy of a natural American harmony, the cage, as Nancy Ruttenburg suggests, "articulates the experience of another vast population of American immigrants whose experience in the New World is based upon a 'frau[d] surpassing in enormity everything which a common mind can possibly conceive' " (*Democratic Personality*, 283). The disembodiment of the African, marked most forcefully by the loss of his eyes to the birds, returns the disembodied music of the Eolian harp to the realm of historical, political – and uniquely Euro-American – violence.

21 Tamanend (corrupted to Tammany) was the name of a Delaware chief who is said to have welcomed William Penn and to have signed the Treaty of Shakamaxon. After the Revolution, Tammany societies sprang up in New York, Philadelphia, and other cities as the common soldiers' alternative to the officers' Society of the Cincinnatus (Norwood, *The Tammany Legend*, 144). The Tammany Society, or Columbian Order of New York City, was formed in 1786 and was the most long-lived and influential of the societies. It practiced pseudo-Native American ceremonials, dressed for significant occasions in "Indian style" and gave its officials pseudo-Native American titles. Aaron Burr became one of the society's most powerful leaders, and it was active in democratic politics well into the nineteenth century (helping to secure full manhood suffrage in New York in 1826 among other things). See Norwood, *The Tammany Legend*, 145–6 and Gustavus Myers, *The History of Tammany Hall*. In a 1938 book (that is itself a remarkable testament to the resilience of the white appropriation of the Native American), Joseph White Norwood explains that "the American ideals of human right to 'life, liberty and the pursuit of happiness,' spring chiefly from original American sources and were developed on American soil for untold centuries before Europeans arrived on this continent . . . These ideals . . . should be known as the first Americans knew them, by a name that completely symbolizes them. This name is TAMANEND" (*The Tammany Legend*, 10). According to Norwood, May 1, or in some cases, May 12 "was set aside on revolutionary calendars as St. Tammany's day and celebrated with festivals in approved Indian fashion" (143).

22 In the preface to the first edition of the novel, Cooper compares his doomed Mohicans to "the feudal princes of the old world [who] fought among themselves, and exercised most of the other privileges of sovereignty" (*Last of the Mohicans*, 2). Interestingly, Cooper compares these Indians with Magua's despicable Iroquois, whom he describes as "the oldest united republic of which the history of North America furnishes any evidence" (3). It is the monarchic Mohican who will bequeath to the young white man (Heyward) the specifically American grandeur of spirit that he will need in order to make the country great. To put it simply, Cooper's novel is a great example of how American political thought regularly repudiated the revolution's introduction of a radically political society and instead looked for some kind of pre-political basis upon which to construct a spirit of American democracy.

23 Freneau invoked the "ancients of these lands," the ghosts of "the painted chief" and the "Indian Queen" even as he was composing his fiercely patriotic poems about the peopling of the New World (see, for example, "The Indian Burying Ground" in Freneau, *Poems*, II, 369–70). His "Prophecy of King Tammany" (in Freneau, *Poems*, II, 187–9) also deserves discussion with respect to this appropriation. Freneau's king foresees the revolution from the moment the white men come ashore and begin the process of displacing his people. It is a fascinatingly confused poem that somehow attempts to align Tammany's death at the hands of white Americans with his status as prophet of the revolution. Here Freneau gives us another displaced sacrifice integral

to the achievement of a republican state (see chapter three below). See too the description of Magawiska in Catherine Maria Sedgwick's *Hope Leslie* (1827): "Her collar –bracelet–girdle–embroidered moccasins, and purple mantle with its rich border of bead work, had been laid aside in prison, but were now all resumed and displayed with a feeling resembling Nelson's, when he emblazoned himself with stars and orders to appear before his enemies, on the fatal day of his last battle" (Sedgwick, *Hope Leslie*, 282).

24 See Galloway, *American Revolution*, and Pearce, *Savagism and Civilization*, among others, for accounts of the extent to which the revolution advanced the displacement and decimation of Native Americans.

25 Another way in which the Indian and the monarch were linked was through the kind of justification for Indian removal that pictured a native in terms of a paradoxically extravagant poverty: in 1795, Massachusetts legislator James Sullivan complained that "five hundred rational animals may enjoy life in plenty, and comfort, where only one savage drags out a hungry existence" (quoted in Pearce, *Savagism and Civilization*, 67).

26 The structure I am describing can be seen at work in as recent a text as the Hollywood film *Mad City* (1998), starring Dustin Hoffman and John Travolta, in which the statue of an Indian chief (who we are told is represented in the act of waving goodbye to and for his exterminated people) is riddled with bullets meant for the working-class hero.

27 Paul Revere's engraving, "America in Distress" (1775), followed an English original but replaced the female Britannia seated on a throne with the image of an Indian princess complete with bow and quiver. While, as Silverman points out, the gesture "reflects many radicals' identification with Indian vigor and militancy" (*A Cultural History*, 320), it also reminds us of the ominous slippage in the American political imaginary between the Native American and the European monarch.

28 Carrol Smith-Rosenberg has written on the "three principal figures" of "discursively constructed negative others" that supported the construction of the new American subject in the revolutionary period: "the white middle-class woman, the American Indian warrior, and the enslaved African American" ("Dis-Covering the Subject," 848–9). Here and throughout this book I will suggest that these groups might be profitably considered alongside the monarchic other.

29 In "A Political Litany," (1775) Freneau calls for revolution to distance America from, among other things, "slaves, that would die for a smile from the throne" (*Poems*, I, 140), and in "On the Emigration . . . " he writes of the European who flees to America where "no proud despot holds him down, / No slaves insult him with a crown" (II, 280). The slave and the monarch, that is to say, belong to the same political imaginary; they are the antithetical but mutually dependent terms of the revolution's defining other. This would be one place to begin making sense of the fact – noted by many African American writers in the early nineteenth century – that days of public celebration in the United States, particularly the fourth of July, were also occasions for

public violence against non-whites: See Prince Hall's 1797 denunciation of "the daily insults" suffered by the black citizens of Boston "much more on public days of recreation" when "we may truly be said to carry our lives in our hands" (quoted in Nash, *Race and Revolution*, 81) and accounts of the fourth of July celebrations in front of the State House Philadelphia in 1805 where, as Gary Nash writes, "dozens of sullen white citizens turned on the free blacks assembled for the festivities and drove them from the square with a torrent of curses and a storm of rocks" (*Race and Revolution*, 81). This repeated event is also recorded in Forten's "Letters from a Man of Colour on a Late Bill Before the Senate of Pennsylvania" (in Nash, *Race and Revolution*, 190).

30 For an extended discussion of this white male body in America see Dana Nelson, *National Manhood*.

31 See Anderson: "The dreams of racism actually have their origins in ideologies of class, rather than in those of nation: above all in claims to divinity among rulers and to 'blue' or 'white' blood and 'breeding' among aristocracies" (*Imagined Communities*, 149). The revolutionary appropriation of monarchic sovereignty would thus also represent an appropriation, for the revolutionary class, of this racism. One way of approaching the failures of the American Revolution, in other words, would be to trace lines of association between the revolution's monarchophobia and its racism. See too C. L. R. James, *The Black Jacobins*, for a nuanced reflection on the relations between class antagonism and the "aristocracy of skin" in revolutionary France.

32 See Catherine Gallagher's discussion of this feature of print (*Nobody's Story*, 62).

33 See Eisenstein, *The Printing Press*.

34 Emerson wrote of the prince who "magnetized the eyes" of men, an image that calls to mind the wily orator of post-revolutionary sentimental culture. Fliegelman writes:

> The rattlesnake's power of "fascination," which is frequently commented upon in late-eighteenth-century natural history, was a natural instance of the threat and fantasy of silent hypnotic control represented in the contemporary debate over mesmerism and romanticized in the sentimental "language of the eyes." The monitorial Mrs. Holmes of *The Power of Sympathy* warned women against seducers who like "some species of American serpents," lock eyes with their prey until "the fascinated bird . . . unable any longer to extend its wings . . . falls into the voracious jaws of its enemy." (*Declaring Independence*, 49)

35 The strict reciprocity of equality and freedom ["the very heart of the ideology of the rights of man or 'bourgeois democracy'"] . . . may be deduced from the conditions in which, in the market, each individual presents himself to the other as the bearer of the universal – i.e. of purchasing power as such. He is a man "without any particular quality," whatever his social status (king or ploughman) and personal wealth (banker or wage-earner). (Balibar, *Philosophy of Marx*, 73–4)

36 See Introduction, note 43 above.

2 CRÈVECOEUR'S REVOLUTIONARY LOYALISM

1 According to Everett Emerson, the English publishers, disposed favorably towards the American cause, chose not to include some of the more aggressively anti-revolutionary papers given them by Crèvecoeur ("Hector St. John de Crèvecoeur," 45). Parts of the letters appeared in American periodicals from 1785 on, but the full text was not published until 1793. By 1805 there were over fifty printings of portions of the book in these American serials. Despite its popularity in Europe, the book itself was out of print in the United States in the nineteenth century and a new edition did not appear until 1904. I am grateful to Scott Slawinski of the University of South Carolina for this information.

2 See Rice, *Le Cultivateur Américain*. While it has been suggested that the French edition is more clearly pro-American and anti-British (and this as a result of Crèvecoeur's experience as a British prisoner in New York on his way back to France), the French edition still includes the pessimistic twelfth letter ("L'Homme des frontiers") that I discuss below. Indeed, despite its differences, the French edition does not finally serve to clarify or simplify the tensions apparent in the original English version. See Emerson's discussion of the French edition, in "Hector St. John de Crèvecoeur."

3 In an 1829 essay on "American Literature," William Hazlitt praised the "vivid and strikingly characteristic" pictures of the *Letters*, that give "not only the objects, but the feelings of a new country." The work of this "Illustrious Obscure," he continued, demonstrates "the power to sympathize with nature," and shows no "fastidious refinement or cynical contempt." "The most interesting part," Hazlitt declared, "is that where he describes the first indications of the breaking-out of the American war – the distant murmur of the tempest . . . his complaints and his auguries are fearful" (Hazlitt, *Complete Works*, 322–3).

4 The *Letters* are dedicated, however, to the Abbé Raynal, one of the most outspoken proponents of a radically extensive republicanism. Raynal's *Philosophical and Political History of the Establishments and Commerce of the Europeans in the Two Indies* (the work praised in Crèvecoeur's dedication) played a significant part in inspiring the leader of the Haitian revolution, Toussaint L'Ouverture (see James, *The Black Jacobins*, 24–5).

5 Rush's comments on loyalists can be found in his *Autobiography* and are excerpted in Richard D. Brown, *Major Problems*, 272–3.

6 See, for example, Nelson, *The American Tory*, Wallace Brown, *The King's Friends*, and Calhoon, *Loyalists*.

7 In this respect, James shares some of his anxiety with Thomas Paine: "If there is any true cause of fear respecting independence," Paine writes, "it is because no plan is yet laid down . . . Men do not see their way out –" (*Common Sense*, 95).

8 James' world would appear to be the one described by James Fenimore Cooper in *The American Democrat*, in which he discusses the advantages of monarchy: "In a monarchy," writes Cooper,

men are ruled without their own agency, and as their time is not required for the supervision or choice of the public agents, or the enactment of laws, their attention may be exclusively given to their personal interest. Could this advantage be enjoyed without the abuses of such a state of things, it would alone suffice to render this form of government preferable to all others. (*The American Democrat*, 118–19)

9 See too, Butler *et al.*:

new social movements often rely on identity-claims, but "identity" itself is never fully constituted; in fact, since identification is not reducible to identity, it is important to consider the incommensurability or gap between them. It does not follow that the failure of identity to achieve complete identification undermines the social movement at issue; on the contrary, that incompleteness is essential to the project of hegemony itself. No social movement can, in fact, enjoy its status as an open-ended, democratic political articulation without presuming and operationalizing the negativity at the heart of identity. (*Contingency*, 1–2)

10 In "The American Belisarius," one of Crèvecoeur's *Sketches of Eighteenth-Century America* (included in the Penguin edition of the *Letters*), S.K., a young frontier farmer, is celebrated as an exemplary independent farmer. His morality and industry are accompanied by a refusal to enter into market relations with traders in the region. Not surprisingly, then, this archetypal American is referred to as "princely" (*Letters*, 411).

11 As I suggested in the introduction, the Bill of Rights is crucial in this respect. As a series of laws against law ("Congress shall make no law"), the amendments are irreducibly at odds with themselves. Just as the self-divided monarch allows for the fantasy of sovereign individual integrity for the colonial farmer, so the self-divided Bill of Rights has allowed for a powerful American fantasy of individual democratic freedom.

12 This picture of patriarchal independence is reinforced by the description of life on John Bertram's farm (see my discussion in chapter one, above).

13 Arendt values the Roman dimension of the American people's veneration of the Constitution as the work of a founding in history, not as God's word or nature's (*On Revolution*, 198–9); the Constitution is respected as a political text, nothing more. Authority in the US, Arendt writes, comes from the Constitution, whose authority derives from "its inherent capacity to be amended and augmented"; we might say that it is a radically textual authorizing power: it calls for interpretation, for new readings, while remaining itself. "The very fact that the men of the American Revolution thought of themselves as 'founders' indicates the extent to which they must have known that it would be the act of foundation itself rather than any other transcendent, transmundane source, which eventually would become the fountain of authority in the new body politic" (*On Revolution*, 204).

14 Unlike the so-called "founding fathers," James is not so sure that the figure of the monarch and the symbolics of that ancient connection are *not* the best possible form of such a grounding principle. It could be that what we have here is further evidence of the fact that Crèvecoeur, unlike the American

revolutionaries, came from a Catholic background (a good Jesuit education) and indeed participated in the erection of a Catholic church in New York after the revolution. Crèvecoeur's farmer, perhaps, lacks the Protestant antipathy towards earthly representatives of divine power. Research suggests that Catholics should have fallen into the category of those who were suspicious of the revolution, i.e. minority groups in the colonies. But although they were slow to take part, Maryland Catholics eventually supported the cause. Perhaps, some have suggested, this only shows a pragmatic sense of where things were going. Nelson concludes that "Adherents of religious groups that were in a local minority were everywhere inclined towards Loyalism" (*The American Tory*, 286). Crèvecoeur's wife, Mehitable Tippet, for example, came from a French Calvinist family that remained loyalist and eventually fled to Nova Scotia. Nelson explains that while most English-speaking descendents of the Hugenots were ardent revolutionaries, those who still spoke French and thus felt more isolated within the colonies tended to suspect the outcome of the revolution (*The American Tory*, 285).

15 Arendt continues, "Certainly no religious fervour but strictly political misgivings about the enormous risks inherent in the secular realm of human affairs" caused them to turn to the "religious belief" in "'future states'" (*On Revolution*, 191). (Franklin's call for prayer in the Constitutional Convention would be one of the best examples of just such a turn.) And if a turn to the fantastic divine father figure can be seen in the hegemonic and legal discourse of the founders, there is, as recent commentators have reminded us, also an immense popular turn towards evangelical Christianity in the post-revolutionary United States. Here too, Brockden Brown's portrait of Theodore Wieland would be germane.

16 Countryman has suggested some of the ways in which we might think of Native American society as having more in common with pre-revolutionary British North America than with the new republic: "the great structural outcome of the Revolution was the Jeffersonian land grid and the lines that defined new states. Neither grid nor states provided room for the conditions that Indians had created between first contact and United States Independence" ("Response," 385). At the same time, as Deloria reminds us, "Indians were also the premier icons of the Revolution, serving simultaneously as representations of an American Self" ("Revolution,"365).

17 Here he blames the laws for "gall[ing] the very necks of those whom they protect" (*Letters*, 211). This is the flipside of the law's power to give new life – another way of indicating legal liberty's relationship to the death (the constitutive death) of the legal subject.

18 The history of official attempts to circumscribe the citizenship of Native Americans is replete with attempts to give a name to the insider–outsider status that the Indian bears, a status at once threatening to white democratic ideology and violent in its effects on native peoples. From 1789 on, American courts and legislatures tried to define Indians as (in the words of the New York Court of Errors in 1823) at once "under our protection" and "not

our subjects." Native Americans have "never . . . been incorporated into the body politic" wrote Judge Charles J. Colcock of the South Carolina Court of Appeals; Indians were "of that class who are said by jurists not to be citizens, but perpetual inhabitants, with diminutive rights"; According to Chief Justice Marshall, Indian tribes were "domestic dependent nations," occupying a "state of pupilage" with respect to the United States (all quotations from Kettner, *The Development of American Citizenship*, 294–6). As James Kettner phrases it, Indian tribes were accorded a "quasi-sovereign character" under American law that never ceased to raise "perplexing theoretical questions concerning the extension of white jurisdiction over their members or territories" (297).

19 To Edward Carrington, January 16, 1787; to James Madison, January 30, 1787 both in Dumbauld, ed., *Political Writings*, 65–7.

20 To William Ludlow, September 6, 1824 (quoted in Pearce, *Savagism and Civilization*, 155).

21 Compare this reference to "sacrifice" to Franklin's which I discuss in the next chapter. See William Hill Brown's 1789 novel, *The Power of Sympathy*, for another version of the coincidence of revolution and horrifying blood alliances.

22 In this regard, we might consider the role of Indian imitation in revolutionary politics (the Boston Tea Party and, in a conservative mode, the false claims about Indian insurgency used to mobilize troops against Shays' rebels in 1787). The Indian can be used to conceal the activities of radicals or conservatives in the revolutionary United States because the Indian is the privileged figure for an outside to law that simultaneously promises the beginning and the end of politics.

3 CITIZEN SUBJECTS: THE MEMOIRS OF STEPHEN BURROUGHS AND BENJAMIN FRANKLIN

1 Quoted in Kammen, ed., *The Origins of the American Constitution*, 370.

2 See Shurr, "Now, Gods," Ziff, *Writing in the New Nation*, and Gura, "Foreword."

3 Laurence Buell has described Burroughs' *Memoirs* as a "quintessential but . . . neglected Yankee autobiography" in which "the vital ingredient is the persona's protean resourcefulness in the face of emergency" (*New England Literary Culture*, 339). More recently, Nancy Ruttenburg has suggested that Burroughs "celebrates rather than bemoans the instability of identity . . . offering his memoirs almost as a manual of how to efface the line between author and character and thereby enjoy an unheard-of existential freedom, increasingly legitimated by a conspicuously Franklinian logic of expedience and liberated from a Franklinian concern for maintaining appearances" (*Democratic Personality*, 271).

4 The scenes of romance that Burroughs particularly enjoyed reading about and consequently appropriating are those in which "I viewed myself at the head of armies . . . and bearing down on all who dared to oppose

me" (*Memoirs*, 5). (Later, when describing the scenes which the prospect of wealth through counterfeiting promised, Burroughs writes: "I felt all the enjoyment of the advantages resulting from property . . . How I should make the rich respect me, and the poor adore me . . . I beheld myself at the head of a people, distributing joy and gladness" [79]).

5 There is much to support such assertions, including the fact that Burroughs wrote a series of essays for the *Long Island Herald*, a Jeffersonian Republican paper that called for "the establishment of the principle of universal benevolence, on the ruins of superstition" (quoted in Cohen, *Pillars of Salt*, 161).

6 Ziff, *Writing in the New Nation*, 61; Buell, *New England Literary Culture*, 340; Cohen, *Pillars of Salt*, 161; Fliegelman, *Prodigals and Pilgrims*, 245; Jones, "Praying Upon Truth," 33. Some of Burroughs' readers have suggested that the critical force of the *Memoirs* lies in its exploitation of anxieties peculiar to a democracy. "Burroughs' career," writes Larzer Ziff,

> presented a gaudy caricature of a democratic society's belief that regardless of origin, through skill and application any man can rise in life . . . Burroughs is a self-confessed deceiver and he cannot offer his career as an explicit example of the injustice of the social ideals that govern democratic America. But the implicit message is there, dramatized by Burroughs' attempts to be what he says he is rather than what he was. The authority of inherited position has been replaced by the authority of public opinion, but the new authority also dilutes reason with prejudice. In the America of Burroughs' *Memoirs*, society is so unfixed by the doctrines of equality and opportunity that it is forced to rely upon appearance as the basis of judgement yet is made uneasy by the sense that there is a reality that does not meet the eye, although it lacks a shared idea of what that reality may be. (*Writing in the New Nation*, 69)

Jay Fliegelman writes that Burroughs is the victim of "a society obsessed with misrepresentation and the deception of the senses as ultimate threats to liberty" (*Prodigals and Pilgrims*, 247), and Burroughs' counterfeiting, he suggests, represented a particularly fearful crime because of "a deep concern lest America itself was counterfeit: an impostor in a world of genuine nations" (247). Finally, Ruttenburg writes that "Burroughs's *Memoirs* celebrates his own radical mutability, his progressive slide into a series of characters fully released from any governing authorial principle, as his emancipation from social and cultural forms that have no inherent legitimacy" (*Democratic Personality*, 271).

7 "Unfortunately," Burroughs writes,

> many novels fell in my way, of that kind, which had a direct tendency to blow the fire of my temper into a tenfold rage . . . Reading and dwelling so much on those romantic scenes, at that early period of life, when judgement was weak, was attended with very pernicious consequences in the operations of my after conduct. Nothing gives the mind of childhood a more unfavourable bias, than a representation of those unnatural characters exhibited in novels and romances. It has a direct tendency to lead the mind from the plain simple path of nature, into the airy regions of fancy; and when the mind is once habituated to calculate on the romantic system, error and irregularity are the common consequences. (*Memoirs*, 4–5)

8 Hence Ruttenburg's accurate though somewhat puzzled conclusion: "Burroughs thus seems to combine a radical destabilization of identity with a

radical populism, whose anonymous, transcendent, and irrepressibly voluble 'we' refuses marginalization" (*Democratic Personality*, 274).

9 This is Godwinian, of course, and as such it is also one of Brockden Brown's abiding concerns.

10 See Minot, *The History of the Insurrections*, and Gross, *In Debt to Shays*.

11 For more on the poverty of Pelham, a town that had a long record of revolutionary patriotism, see the account of the town in Kaufman, ed., *Shays' Rebellion*.

12 The same year his *Stephen Burroughs's Sermon, Delivered in Rutland, on a Hay Mow, to his Auditory the Pelhamites* was also published in Hanover. Although the fiction of this sermon's delivery asserts that it was given in 1784, the event that it alludes to, Shays' rebellion, occurred in 1786 and 1787. For a version of this sermon see Parmenter, *History of Pelham*, 337–40.

13 See Davidson, *Revolution and the Word*, 257–8, on the Connecticut Wits who mocked the "anarchist" Shaysites. Buell also notes that the mode of "contempt for formal learning" that he recognizes in Burroughs as part of a Yankee tradition, resembled the manner in which Federalist satire viewed Thomas Jefferson's philosophical researches (*New England Literary Culture*, 341).

14 Franklin, too, mocked the Shaysites in an anonymous article for the *American Museum* (February 1787) in which he reproduced accounts of the farmers' appetite for "sugar, coffee, gauzes, silks, feathers, and the whole life of baubles and trinckets" (quoted in Smith-Rosenberg, "Dis-Covering the Subject," 854–5).

15 Fliegelman writes: "Like Franklin, Burroughs and his friends see paper money as the symbol of a new age of invention and reconceived values, as the great new fiction of the age" (*Prodigals and Pilgrims*, 247). At the same time, he contests that "In a society obsessed with misrepresentation and the deception of the senses as ultimate threats to liberty, the counterfeiter, like the Jacobin for whom he is an analogue, cannot be tolerated" (247). Where Fliegelman sees the threat of the Jacobin, I am suggesting the presence of a neo-monarchical gesture. This is less a point of contention, however, than a point of convergence: it is the relationship between the absolute monarch and the anarcho-Jacobin that Burroughs gives us to contemplate. Similarly, one could argue that by claiming the right to ordain himself as Pelham's minister, Burroughs was undermining elite authority or mimicking a royal appropriation of divine sanction.

16 The arguments that Lysander and Burroughs use to defend their schemes of deception, repeat in almost all their major terms the kind of arguments that had been used for many years by merchants and businessmen to deter sovereign or parliamentary interference in the marketplace (Lysander's claim, that "Money, of itself, is of no consequence, only as we, by mutual agreement, annex to it a nominal value, as the representation of property," echoes Nicholas Barbon in 1696, who wrote that "Things have no value in themselves . . . it is opinion and fashion brings them into use, and gives them a value" (quoted in Appleby, "Locke," 72). In 1695, faced with a

severe shortage of coin, the English parliament considered calling in clipped silver coins and reminting them with a devaluation of 25 percent, i.e. with 25 percent less silver denominated for each coin. The merchants and entrepreneurs who contributed to the heated debate which followed, defended a theory of money as a medium of exchange, separable from the intrinsic value of any precious metal. James Hodges, for example, suggested that "Silver, considered as Money, hath, speaking properly, no real intrinsick value at all," for "the whole value that is put upon Money by Mankind, speaking generally, is extrinsick to the money." "As many used to say," wrote another commentator, "if it was Leather, if it would pass, it would serve" (quoted in Appleby, "Locke," 67–8). The point here is that Burroughs and Lysander do not participate in a popular resistance to crown control of the economy but in the *laissez-faire* mystique of the market's sovereignty, a discourse that was as opposed to parliamentary legislative interference as it was to the crown's authority. Lysander and Burroughs, that is to say, participate fully in that democratic-capitalist displacement whereby the monarch's sublime transcendence of history (via the concept of the two bodies) has been transferred to the commodity and, in particular, to that preeminent commodity (Marx's "universal commodity," *Capital*, 102): money.

17 Burroughs writes, "We are too apt to be governed by the opinion of others" (*Memoirs*, 1–2). Later he notes, "As to my own sentiments of religion, you may find them comprised in the following line from Pope: 'An honest man's the noblest work of God'; and this honesty consists in following the law of our own mind, without depending on the dogmas of others" (358).

18 Balibar continues:

> to understand that this subject (which the citizen will be *supposed* to be) contains the paradoxical unity of a universal sovereignty and a radical finitude, we must envisage his constitution – in all the historical complexity of the practices and symbolic forms which it brings together – from *both* the point of view of the State apparatus and that of the permanent revolution. This ambivalence is his strength, his historical ascendancy. ("Citizen Subject," 55)

See too Balibar's "Subjection and Subjectivation" and *The Philosophy of Marx*.

19 Conner writes of Franklin's revealing antipathy towards mobs which "serve as haunting reminders of the fate that lurked in the shadows, waiting to seize the society which turned aside from the virtuous quest" (Poor Richard's Politicks, 111). Needless to say, Franklin provides plenty of evidence to suggest that his political virtue required the very lurking in the shadows that is here associated with popular mobocracy.

20 For more on Franklin's "intrigues with low women" and the implications for his son, William (the ostensible addressee of the first part of the *Autobiography*,) see Shurr, "Now, Gods."

21 See Warner, *The Letters of the Republic*, 190, n. 18.

22 In his landmark study of Franklin and Cotton Mather, Mitchell Breitwieser writes of the Franklinian self that "stands in detached constraining opposition to erotic and aesthetic feeling, to intensities of interest, to unreflective

devotion, and to political sentiments that seem to go contrary to what has been deemed the universal interest" (Cotton Mather and Benjamin Franklin, 8). Breitwieser points out that for Franklin this self succeeded by appearing to unite the self that governs with the self that is governed. By putting Franklin next to Burroughs, I want to compare this political fantasy with that of a subjectivity that coincides with itself only in an experience of singular freedom from law.

23 Jacques Derrida asks: "How are we to reconcile the act of justice that must always concern singularity, individuals, irreplaceable groups and lives, the other or myself *as* other, in a unique situation, with rule, norm, value or the imperative of justice which necessarily have a general form, even if this generality prescribes a singular application in each case?" ("Force of Law," 949).

24 Commenting on the Futurists' celebration of technologically enhanced modern warfare, in which "War is beautiful because it initiates the dreamt-of metalization of the human body," Benjamin warned of the appeal and the danger of an over-identification with the formally disembodied State ("The Work of Art," 241–2).

25 Nancy, *Sense of the World*, 104. Nancy continues: "In a sense, the citizen does nothing other than share with his/her fellow citizens the functions and signs of citizenship, and in this 'sharing' his/her being is entirely expressed." There would be something autoteleological about this citizenship, "where the *autos* would be utterly deprived of all interiority, without relation either to what we designate as the 'private sphere' or to what we call 'the nation'" (104).

26 Franklin's (and the convention's) investment in secrecy here finds its antithesis in the First Amendment's suggestion that citizens need keep no secrets in the United States. Anti-federalists were quick to jump on Franklin's words, particularly after the Boston Gazette published the speech on December 3. One aggressively patronizing writer to the newspaper suggested that out of "tenderness to the infirmities of age" and respect for Franklin's former accomplishments, the "puerile speech" should have been left "concealed beneath the roof where the liberties of America have been relinquished" (quoted in Bailyn, ed., *Debate on the Constitution*, I, 1138).

27 This self-deprecation may even have been supplemented by Franklin's decision not to stand and read the speech himself but to delegate this task to James Wilson. There has been some scholarly difference of opinion over whether or not Franklin's health or his wit should be held responsible for this self-concealment. See Oberg, "'Plain, insinuating, persuasive,'" and Carr, *The Oldest Delegate*.

28 God is the master figure, after all, of what Warner calls the "non-empirical agency" of print. Indeed, one could show, by comparing the text of Franklin's call for prayer in the convention (June 28, 1787) with his speech at the conclusion (September 17), that the sacrifice of opinion is Franklin's direct substitution for the invocation of God that the convention voted to bypass. "Without His concurring aid," pleaded Franklin (and recalling John Winthrop), "we shall succeed in this political building no better than the

builders of Babel: we shall be divided by our little partial local interests; our projects will be confounded, and we ourselves shall become a reproach and bye word down to future ages" (Franklin, *Writings*, 1139). Opinion and God are linked, in other words, via the category of the irreducibly singular (see Derrida, "Force of Law," 1023).

29 By 1837, Harriet Martineau will be complaining that "the worship of opinion is, at this day, the established religion of the United States" (*Society in America*, III, 7).

30 Compare Franklin here with Malcolm X talking to supporters in 1964:

> Whether we are Christians or Muslims or nationalists or agnostics or atheists, we must first learn to forget our differences. If we have differences, let us differ in the closet; when we come out in front, let us not have anything to argue about until we get finished arguing with the man. If the late President Kennedy could get together with Khrushchev and exchange some wheat, we certainly have more in common with each other than Kennedy and Khrushchev had with each other. ("The Ballot," 2543)

31 In *Federalist* no. 10, Madison refers to a wise representative as one who would be "least likely to sacrifice [the true interest of their country] to temporary or partial considerations" (*Federalist Papers*, 126). This use of the word "sacrifice" when compared with Franklin's reminds us that there are two important senses of this term, one (which I will call "pagan") implies a violence that merely destroys; the other (which we could call "Christian") suggests a violence that precipitates an afterlife. The two senses, of course, will not leave each other alone.

32 For more on the stylistic achievements of the speech see Oberg, " 'Plain, insinuating, persuasive.' "

33 The political and public consequences of the sacrifice Franklin calls for are a structure whose status as real or apparent is indeterminable. The sacrifice, in other words, deconstructs the opposition between the constative and the performative (their apparent unanimity will also be indistinguishable from real unanimity): "the law is transcendent, violent and non-violent," Derrida writes, "because it depends only on who is before it – and so prior to it –, on who produces it, founds it, authorizes it in an absolute performative whose presence always escapes him" ("Force of Law," 993).

34 It should come as no surprise to learn that this extravagantly intimate discourse on secrecy and sacrifice was in wide public circulation upon the immediate conclusion of the convention. Two days after the remarks had been delivered, the *Pennsylvania Gazette* reported that, as Barbara Oberg tells us, "Franklin had made an address that was 'truly pathetic, and extremely sensible. The concurrence of this venerable patriot in this Government, and his strong recommendation of it, cannot fail of recommending it to all his friends in Pennsylvania'" (" 'Plain, insinuating, persuasive,' " 181).

35 Rush is quoted in Oberg, " 'Plain, insinuating, persuasive,' " 178. Guillotin used the phrase, "l'âme de la Convention" in a February 2, 1788 letter to Franklin (see Oberg, " 'Plain, insinuating, persuasive,' " 178). "The founder

of the spirit of a people, one could show, always has the figure of a *revenant-survivant*, a ghost-survivor" (Derrida, *Specters of Marx*, 146).

36 Oberg points out that the speech is ostensibly addressed to the convention's chair, George Washington, but that the frequent uses of the address "Sir" nevertheless work to gender the audience and include all the delegates within a particular fraternal circle.

37 As Michael Warner puts it, the Constitution works by ensuring that "the people are always coming across themselves in the act of consenting to their own coercion" (*The Letters of the Republic*, 112). Franklin's character recalls his own youthful self in the *Autobiography*, when he writes of his decision to abandon vegetarianism when confronted by a tempting plate of seafood: "So convenient a thing it is to be a *reasonable Creature*, since it enables one to find or Make a Reason for everything one has a mind to do" (*Autobiography*, 39).

38 The idea that only the privileged (in this case, the white male founders) know how to keep secrets could also be approached by way of a reading of Frederick Douglass' *Narrative of the Life of Frederick Douglass, An American Slave*, which not only tries to teach Northerners about the culture of secrecy practiced and exploited by slaves, but does so while keeping the fact that a lesson is being given (by a black man to white people!) secret from the students.

39 One hundred years later, Burroughs was still leaving a bad taste in the mouth of Pelham's historian, C.O. Parmenter, who writes,

> the people of Pelham had been through the hard struggle of the Revolution and had responded to all calls as promptly as it was possible for them to do; they were patriotic, but they were not possessed of abundant wealth and the long years of war had borne heavily upon them. The war had but recently ended when in 1786, they were humiliated as well as angered by a four or five months' experience with Stephen Burroughs, a wolf in sheep's clothing, who came among them as a supplyer when without a settled minister. (*History of Pelham*, 156)

40 For another take on some of these questions, see Bryce Traister's discussion of the libertine in the early republic: "Americans thus found their own fascination with the paradoxes of revolutionary agency embodied in the figure of the oddly passive yet still animated libertine, a male figure at once fiercely independent but insufficiently so" ("Libertinism and Authorship," 8).

41 Speaking out of a more explicitly Marxist discourse, we might say that this secret is the secret of the dialectical relation of forces at play in every moment of democratic politics. There is a direct correlation between what I am attempting to formulate here with respect to the American subject of democracy and what Marx's thought would suggest about the irreconcilable contradictions of capitalism: "*In reality, there are always two overlapping collectives* of workers, made up of the *same* individuals (or almost) and yet incompatible: a capital-collective and a proletariat-collective. Without the latter, engendered by the resistance to capitalist collectivization, the capitalist 'autocrat' could not himself exist" (Balibar, *Philosophy of Marx*, 101).

4 AN EPISTEMOLOGY OF THE BALLOT BOX:
BROCKDEN BROWN'S SECRETS

1 Jay Fliegelman, whose line on Brown is by no means a narrow one, writes of *Wieland's* "terrifying post-revolutionary account of the fallibility of the human mind and, by extension, of democracy itself," and of that novel's sensitivity to "larger fears about the Jacobinization of the impressionable American mind" ("Introduction," vii, xi).

2 "England's constitution," wrote Thomas Paine, was suited "for the dark and slavish times in which it was erected." On the other hand, of the American experiment, he proclaimed, "the sun never shone on a cause of greater worth" (*Common Sense*, 82).

3 Richard Buel is not alone in describing the period in terms of a "mood of grim foreboding" that hung over the early republic on account of the "specter[s]" of " 'great secrecy' " frequently conjured up by wary politicians (*Securing the Revolution*, 174–5). Linda Kerber refers to the early national period as "one of the most intellectually traumatic in modern times" (*Federalists in Dissent*, xxi). See too the first chapter of Christophersen, *The Apparition in the Glass*.

4 Robison's book was printed in Edinburgh in 1797 and reprinted in New York the following year.

5 Curiously, Robison's book is one of the documents circulated by contemporary militia movements in the United States. What ought we to do with the fact that the leading New England clergyman, Yale President, and notorious denouncer of secret internal threats to the nation, Timothy Dwight, in some sense "passed on" John Robison's book to the Oklahoma City bomber, Timothy MacVeigh?

6 Madison maintained a careful secrecy concerning the progress of the new Constitution. His use of a cipher with which to communicate secretly with Jefferson, however, would also seem to be evidence of a certain delight in secrecy. See Brant, *James Madison*, 188. The code was later decoded for posterity by Jefferson's secretary.

7 Furthermore, the debates in Congress for September 26 and 27, the days devoted to discussion of the proposed Constitution drawn up in Philadelphia, were officially censored from the Records.

8 George Mason wrote of the need to "keep our doors shut" in order to protect "the public eye" from the "crude and indigested" shapes which the "business" might at first assume (Farrand, ed., *Records*, III, 28). The reference to "closed doors" and "out of doors" picks up on the phrase frequently used in this period to designate the sovereign people in their capacity as ultimate source of legitimate political power. In much revolutionary rhetoric, the people were only to be found "out of doors," at the site of an excess that could not be contained by any structure, the site of actions open to the light of the sun that Thomas Paine liked to refer to as shining upon the American cause (*Common Sense*, 82). The motif of the door also recurrs in one of Madison's more nervous missives from the convention: "The labor is great indeed," he

told William Short, "whether we consider the real or imaginary difficulties within doors or without doors" (Farrand, ed., *Records*, iii, Appendix A, 37).

9 Of course, some of the debates taking place behind the convention's closed doors concerned precisely the shape of a "man," what counts as a person, and the astonishing possibility of "three-fifths of a person." For an excellent discussion of this debate, see Finkelman, "Slavery," 188–225. Racist and pro-slavery rhetoric hardly needed a cloak of secrecy in late-eighteenth-century America; nevertheless, there is an important relationship signaled by the coincidence of the convention's desperate secrecy and the issue of slavery that made up part of the discussion. The "crude matter" of the relationship between the slave's gothic body (three-fifths of a person) and the constitutional citizen's body (five-fifths of a person?) needed to be kept secret in the name of a fantasy of sovereign individuality that owes everything to the aura of monarchism.

10 For more on the word "crude" that crops up repeatedly in these accounts of the convention, see Wills, *Explaining America*, 243–4. As a term often used in scientific discussions of the chemistry of digestion, "crude" both signaled the founders' relationship to Scottish scientific analogizing in political discourse, and went some way towards producing political voice (the unanimous voice of the convention) as a form of *ventriloquism* (literally, a speaking from the stomach).

11 If we were looking for a way to read some kind of erotics into the monumentally cerebral (some would say "dry") history of the formation of the Constitution, we might begin here with this secret yielding to the other's force.

12 "It seems that the law as such should never give rise to any story. To be invested with its categorical authority, the law must be without any history, genesis, or any possible derivation. That would be *the law of the law*" (Derrida, "Before the Law," 191).

13 The possibility of a wholly fleshly "body politic" that Miller's account suggests, is surely as fantastic and undesirable as the ghostly citizen of his gothic imagination. Miller's take on these matters has recently been echoed at some length by Dana Nelson, who writes of the "virtualization" of democracy under the Constitution, and who quotes (without qualification) C. Douglas Lummis' claim that the revolution is at its most revolutionary where "the polity has broken down naturally [*sic*] into units small enough that the people can confront one another in genuine communities" (quoted in Nelson, *National Manhood*, 33). This fetishization of the "genuine community" is, to say the least, surprising. Nelson herself notes (while discussing Jefferson's scientific racism) that "strategies of splitting and excorporation are psychologically corollary to desires that are about engulfment and *in*corporation" (54).

14 Samuel Beer suggests that this position is Machiavellian first. The expanding public was, according to Machiavelli, made "unwieldy" and hard to "manage" by the "animosities and tumults" of too many participants (quoted in Beer, *To Make a Nation*, 90). "The fundamental problem," Beer writes, "was not class conflict but pluralism" (90). As Beer helps us to see, this position

shares assumptions with those political theories that justify dictatorial rule on the grounds that, as Thomas Aquinas wrote, "many, as such, seek many things, whereas one attends only to one" (Beer, *To Make a Nation*, 91).

15 Of course, even Beer's formulation cannot help reproducing difference in the course of trying to name a self-identical purity: "self-sacrificing virtue" is no less troubled by difference than self-love. See my discussion of (self-) sacrifice in the convention in chapter three.

16 I think it would be possible to show that it is this primary self-difference at work in Madison's theory that gets called "blockage" in his theory of the constitutional State by such scholars as Robert Dahl. See Dahl's *A Preface to Democratic Theory*.

17 One might also consider here Madison's remarks on irreducible "sources of . . . obscurity" in the domains of language and the natural sciences in the fascinating (and very un-Hamiltonian) *Federalist* no. 37.

18 This ambiguated singularity of the source and recipient of political authority is registered in other ways in *The Federalist Papers*. In arguing for the Constitution as a means of making national politics a popular politics, Alexander Hamilton writes of "the persons of the citizens – the only proper objects of government" (*Federalist* no. 15, 149). In *Federalist* no. 39, Madison writes of republican government as one which "derives all its powers directly or indirectly from the great body of the people" (255). As "object" *and* origin of political power, the people are registered here (and elsewhere) in strikingly awkward formulations: "the persons of the citizens" or "the great body of the people."

19 Similarly, the concept of the division of powers will be translated under constitutional republicanism into a separation not designed to represent differences between classes of subjects but to institutionalize separation itself as a means to limit the possibility of representative tyranny. J. G. A. Pocock writes: "[separation of powers] ensured that the representatives could not corruptly consolidate themselves to monopolize the government. We have seen how separation of powers emerged with conjoint sovereignty to give parliamentary monarchy its republican shadow; in this way too the oppositions of eighteenth-century Britain left their legacy to the American republic" (*Virtue, Commerce, and History*, 271). It is for its literary exploration of precisely these kind of "shadows" and monarchic "legacies" that Brown's work remains vital. Secrecy and separation are of course etymologically related (*Oxford English Dictionary*: "Secret fr. L *Secretus*, past part. of *secernere* to separate").

20 Nash describes newspapers in New York in the first half of 1776 that were "filled with articles proposing annual assembly elections, rotation of offices, secret balloting, universal adult male suffrage, equal apportionment, popular election of local officials, and the abolition of slavery and imprisonment for debt" (*Urban Crucible*, 374).

21 See too Nash: "It was precisely the massive political arm twisting which viva voce voting allowed that led in 1769 to an all-out effort by New York's popular leaders and their laboring-class supporters to substitute a

system of secret balloting such as had been used for decades in Boston and Philadelphia" (*Urban Crucible*, 366–7). A 1769 meeting in New York City "to protest the abuses of open voting and to advocate the secret ballot " was held, Williamson notes, "under the shadow of the Liberty Pole" (*American Suffrage*, 77–8), and defenders of voice voting, "who understood clearly what they stood to lose if electoral procedures were changed . . . fought back" (Nash, *Urban Crucible*, 367). In New Jersey, the switchover from viva voce to ballot voting was on a slow, county-by-county basis until 1797, when a law to enforce uniformity of procedure throughout the state was passed. See the Newark *Centinel of Freedom*, March 15, 1797.

22 The anti-democratic dimension of dominant sentimental discourse in this period is given some focus here by critics of the secret ballot who defended the viva voce system for providing that "every Elector is at Liberty to declare the Sentiments of his Heart publicly, which is the Glory of the British Constitution" ("J.W., a Squinter on Public Affairs," *Connecticut Courant*, March 5, 1770, quoted in Williamson, *American Suffrage*, 42). One could also think of the transition from viva voce to written ballot voting as paralleling the transfer of cultural fascination from the theatre to the novel in the course of the eighteenth century.

23 This fear, of course, lay behind the classic defense of property restrictions on the franchise. In the oft quoted words of William Blackstone, these restrictions worked to exclude "such persons as are in so mean a situation that they are esteemed to have no will of their own. If these persons had votes, they would be tempted to dispose of them under some undue influence or another" (from the *Commentaries on the Laws of England*, 1765, quoted in Keyssar, *The Right to Vote*, 10). Keyssar notes that those who adopted Blackstone's line of argument were just as likely to restrict the franchise on the grounds that "such persons" had too much will: "If men without property could vote, reflected the judicious conservative, John Adams, 'an immediate revolution would ensue' " (*The Right to Vote*, 11).

24 While Michael Warner's very influential study, *The Letters of the Republic*, argues for the interpretive importance of "print culture" for any understanding of late-eighteenth-century America, his argument frequently acknowledges that many of the features assigned to "print" function just as pertinently when considered under the more general rubric of writing. Moreover, it is writing's relationship to secrecy that I find most interesting in Warner's claim that "writing became the hinge between a delegitimizing revolutionary politics and a nonrevolutionary, already legal signification of the people; it *masked* the contradiction between the two" (*The Letters of the Republic*, 104, my emphasis).

25 Derrida points out that for Rousseau in the *Contrat social*, "the instance of writing must be effaced to the point where a sovereign people *must not even write to itself*, its assemblies must meet spontaneously, without 'any formal summons' " (*Of Grammatology*, 302).

26 For Rousseau's analysis see the *Contrat social* in *Oeuvres complètes*, III: 351–470. Montesquieu explicitly addressed the question of secret voting in *The Spirit of the Laws*. "Here," he writes,

is what must be thought about it: When the people cast votes, their votes should no doubt be public; and this should be regarded as a fundamental law of democracy. The lesser people must be enlightened by the principal people and subdued by the gravity of certain eminent men . . . But votes cannot be too secret in an aristocracy when the body of nobles casts the votes, or in a democracy when the senate does so, for here the only issue is to guard against intrigues. (14)

In other words, secrecy and political *equality* should go hand in hand.

27 Brown began work on his "Memoirs of Carwin" while *Wieland* was still in press, and Alexander Cowie has argued that "Memoirs of Carwin" was intended "as a sequel or an interpolated addition to *Wieland*." "It probably should not," he adds, "be read as a prologue" ("Historical Essay,"337). Near the end of *Wieland*, Carwin makes reference to having sought "retreat in the wilderness" from the wild events of *Wieland*, where he "might henceforth employ myself in composing a faithful narrative of my actions." "I designed it," he adds, "as my vindication from the aspersions that had rested on my character, and as a lesson to mankind on the evils of credulity on the one hand, and of imposture on the other" (*Wieland*, 212). In the preface ("Advertisement") to *Wieland*, the author writes: "The memoirs of Carwin alluded to at the conclusion of the work, will be published or suppressed according to the reception which is given to the present attempt" (3).

28 Brown's story shares something, in other words, with those American stories of formative disobedience that I discussed in chapter three: Franklin's accounts of his quarrels with his father and brother in the *Autobiography* and Stephen Burroughs' story of petty theft and deception at the start of his "notorious" *Memoirs*.

29 In fact, it is difficult to decide, finally, if the specters and goblins he is afraid of are not displaced indications of the disconcerting paradoxicality of Carwin's experimental detour: going into the wilderness in order to stay within the law. Something of this paradoxicality seems to be registered in Brown's own attitude towards the practice of law. His friend and biographer William Dunlap wrote that the young Brown gave up the profession his family had encouraged him to train for because "he could not reconcile it with his ideas of morality to become indiscriminately the defender of right or wrong; thereby intimating, if not asserting, that a man must, in the practice of the law, not only deviate from morality, but become the champion of injustice" (*The Life of Charles Brockden Brown*, 40).

30 Compare Carwin here to Franklin's Poor Richard (discussed in chapter three) listening to his own maxims uttered by another and "benefit[ting] from the echo."

31 The importance of the "Mohock" reference in this passage deserves its own study. The "indifference" of this choice in the mediation of Carwin's revolutionary anxiety could be interestingly compared with, for example, the use of Indian imitation in the Boston Tea Party and the false alibi of Indian insurgency used by the Confederate government to justify sending financial aid to those attempting to suppress Shays' rebellion, the symbolic exploitation of Native Americans in patriotic poems and plays, the revolutionary arrogation

of Chief Logan's speech to the British, etc. The figure of the Native American emerges here as a particularly economic revolutionary device. While helping to mask acts of unsettling violence, the appropriated Indian also registers, once again, the revolution's yearning for an origin "out of doors." See Silverman: "The use of Indian costumes [in the Boston Tea Party] did not constitute a premiere: Colonists in the South dressed up as Indians during Saint Tammany Day festivities; the ship *Gaspee* had been burned in 1772 by Rhode Islanders in Indian dress, such costumes serving at once as disguises and as assertive revelations of new identities" (*A Cultural History*, 249).

32 Carwin exemplifies, for me, the correspondences between Burroughs and Franklin that I discussed in chapter three. He breaks from his father and sets out on a life which, dependent as it is upon his deceptive vocal accomplishment, is always potentially criminal and anti-social. At the same time, his discovery of the efficacy of ventriloquism marks him as decidedly Franklinian.

33 For more on *Edgar Huntly* see my "Sleep-Walking Out of the Revolution."

34 On the importance of the voice and public speaking in revolutionary America, see Fliegelman, *Declaring Independence* and Looby, *Voicing America*.

35 Thus when Brown brings Carwin to bear on the young Americans in *Wieland*, he gives a twist to the popular, xenophobic identification of threats to the new nation with European corruption: what the United States fear and thrill to, Brown's work suggests, is an alienated return of their revolutionary selves.

36 One might compare this society with any one of a great number of secret societies and clandestine colleges that proliferated in Europe in the second half of the eighteenth century, including Sade's fictional "*Société des Amis du Crime*" about which Maurice Blanchot writes: "the possibility of betrayal is forever present: between accomplices there is a constantly mounting tension, so much so that they ultimately feel themselves less bound by the oath that unites them than by the mutual need to violate this oath" ("Sade,"47).

37 One could dwell here on the Godwinian motifs in Ludloe's philosophy. For example, his commitment to the justice of "spontaneity," his antipathy towards contracts and promises, his veneration of "sincerity," and his commitment to a "new model of society" grounded in rational enquiry. His library also contains "Aristotle's republic, the political romances of Sir Thomas Moore, Harrington, and Hume" and other works on "political economy and legislation," in all of which Ludloe found "nothing but error and absurdity" (*Wieland*, 298).

38 See Brown's "Remarks on Mysteries" from his *Literary Magazine* 6 (October 1806) as reproduced in Weber, ed., *Literary Essays and Reviews*, 176–7. Brown writes: "Mysterious fraternitites seem to have abounded in all ages. In many cases, this mystery has been prompted by considerations of personal safety; but, in many cases, also, societies have been formed merely for the pleasure of having a secret, and of obtaining that importance in the eyes of others, which the possession of a secret is sure to confer" ("Remarks on Mysteries,"177).

39 Ludloe's society, like the American Constitutional Convention discussed in chapter three, demonstrates a crucial relationship to sacrifice.

40 And along with secrets, the sect would do away with the various arts of delusion (rhetorical persuasion) that are, not surprisingly, associated with the "seductive and bewitching powers of women" (*Wieland*, 292).

41 The contradictions and complexities of Ludloe's society are not out of line, I would suggest, with those of Freemasonry, one of the possible models for Ludloe's sect. See Steven C. Bullock's work. In a review of books on Freemasonry, Bullock notes that Masonic lodges can be thought of (as Margaret Jacon suggests) in terms of their contribution to the development of modern democratic politics (Masonry was "the most avowedly constitutional and aggressively civic" of modern social organizations [quoted in Bullock, "Review Essay," 87]) or in terms of their "connection to antiquity" ("the national grand lodges were headed by nobles and royals appointed for life"; "What distinguishes Masonry," Bullock writes, "is not its constitutions but its religious character and its link to public honor" ("Review Essay," 88).

42 And since the ventriloquism begins with Indian imitation, we could add that Carwin's subjectivity is also in debt to the native American Indian.

43 The story was published anonymously, but Alfred Weber's critical notes in his invaluable collection of Brown's stories provide overwhelming evidence to support Brown's authorship. Readers familiar with Brown's work would quickly recognize his style in this story (bouts of awkwardly pedantic syntax, structural assymetry, the persistent threat of complete narrative collapse, all-in-all the breathless sense of an untrained literary sensibility trying to keep up with a tireless philosophical imagination). I would even go so far as to say that "A Lesson on Concealment" gives us a perfectly distilled, pocket-sized Brown.

44 See Brown's comments on *Clarissa* in this regard, in *Literary Essays and Reviews*, ed. Weber, 100–2.

45 See Michael Warner's discussion, in *The Letters of the Republic*, of the "obscurity of agency" that was crucial to the effectiveness of the Constitution. For Warner it is print culture in particular that guaranteed this obscurity of agency. But Brown, intriguingly, often likes to exploit an obscurity of agency in voice, as if to delimit the unsettling and revolutionary potential of this obscurity.

46 And it might be worth thinking here about how frequently patriotic discourse tells us that American revolutionaries *loved* liberty: it is not enough simply to entertain a reasoned acceptance of a more appropriate political order.

47 See too Fritz Fleischmann's discussion of the story in *A Right View of the Subject*. Mary's perspective in the story, Fleischmann suggests, "exposes a complicity in injustice among these men" (102).

5 LUXURY, EFFEMINACY, CORRUPTION: IRVING AND THE GENDER OF DEMOCRACY

1 Quoted in Williamson, *American Suffrage*, 279.

2 Note the gendered contrast between writing (the "name" of master) and clothing (the petticoat) in this response.

3 See James Sullivan's letter to Elbridge Gerry on this matter and Adams' long reply to Sullivan (May 26, 1776), both in volume IV of *The Papers of John Adams*, 208–13.

4 A number of towns rejected the 1778 version of the Massachusetts State Constitution on the grounds that, among other things, it excluded Negroes from the suffrage. The vote should be given, said the people of Upton, to "every freeman twenty one years of age possessed of suitable property . . . without regard to Nation or Colour, seeing all Nations are made of one blood" (quoted in Handlin and Handlin, eds., *The Popular Sources of Political Authority*, 263). For more on the history of voting qualifications see Keyssar, *The Right to Vote*, Williamson, *American Suffrage*, and Dinkin, *Voting in Revolutionary America*.

5 That freeholders in land were the backbone of the state was a classical political idea having roots in Aristotle, Cato, Cicero, and the Renaissance. Montesquieu and Blackstone reasserted the point. James Harrington called for a widening of the franchise in eighteenth-century England at the same time as he called for an institution of secret balloting, suggesting a link between the end of land-based political will and the institution of secrecy at the site of the expression of political will. See chapter four.

6 *General Statutes of New Jersey 1709–1895*, XXII, quoted in Turner, "Women's Suffrage," 166 n.6. "Clear estate" excluded married women who could not own anything in clear estate. The 1797 election law dropped this requirement.

7 For a detailed discussion of the franchise in the revolutionary era see Keyssar, *The Right to Vote*, 8–25.

8 The Society of Friends had a history of proposing equality of women with men. See Soderlund, "Women's Authority." "Lucretia Mott and her fellow Quaker activists had behind them almost two centuries of female participation in the leadership of their faith when in 1848 they helped to draw up the Declaration of Sentiments for the convention at Seneca Falls" (722). There is some confusion among historians, however, as to whether it was Quaker *John* Cooper (who drafted the original 1776 constitution) or *Joseph* Cooper in 1790, who deserves the credit for this enfranchisement (see Klinghoffer and Elkin, "The Petticoat Electors," 168 n. 21).

9 Quoted in Klinghoffer and Elkin, "The Petticoat Electors," 174.

10 As late as 1953, one history of voting in New Jersey maintained (despite lack of convincing evidence) that women never exercised the vote of their own volition (McCormick, *The History of Voting in New Jersey*, 97–111). On the other hand, Joan Gunderson refers to New Jersey women who "quietly assumed their independence by voting" in elections in the 1790s ("Independence," 66). Gunderson's useful article discusses the relationship between marriage and independence as it was thought through (or more often *not* thought through) during the revolutionary era. She suggests that the very rhetoric of independence that drove the revolution served to exclude married women from the post-revolutionary political process because their independence was compromised by marriage. Concluding her discussion with a reference to the Seneca Falls Declaration (1848) and its assumption of the revolutionary

language of independence and political right, Gunderson writes: "The independence/dependence framework that had been so much a part of the political thought of the American Revolution contained both the chains of bondage and the keys to a long struggle for freedom for women" (77). The length of this struggle, not to mention the inconsistencies espoused at every moment ought to direct us, I would suggest, towards rethinking the investment in independence in the first place. Women's "dependent" subjectivity, as Gunderson herself notes, represented, for revolutionary men, a trace of monarchic subjectivity in the new republic. Repudiating women's political authority was part of the discourse of monarchophobia and, as such, also part of the revolutionary refusal to think through the relationship between (not just the opposition of) democracy and monarchism. For more on women's political participation in revolutionary New Jersey see Klinghoffer and Elkin, "The Petticoat Electors."

11 See too the newspaper accounts referred to by Turner: *The New Jersey Journal* for October 18, 1797 (published in Elizabeth) and the *Newark Centinel* of the same day.

12 Linda Kerber points out that in another instance (that of the treason statute as drafted by the Continental Congress) women were carefully included by a reference to "all persons abiding within any of the United Colonies" (*Women of the Republic*, 121).

13 Wright is drawing on Thomas S. Griffiths, *A History of Baptists in New Jersey* (1904). Wright also quotes Griffiths on the story that "Governor Pennington is said to have escorted a 'strapping negress to the polls where he joined her in the ballot' " (Wright, *Negro Suffrage*, 173). This insistent embodiment of the black woman in question constitutes an example of the kind of anxiety about citizenship that this chapter seeks to address.

14 A long-running debate over whether or not black freemen had the right to vote also took place in Pennsylvania. See Turner, 176 n. 48. Also see debates in Massachusetts in 1778 and 1779 (Boston's *Independent Chronicle*, April 9, 1778, September 23, 1779; and the *Boston Continental Journal*, January 8, 1778.)

15 W. H. Shaw (*History of Essex Counties, New Jersey* [Philadelphia, 1884]), quoted in Turner, "Women's Suffrage," 182.

16 See the *Centinel*, November 24, 1807.

17 See Wright, *Negro Suffrage*, 180–1, on the petitions to the New Jersey legislature in 1841 and 1842.

18 Turner suggests that the amendment of the law in 1807 was not directed "primarily" against women, but was "intended to exclude all classes who held the privilege doubtfully" ("Women's Suffrage,"185).

19 See the debates in the New Jersey Legislature (*Journals of the Legislative Council*, November 14, 1807). For more on the categories of exclusion worked out by nineteenth-century Americans, see Keyssar, *The Right to Vote*, 54–67: "By the early 1850s," Keyssar concludes, "several groups or categories of men (and one group of women) had lost the political rights they possessed a half century earlier. Although the franchise on the whole had been broadened, new barriers were erected, targeting specific – and smaller – populations" (67).

20 Mrs. Carter replies: "If the law should exclude from all political functions every one who had a mole on his right cheek, or whose stature did not exceed five feet six inches, who would not condemn, without scruple, so unjust an institution? Yet, in truth, the injustice would be less than in the case of women" (*Alcuin*, 68).

21 As Robert Ferguson points out,

> when the American woman actually finds a place in early drafts of the constitution, it is as a fugitive slave. "If any Person bound to service or labor in any of the United States shall escape into another State," ran the original and unanimous language of August 29th, "He or She shall not be discharged . . . but shall be delivered up to the person justly claiming their service or labor." ("The Limits of Enlightenment," 496–7)

> The Committee of Style revised this passage, substituting the "he or she" for a simple and direct negative subject (the phrase is Ferguson's): "No person legally held to service." This is a striking instance of the threatening grammar of conjunction that I have been discussing: one might have thought that the slave subject was not entitled to the gender-neutral subjectivity that the ideal democratic citizen claims. But in fact the mere presence of gender distinction anywhere in the document appears to trouble not just the "style" of the text but the very fantasy of citizenship in which it is so powerfully invested.

22 Klinghoffer and Elkin are very useful on the specific party dynamics that contributed to the passage of the 1807 election law. In particular they point to the split within the Republican party between the "liberal" members who defended a broad franchise and a new "moderate" faction that advocated restrictions ("The Petticoat Electors,"186–7). Through a complicated series of events the liberal republicans agreed to support measures to prevent non-taxpayers and aliens from voting, a move which required Republicans to counter lost votes by pursuing the disenfranchisement of women and blacks (who had tended to vote Federalist) (188). Klinghoffer and Elkin go so far as to claim, however (in an astonishing example of post-feminism?), that "the growth of gender ideology was not the reason for the disenfranchisement of women. Power politics was" (192). The complexity of the political situation should not blind us to the effective presence in this period of a general desire on the part of propertied white men to restrict the franchise to propertied white men.

23 This form of revolutionary idealism is on display as early as 1775, when Freneau wrote of the American soldier: "No fop in arms, no feather on his head, / No glittering toys the manly warrior had, / His auburne face the least employ'd his care, / He left it to the females to be fair" ("A REVERIE. By a SOLDIER," quoted in Silverman, *A Cultural History*, 286).

24 "I fear chiefly lest my expression not be extra-vagant enough, may not wander far enough beyond the narrow limits of my daily experience . . . I desire to speak somewhere without bounds" (Thoreau, *Walden*, 209).

25 Marriage suggests the horrifying image of two people in the voting booth, reminding us among other things that democratic idealism might have a

particular problem with sexuality. The ballot box/voting booth and the marriage bed both give a secret space to something having to do with reproduction.

26 In Carol Pateman's analysis this would be the fraternal version of feudalism's paternal patriarchy (*The Sexual Contract*, 3).

27 As Kerber points out, marriage was generally thought of and written about as a means of accomplishing what English common law called "unity of person." The unified person left standing was generally male (*No Constitutional Right*, 28).

28 The liberation scene in Equiano's narrative (1789) explicitly contrasts the African, deliriously grasping the piece of paper that grants him freedom, with the two white men (his owner and a friend), whose power to free Equiano corresponds with a discourse of arbitrary generosity that revels in its own sovereign freedom from law and compulsion. Noting the master's initial reluctance to "sell" Equiano back to himself, the captain of the ship on which Equiano had earned his money intervenes: " 'Come, come,' said my worthy captain, clapping my master on the back, 'Come, Robert, (which was his name), I think you must let him have his freedom' " (*The Interesting Narrative*,135).

29 One could even argue that democrats were particularly hostile towards marriage and its relationship to the political since monarchism's history was so visibly a history of marriage's relationship to corrupt, family-based power. See Paine's essay on monarchism, "An Essay for the Use of New Republicans."

30 Lincoln made this point in 1857, taking issue with Stephen Douglas' suggestion that American attitudes towards the black man had improved since 1776: "This assumption is a mistake," writes Lincoln,

> as a whole, in this country, the change between then and now is decidedly the other way; and their ultimate destiny has never appeared so hopeless as in the last three or four years. In two of the five states – New Jersey and North Carolina – that then gave the free negro the right of voting, the right has since been taken away; and in a third – New York – it has been greatly abridged; while it has not been extended, so far as I know, to a single additional state, though the number of states has more than doubled. ("Speech," 178)

31 One should also consider the poor as another example of compromised independence, an example that figured importantly in debates over the franchise and one which, as Edmund Morgan has persuasively argued, was crucially displaced in America onto the persons of slaves:

> In the republican way of thinking as Americans inherited it from England, slavery occupied a critical, if ambiguous position: it was the primary evil that men sought to avoid for society as a whole by curbing monarchs and establishing republics. But it was also the solution to one of society's most serious problems, the problem of the poor. Virginians could outdo English republicans as well as New England ones, partly because they had solved the problem: they had achieved a society in which most of the poor were enslaved. (*American Slavery*, 381)

32 Cathy Davidson, on the other hand, suggests that "Rip" captures the impact
    of the revolution for "most Americans" who, like the "Connecticut farmer"
    (Davidson's exemplary "ordinary American" on this occasion), "still had to
    worry about tilling unyielding soil, milking cows, feeding a growing family –
    facts of life that remained, for most Americans, more present and more
    pressing than the political considerations and compromises whereby the
    Constitution was being forged somewhere in Philadelphia behind locked
    doors" (*Revolution and the Word*, 39).
33 Jeffrey Rubin-Dorsky, glossing Haskell Springer, tries to account for the
    narrative's performance of its own fictionality in this way: "It is possible
    that Irving is engaging here in what Haskell Springer calls a 'technique of
    self-contradiction' – the 'story proper and the comments upon the tale'
    exert pressures in 'opposite directions,' so that together they wind up
    asserting the 'reality' of seemingly unreal events – to alert the reader to the
    essentially fictional character of this world" (*Adrift in the Old World*, 112).
34 "Rip Van Winkle" appeared in *The Sketch Book* immediately following a
    piece entitled "The Wife." The bachelor narrator of this classic example of
    republican domestic ideology praises the wife who supports her husband
    through any misfortune:

    And indeed, I have observed that a married man falling into misfortune is more
    apt to retrieve his situation in the world than a single one; partly because he is more
    stimulated to exertion by the necessities of the helpless and beloved beings who
    depend upon him for subsistence; but chiefly because his spirits are soothed and
    relieved by domestic endearments, and his self-respect kept alive by finding, that
    though all abroad is darkness and humiliation, yet there is still a little world of love
    at home, of which he is the monarch. (*History*, 760)

    As Judith Fetterley points out, "The German tale on which [Irving] based
    'Rip' has no equivalent for Dame Van Winkle; she is Irving's creation and
    addition" (*The Resisting Reader*, 3).
35 There is a direct correlation between Vedder, the mountains, and the Native
    American: all of these figures indicate a sovereign silence that has everything
    to do with an aestheticization of death. This aesthetic can also be thought
    of in terms of what Laura Murray calls an "aesthetic of dispossession."
36 Etienne Balibar writes: "The fact that the order to which he [the subject]
    'responds' [with his "obedience"] comes to him from *beyond* the individual
    and the mouth that utters it is constitutive of the subject" ("Citizen
    Subject," 41). A crucially nostalgic (and of course misogynist) repudiation
    of "the mouth that utters" is dramatized in Irving's story. It is in fact the
    utter repudiation of "the mouth which utters" in favor of the smoke that
    hovers above and around its audience that marks Rip as belonging to the
    order of the monarchical subject. It is with its abjection of Dame Van
    Winkle's mouth (often her tongue) that this story (or at least its privileged
    central character) marks its resistance to the order of the citizen-subject,
    the subject of democracy. And it is perhaps not surprising that this too
    should mark the site of the story's tiresome misogyny.

37 Martin Roth points out that "petticoat" government and "democratic" government were associated throughout the eighteenth century in British political satire: "Petticoat government was a popular burlesque fiction for the situation of the parliamentary ruler in Arbuthnot's *John Bull* and its many imitators, and the Punch and Judy farces, which usually had a political level" (*Comedy and America*, 158).

38 Recall the suggestion (made in debates over the franchise in 1797) that reform would, among other things, restore "quiet" to New Jersey politics (see Turner, "Women's Suffrage," 184–5, quoted on p. 147 above).

39 Consider, in this regard, John Adams' suggestion for a Great Seal for the new United States: "Hercules, as engraved by Gribeline . . . resting on his Clubb. Virtue pointing to her rugged Mountain, on one Hand, and perswading him to ascend. Sloth, glancing at her flowery Paths of Pleasure, wantonly reclining on the Ground, displaying the Charms both of her Eloquence and Person, to seduce him into Vice" (quoted in Silverman, *A Cultural History*, 321–2).

40 In *National Manhood*, Nelson repeatedly identifies a gendered distinction in the early United States between a masculine political fraternity and its messily embodied feminine other(s). Thus, in *The Federalist Papers*, "Publius's key argumentative strategy is to compare the ideal, masculine political body provided by the Constitution to a feminine, disorderly body allegedly created by the Articles of Confederation. That latter 'body' is governed by weakness and passion . . . It is mobbish and disorderly . . . even deviant" (*National Manhood*, 42).

41 As Martin Roth explains, the basis for the story was to be found in Irving's *History of New York* (1809) in a chapter devoted to Stuyvesant's voyage up the Hudson, "which was also an allegory of the failure of the imagination in America" (*Comedy and America*, 155).

42 Donna Hagensick comments that *Salmagundi* paved the way for Irving's *A History of New York* "in which many of the same failings of democracy (from Irving's viewpoint) are attacked with greater perfection" ("Irving," 183). Irving participated in his family's "distinctly Federalist ideology," writes Hagensick: "Broadly this meant endorsing the political ideas of Alexander Hamilton, while opposing those of Thomas Jefferson. More specifically it meant favoring nationalism over sectionalism; commercialism over agrarianism; and, the rights of wealth and property over the rights of the common people or mob" (181).

43 In a later letter (April 25, 1807), Irving's Mustapha refers to congress as "the 'mother of all inventions'; and a most fruitful mother it is let me tell thee, though its children are generally abortions" (*History, Tales and Sketches*, 182).

44 "If women are bad because they are portrayed as governmental, government is bad because it is portrayed as female," is how Judith Fetterley puts it (*The Resisting Reader*, 6).

45 Rip himself, Fetterley points out, "rejects the conventional image of masculinity and behavior traditionally expected of an adult male and identifies himself with characteristics and behaviors assumed to be feminine

and assigned to women. Thus, the figure who 'presides over the birth of the American imagination' is in effect a female-identified woman-hater" (ibid., 5). Fetterley, somewhat surprisingly, goes on to ignore this crossover, however, and instead insists on the fact that "the opposition between Rip and Dame is extended to women and men in general" (5). Thus she concludes that there is no way for a woman to read "Rip Van Winkle" without experiencing the act as "disastrous." ("The woman who reads 'Rip Van Winkle' finds herself excluded from the experience of the story. She is no part of the act of resistance, nor does she recognize herself in that which is being resisted," 10.) Fetterley's insightful reading both exposes – and retreats from – some of the story's most useful ambiguities. Hence she notes that the "divided" female reader finds her most appropriate description in Rip's words upon returning to the village: "I'm not myself – etc." But she stops before dwelling at more length on this strange, gender-troubling alignment. Rip is never more real in this story than in this brief but critical identity crisis.

46 In his *History of New York*, Irving refers to Governor William Kieft, who is associated with disruptive democratization in New Amsterdam and with submitting to a species of government at home "neither laid down in Aristotle, nor Plato; in short, it partook of the nature of a pure unmixed tyranny, and is familiarly denominated *petticoat* government" (518).

47 It is important to remember that degraded speech is often associated both with effeminacy and, of course, with the literary. Thus, to take only one small example, critics of an attempt to found a new theatre in Charleston, South Carolina in 1773 referred to the ongoing economic struggle with Great Britain and warned that those who subscribed to the new theatre at such a pressing time "wish to see us effeminized or tamed into vassals, fit for Despotism" (quoted in Silverman, *A Cultural History*, 250).

48 Christopher Looby has a different take on this in *Voicing America*. He suggests (taking his cue from Martin Roth) that Irving, in the *History of New York* and in "Rip" was engaged in a "deconstruction of the epistemological assumptions and causational structures of historical writing" and that this deconstruction "was meant to diminish the power of accumulated historical understanding, to destroy precedent, and reopen historical time to creative possibilities" (93). This description, however, only confirms my sense that Irving's energies are entirely anxious energies: his satire bears all the trademarks of an anarchic resignation, a turning away from the possibilities of history and politics in the name of a generally aggressive uncertainty about how exactly to think about the relationship between political discourse and historical truth. Dame Van Winkle is the primary figuration of the enactment of this anxiety as violence. A similar dynamic is at work in Irving's aggressively gendered and all too predictable dismissal of the endless verbosity of American politics in the "Mustapha Rub-a-Dub-Keli Khan" letters in *Salmagundi* (1807–8).

49 It is only as subjects of a Franklinian investment in the authority of a pseudonymous (or anonymous) voice that we can come to root for the insistently un-Franklinian Rip. Rip, in fact, has a lot in common with

Stephen Burroughs, who not only fails to settle down to any kind of productive, socially acceptable labor in New England, but ends up, like Rip, disappearing into the social rehearsal of his own story. Also, like Burroughs (and once again displaying a kind of pathological literalization of Franklin's textual disappearing acts), Rip's return includes moments of disorienting insubstantiality: "God knows...I'm not myself – I'm somebody else – that's me yonder – no – that's somebody else got into my shoes" ("Rip Van Winkle," 781). This is after seeing his grown-up son loafing against a tree much as he himself was inclined to do before the revolution.

50 Philip Young refers to Rip as "Lazarus come from the dead, come back to tell us all" ("Fallen From Time," 84). In an affectionate registration of the identification between Rip and the nominal author of the story, Jeffrey Rubin-Dorsky writes of a "totally unaggressive" Rip, who "poses no threat to the business of post Revolutionary America." "In fact," Rubin-Dorsky continues,

> he becomes a great favorite with "the rising generation," since he has something to tell them about the past which, contrary to the America Irving knew, they apparently value. Thus, with its depiction of the anxiety of estrangement transformed into the ease of acceptance, "Rip Van Winkle" weaves Irving's desire for a settled life (as chronicler) into the fabric of his story. (*Adrift in the Old World*, 110)

51 For that comic spirit which is without any infusion of gall, which delights in what is ludicrous rather than ridiculous (for its laughter is not mixed with contempt), which seeks its gratification in the eccentricities of a simple, unrefined state of society, rather than in the vicious follies of artificial life; for the vividness and truth with which Rip's character is drawn, and the state of society in the village where he lived, is depicted; and for the graceful ease with which it is told, the story of Rip Van Winkle has few competitors. (Brevoort, "Review," 47)

52 "Irving stood at the headwaters of an American stream which flowed finally in many directions" (Leary, "Washington Irving," 191).

53 Hedges writes: "Irving seems to me to be a very complicated kind of American, an extremely ambivalent, uneasy, uncertain American, in some ways a very lonely American...Irving, I think, was an American torn between romantic and classical attitudes, uncertain of the role and function of the writer in a commercial society" ("The Theme of Americanism," 780).

54 Even as he can also be taken for a spy in America: "Here a general burst from the bystanders – 'A tory! A tory! A spy! A refugee! Hustle him! Away with him!'" ("Rip Van Winkle," 1256).

55 Interestingly, despite a general tendency to distance himself from Jeffersonian or democratic politics in the new republic, Irving wrote in 1838 (in a letter to Gouverneur Kemble):

> As far as I know my own mind, I am thoroughly a republican, and attached...to the institutions of my country; but I am a republican without gall, and have no bitterness in my creed. I have no relish for puritans either in religion or politics, who

are for pushing principles to an extreme ... Ours is a government of compromise. We have several great and distinct interests bound up together, which, if not separately consulted and severally accommodated may harass and impair each other. (Quoted in Hagensick, "Irving," 180)

56 Fliegelman suggests that there is something of Thomas Paine in Rip's lamentations about his wife (*Prodigals and Pilgrims*, 293 n.5). This conflation of Rip and Paine confirms one of my repeated suggestions, namely, that a certain strand of revolutionary discourse was fully compatible with monarchic subjectivity: Paine's antipathy towards the marriage contract and this story's demonization of the tongue-lashing wife both participate in a resistance to politics as the groundless ground of the democratic social order.

57 In a very different reading of the story, Martin Roth argues that

"Rip Van Winkle" is a story of the artistic imagination ... The responsibility of the artist as conceived by Washington Irving ... and imposed upon Rip Van Winkle, was nothing less than to prevent the American Revolution: effectively, to fight history, in order to allow the imagination to flourish in America ... the dramatization of that responsibility and that failure resulted in Irving's finest American tale. (*Comedy and America*, 159, 161)

58 Affection for the character of Rip can be heard in Philip Young's reference to the tale's "extraordinary picture of the self arrested in a timeless infancy" that appeals " to the child and primitive in everyone" but that conflicts "with the adult and rational perception that we do indeed grow old, that time and history never stop." "In much the same way," Young concludes, "our affection for Rip himself must oppose our reluctant discovery that as a man we cannot fully respect him" ("Fallen From Time," 84). It is not clear how, as a woman, we should feel about this Rip. Terence Martin writes that "the tale dramatizes Rip's loss of identity, and, by inference, the loss of identity of the imaginative function. Rip's miraculous sleep has left him ignorant of the American Revolution – the magical, the marvelous, the imaginative, and the indolent have had no place in the founding of the new republic" ("Rip," 60).

AFTERWORD: THE REVOLUTION'S LAST WORD

1 Jonathan Arac locates Cooper's work within the genre of the "national narrative," a genre that was "part of the process by which the nation was forming itself and not merely a reflection of an accomplished fact" ("Establishing National Narrative," 608).

2 Kammen, *A Season of Youth* (especially chapter 6).

3 Cooper's comment came in a letter in which he compared his impatience with *Precaution*, his first novel, and his preference for *The Spy* (quoted in Charles Hansford Adams, "The Guardian of the Law," 42).

4 "Letter to an American Lady" (1823), in Dekker and McWilliams, eds., *Fenimore Cooper*, 67–8.

5 See Kammen, *A Season of Youth*. Clark surmises that *The Spy*'s popular success was an indication of the extent to which it was "in tune with the nation's ambiguous desire for independence, democracy, individualistic freedom and the right to amass property without fear of expropriation" ("Rewriting Revolution," 198).

6 Arac goes on to claim that Balzac (an admirer of Cooper) inherited some of this "democratic" attention to the "trivial and socially discredited" despite his royalist political sympathies ("Establishing National Narrative," 617).

7 Quoted in Brockden Brown, "Review of An Oration," 57.

8 See Cooper's 1831 introduction in the Penguin edition, 5. See too Wayne Franklin's introduction to this edition. Gilmore makes the point that this fascination with patriotism's distance from the marketplace rewrites the "effort to come to terms with his own feelings about engaging in the commerce of literature" ("James Fenimore Cooper," 682).

9 Birch, in other words, was one of the figures Cooper constructed in order to answer what, according to Philip Gould, was one of the most anxious questions of the early national period: "What was the status of Revolutionary 'zealotry' in a post-Revolutionary world?" (*Covenant and Republic*, 171).

10 Quoted in Bakeless, *Turncoats*, 170. O'Toole also points out that those who had early shown their sympathies for the revolution ruled themselves out as candidates for undercover espionage work: "To recruit those individuals whose lack of pre-war political activity now made them most useful as spies, Washington saw that he would probably have to offer the inducement of money; even some of those who had lately acquired a degree of Patriot ardor required some monetary inducement to risk the gallows" (*Honorable Treachery*, O' Toole, 370).

11 Gilmore suggests, however, that the focus on a story necessarily known only to a select few suggests "the novelty of Cooper's perspective on historical knowledge: once a common heritage, past deeds are now secrets known only to a few." "In effect, Cooper is privatizing or subjectivizing history," Gilmore continues, a strategy "in keeping with the temper of an ever more buoyant and individualistic society" ("James Fenimore Cooper," 680–1).

12 See too Paine's "Dialogue between the Ghost of General Montgomery Just Arrived from the Elysian Fields; and an American Delegate, in a Wood near Philadelphia" (Philadelphia 1776), in which the early revolutionary war hero says "I live in a world where all political superstition is done away. The king is the author of all the measures carried on against America" (quoted in Silverman, *A Cultural History*, 324). A post-revolutionary United States is indistinguishable here from a life after death.

13 See chapter four above for more on these questions.

14 Caesar's status in the novel might be considered alongside the tortuous attempts to categorize the status of African Americans as soon as they ceased to be completely circumscribed by the laws of slavery. As James Kettner writes:

> Free Negroes appeared to occupy a middle ground in terms of the rights they were allowed to claim in practice, a status that could not be described in the traditional

language of slave, alien, or citizen . . . "free Negroes," wrote Judge Colcock of South Carolina, were "not aliens," but neither had they "become incorporated into the body politic." One judge attempted to solve the problem by referring to free blacks as "quasi citizens, or at least denizens," while Mississippi's highest court preferred the term "alien strangers." (Kettner, *The Development of American Citizenship*, 319–20)

In 1963, Martin Luther King referred to the African American as "an exile in his own land" ("I Have A Dream," 1423), a phrase that could be applied to Harvey Birch, thereby further complicating the exact relationship between the marginalized Caesar and the heroicized Birch.

15 "Birch is less a renegade than an emanation of Washington's will, the embodiment of those pure qualities of infertility, sacrifice and freedom at the heart of the Washington mythos" (Wallace, "Cultivating an Audience,"51).

16 In an intriguing extension of this play of signatures, the manuscript narrative of the shoemaker, Enoch Crosby, one of the most successful of all counter-intelligence agents in the revolutionary war and the figure who bears most resemblence to Cooper's Birch, was only signed late in Crosby's life after he had come forward to identify himself as the spy in question. This claim was in turn supported by numerous affidavits from respectable associates of Crosby's. See Bakeless, *Turncoats*, 136–7. Cooper always denied that Crosby was the model for his novel despite the many similarities.

Bibliography

A Rising People: The Founding of the United States, 1765–1789: a Celebration from the Collections of the American Philosophical Society, the Historical Society of Pennsylvania, the Library Company of Philadelphia. Philadelphia: Library Company of Philadelphia, 1989.

Adams, Abigail and John. *The Book of Abigail and John: Selected Letters of the Adams Family, 1762–1784.* Ed. L.H. Butterfield *et al.* Cambridge, MA: Harvard University Press, 1975.

Adams, Charles Hansford. *"The Guardian of the Law:" Authority and Identity in James Fenimore Cooper.* University Park: Pennsylvania State Press, 1990.

Adams, John. *The Works of John Adams.* Ed. Charles Francis Adams. 10 vols. Boston: Little Brown, 1850–6.

The Adams–Jefferson Letters: The Complete Correspondence Between Thomas Jefferson and Abigail and John Adams. Chapel Hill: University of North Carolina Press, 1959.

The Papers of John Adams. Ed. Robert J. Taylor *et al.* 10 vols. Cambridge, MA: Harvard University Press, 1977–.

The Political Writings of John Adams. Ed. George A. Peek. New York: Macmillan, 1985.

Aderman, Ralph M., ed. *Critical Essays on Washington Irving.* Boston, MA: G.K. Hall and Co., 1990.

Allen, Gay Wilson and Roger Asselineau. *An American Farmer: The Life of St. John de Crèvecoeur.* New York: Penguin, 1987.

Anderson, Benedict. *Imagined Communities: Reflections on the Origin and Spread of Nationalism.* London: Verso, 1996.

Anderson, Perry. *Lineages of the Absolutist State.* London: New Left Books, 1974.

Appleby, Joyce. *Liberalism and Republicanism in the Historical Imagination.* Cambridge, MA: Harvard University Press, 1992.

"Locke, Liberalism, and the Natural Law of Money." In *Liberalism and Republicanism in the Historical Imagination.* Cambridge, MA: Harvard University Press, 1992. 58–89.

Arac, Jonathan. "Establishing National Narrative." In *The Cambridge History of American Literature*, vol. II. Ed. Sacvan Bercovitch. Cambridge: Cambridge University Press, 1995. 607–28.

Arendt, Hannah. *On Revolution.* 1963. Reprint, New York: Penguin, 1990.

Atwood, J. Brian. "Fragile – But Democratic." *New York Times* (June 30, 1995). A27.

Bailyn, Bernard. *The Ideological Origins of the American Revolution.* Cambridge, MA: Belknap Press of Harvard University Press, 1967.

ed. *The Debate on the Constitution.* 2 vols. New York: Library of America, 1993.

Bakeless, John. *Turncoats, Traitors and Heroes: Espionage in the American Revolution.* 1959. Reprint, New York: Da Capo, 1998.

Balibar, Etienne. "Citizen Subject." In *Who Comes After the Subject?* Ed. Eduarda Cadava *et al.* New York: Routledge, 1991. 33–57.

"Subjection and Subjectivation." In *Supposing the Subject.* Ed. Joan Copjec. London: Verso, 1994. 1–15.

The Philosophy of Marx. London: Verso, 1995.

Ball, Terence and J.G.A. Pocock, eds. *Conceptual Change and the Constitution.* Lawrence: University Press of Kansas, 1988.

Banning, Lance. *Jefferson and Madison: Three Conversations from the Founding.* Madison: Madison House, 1995.

Beard, James Franklin. "Cooper and the Revolutionary Mythos." *Early American Literature* 11 (1976): 84–104.

Becker, Carl L. *The Declaration of Independence: A Study in the History of Political Ideas.* 1922. Reprint, New York: Vintage, 1958.

Beer, Samuel H. *To Make A Nation: The Rediscovery of American Federalism.* Cambridge, MA: Harvard University Press, 1993.

Benjamin, Walter. "The Work of Art in the Age of Mechanical Reproduction." In *Illuminations: Essays and Reflections.* Ed. Hannah Arendt. New York: Schocken, 1969. 217–51.

"Theses on the Philosophy of History." In *Illuminations: Essays and Reflections.* Ed. Hannah Arendt. New York: Schocken, 1969. 253–64.

"Critique of Violence." In *Reflections: Essays, Aphorisms, Autobiographical Writings.* Ed. Peter Demetz. New York: Shocken, 1978. 277–300.

Berthoff, Warner B. "'A Lesson on Concealment': Brockden Brown's Method in Fiction." *Philological Quarterly* 37 (1958): 45–57.

Blanchot, Maurice. "Sade." In *The Complete Justine, Philosophy in the Bedroom and Other Writings,* by The Marquis de Sade. Compiled and translated by Richard Seaver and Austryn Wainhouse. New York: Grove Press, 1965. 37–72.

Bogin, Ruth. "'The Battle of Lexington': A Patriotic Ballad by Lemuel Haynes." *William and Mary Quarterly* 42:4 (1985): 499–509.

Boyd, Steven R. "The Contract Clause and the Evolution of American Federalism, 1789–1815." *William and Mary Quarterly* 44.3 (1987): 529–48.

Brant, Irving. *James Madison: The Virginia Revolutionist.* New York: Bobbs-Merrill, 1941.

Breitwieser, Mitchell. *Cotton Mather and Benjamin Franklin: The Price of Representative Personality.* Cambridge: Cambridge University Press, 1984.

Brevoort, Henry Jr., "Review of *The Sketch Book* No. 1 by Washington Irving." In *Critical Essays on Washington Irving*. Ed. Ralph M. Aderman. Boston, MA: G.K. Hall and Co., 1990. 46–7.

Brown, Charles Brockden. *Alcuin*. Albany, NY: New College and University Press, 1987.

"A Lesson on Concealment." In *"Somnambulism" and Other Stories*. Ed. Alfred Weber. New York: Peter Lang, 1987. 53–102.

"Objections to Richardson's Clarissa." In *Literary Essays and Reviews*. Ed. Alfred Weber *et al*. New York: Peter Lang, 1992. 100–2.

"Remarks on Mysteries." In *Literary Essays and Reviews*. Ed. Alfred Weber *et al*. New York: Peter Lang, 1992. 176–7.

"Review of An Oration on the Death of General Washington by Governeur Morris." In *Literary Essays and Reviews*. Ed. Alfred Weber *et al*. New York: Peter Lang, 1992. 56–69.

"Walstein's School of History." In *Literary Essays and Reviews*. Ed. Alfred Weber *et al*. New York: Peter Lang, 1992. 31–8.

Wieland and Memoirs of Carwin, Kent, OH: Kent State University Press, 1993.

Brown, Richard D. ed. *Major Problems in the Era of the American Revolution, 1760–1791*. Lexington, MA: D.C. Heath and Company, 1992.

Brown, Wallace. *The King's Friends: The Composition and Motives of the American Loyalist Claimants*. Providence, RI: Brown University Press, 1965.

Buel, Richard. *Securing the Revolution: Ideology in American Politics, 1789–1815*. Ithaca, NY: Cornell University Press, 1972.

Buell, Lawrence. *New England Literary Culture: From Revolution Through Renaissance*. Cambridge: Cambridge University Press, 1986.

Bullock, Steven C. "The Revolutionary Transformation of American Freemasonry, 1752–1792." *William and Mary Quarterly* 47 (1990): 347–69.

"Review Essay – Initiating the Enlightenment?: Recent Scholarship on European Freemasonry." *Eighteenth-Century Life* 20 (1996): 80–92.

Burroughs, Stephen. *Memoirs of Stephen Burroughs*. Boston: Northeastern University Press, 1988.

Burnett, Edmund Cody. *The Continental Congress*. New York: W.W. Norton and Co., 1964.

Butler, Judith, Ernesto Laclau, and Slavoj Zizek. *Contingency, Hegemony, Universality: Contemporary Dialogues on the Left*. London: Verso, 2000.

Calhoon, Robert M. *The Loyalists in Revolutionary America, 1760–1781*. New York: Harcourt Brace Jovanovich, 1973.

Cappon, Lester J., ed. *The Adams-Jefferson Letters: The Complete Correspondence Between Thomas Jefferson and Abigail and John Adams*. 2 vols. (Published for the Institute of Early American History and Culture at Williamsburg, VA.) Chapel Hill: University of North Carolina Press, 1959.

Carr, William George. *The Oldest Delegate: Franklin in the Constitutional Convention*. Newark: University of Delaware Press, 1990.

Christophersen, Bill. *The Apparition in the Glass: Charles Brockden Brown's American Gothic*. Athens: University of Georgia Press, 1993.

Clark, Robert. "Rewriting Revolution: Cooper's War of Independence." In *James Fenimore Cooper: New Critical Essays*. Ed. Robert Clark. London: Vision Books, 1985. 187–205.

Cohen, Daniel A. *Pillars of Salt, Monuments of Grace: New England Crime Literature and the Origins of American Popular Culture, 1674–1860*. Oxford: Oxford University Press, 1993.

Conner, Paul W. *Poor Richard's Politicks: Benjamin Franklin and His New American Order*. New York: Oxford University Press, 1965.

Cooper, James Fenimore. *The Last of the Mohicans*. New York: Penguin, 1986.
The American Democrat. New York: Penguin, 1989.
The Spy: A Tale of the Neutral Ground. New York: Penguin, 1997.
Notions of the Americans: Picked Up By A Travelling Bachelor. Ed. Gary Williams. Albany, NY: State University of New York Press, 1991.

Countryman, Edward. *The American Revolution*. 1985. Reprint, New York: Hill and Wang, 1994.
"Indians, the Colonial Order, and the Social Significance of the American Revolution." *William and Mary Quarterly* 53.2 (1996): 342–62.
"Response." *William and Mary Quarterly* 53.2 (1996): 379–86.

Cowie, Alexander. "Historical Essay." In Charles Brockden Brown. *Wieland and Memoirs of Carwin*. Kent, OH: Kent State University Press, 1977. 311–48.

Crane, Verner. *Benjamin Franklin's Letters to the Press, 1758–1775*. Chapel Hill: University of North Carolina Press, 1950.

Crèvecoeur, J. Hector St. John de. *Letters From an American Farmer and Sketches of Eighteenth-Century America*. Ed. Albert E. Stone. New York: Penguin, 1986.

Cunningham, Noble E. *In Pursuit of Reason: The Life of Thomas Jefferson*. New York: Ballantine, 1987.

Dahl, Robert. *A Preface to Democratic Theory*. Chicago: University of Chicago Press, 1956.

Davidson, Cathy N. *Revolution and the Word: The Rise of the Novel in America*. New York: Oxford University Press, 1986.

Deloria, Philip J. "Revolution, Region, and Culture in Multicultural History." *William and Mary Quarterly* 53.2 (1996): 363–6.

De Man, Paul. *Allegories of Reading: Figural Language in Rousseau, Nietzsche, Rilke, and Proust*. New Haven, CT: Yale University Press, 1979.
The Resistance to Theory. Minneapolis: University of Minnesota Press, 1986.

Dekker, George and John P. McWilliams, eds. *Fenimore Cooper: The Critical Heritage*. London: Routledge and Kegan Paul, 1973.

Derrida, Jacques. *Of Grammatology*. Trans. Gayatri Chakravorty Spivak. Baltimore, MD: Johns Hopkins University Press, 1976.
"Declarations of Independence." *New Political Science* 15 (1986): 7–17.
Limited Inc. Evanston, IL: Northwestern University Press, 1988.
"The Force of Law: The 'Mystical' Foundation of Authority." *Cardozo Law Review* 2.5–6 (1990): 919–1046.

"Before the Law." In *Acts of Literature*. Ed. Derek Attridge. New York: Routledge, 1992. 181–220.

"'This Strange Institution Called Literature': An Interview with Jacques Derrida." In *Acts of Literature*. Ed. Derek Attridge. New York: Routledge, 1992. 33–75.

Specters of Marx: The State of the Debt, the Work of Mourning, and the New International. New York: Routledge, 1994.

The Gift of Death. Trans. David Wills. Chicago: University of Chicago Press, 1995.

Dinkin, Robert J. *Voting in Revolutionary America: A Study of Elections in the Original Thirteen States, 1776–1789*. Westport, CT: Greenwood Press, 1965.

Douglass, Frederick. "What to the Slave Is the Fourth of July?: An Address Delivered in Rochester, New York, on 5 July 1852." In *Call and Response: The Riverside Anthology of the African American Literary Tradition*. Eds. Patricia Liggins Hill *et al.* New York: Houghton Mifflin, 1998. 320–35.

Downes, Paul. "Sleep-Walking Out of the Revolution: Brown's *Edgar Huntly*." *Eighteenth-Century Studies* 29:4 (1996): 413–31.

Dunlap, William. *The Life of Charles Brockden Brown*. Philadelphia, PA: James P. Parke, 1815.

Dwight, Timothy. *Travels in New England and New York*. New Haven, CT: 1821.

Edgeworth, Maria. "Letter to an American Lady." In *Fenimore Cooper: The Critical Heritage*. Eds. George Dekker and John P. McWilliams. London: Routledge and Kegan Paul, 1973. 67–8.

Eisenstein, Elizabeth L. *The Printing Press as an Agent of Change: Communications and Cultural Transformations in Early Modern Europe*. Cambridge: Cambridge University Press, 1979.

Elkins, Stanley and Eric McKitrick. *The Age of Federalism: The Early American Republic, 1788–1800*. New York: Oxford University Press, 1993.

Elliot, Jonathan, ed. *The Debates in the Several State Conventions, on the Adoption of the Federal Constitution, as Recommended by the General Convention at Philadelphia in 1787*. Philadelphia: Lippincott, 1881.

Emerson, Everett. "Hector St. John de Crèvecoeur and the Promise of America." In *Forms and Functions of History in American Literature: Essays in Honor of Ursula Brumm*. Ed. Winfried Fluck *et al.* Berlin: E. Schmidt, 1981. 44–55.

Emerson, Ralph Waldo. "Self-Reliance." In *Essays: First and Second Series*. New York: Library of America, 1990. 27–52.

Equiano, Olaudah. *The Interesting Narrative and Other Writings*. New York: Penguin, 1995.

Esch, Deborah. *In the Event: Reading Journalism, Reading Theory*. Stanford, CA: Stanford University Press, 1999.

Farrand, Max, ed. *The Records of the Federal Convention of 1787*. 3 vols. New Haven, CT: Yale University Press, 1911.

Ferguson, Robert. "The Limits of Enlightenment." In *The Cambridge History of American Literature*, vol. 1. Ed. Sacvan Bercovitch. New York: Cambridge University Press, 1994. 496–537.

"The Commonalities of *Common Sense.*" *William and Mary Quarterly*, 3rd series, 57:3 (2000): 465–504.

Fern, Fanny. "Independence." In *Ruth Hall and other Writings*. Ed. Joyce W. Warren. New Brunswick, NJ: Rutgers University Press, 1988. 314–15.

Fetterley, Judith. *The Resisting Reader: A Feminist Approach to American Fiction*. Bloomington: Indiana University Press, 1977.

Fiedler, Leslie A. *Love and Death in the American Novel*. New York: Stein and Day, 1966.

Finkelman, Paul. "Slavery and the Constitutional Convention: Making a Covenant with Death." In *Beyond Confederation: Origins of the Constitution and American National Identity*. Eds. Richard Beeman *et al.* Chapel Hill: University of North Carolina Press, 1987. 188–225.

Fischer, David Hackett. *Paul Revere's Ride*. New York: Oxford University Press, 1994.

Fleischmann, Fritz. *A Right View of the Subject: Feminism in the Works of Charles Brockden Brown and John Neal*. Erlangen: Palm and Enke, 1983.

Fliegelman, Jay. *Prodigals and Pilgrims: The American Revolution Against Patriarchal Authority, 1750–1800*. Cambridge: Cambridge University Press, 1982.

"Introduction." In Charles Brockden Brown. *Wieland and Memoirs of Carwin the Biloquist*. New York: Penguin, 1991. vii–xliv.

Declaring Independence: Jefferson, Natural Language, and the Culture of Performance. Stanford, CA: Stanford University Press, 1993.

Foner, Eric. *Thomas Paine and Revolutionary America*. New York: Oxford University Press, 1976.

Ford, Paul Leicester, ed. *Pamphlets on the Constitution of the United States, Published During its Discussion by the People, 1787–88*. Brooklyn, 1888.

Forten, James. *Letters From A Man of Colour on a Late Bill Before the Senate of Pennsylvania*. Philadelphia PA, 1813. In Gary B. Nash. *Race and Revolution*. Madison, WI: Madison House, 1990. 190–8.

Foucault, Michel. *Discipline and Punish: The Birth of the Prison*. New York: Vintage, 1979.

Franklin, Benjamin. *The Autobiography and Other Writings*. New York: Penguin, 1986.

Writings. New York: Library of America, 1987.

Franklin, Wayne. "Introduction." In James Fenimore Cooper. *The Spy: A Tale of the Neutral Ground*. New York: Penguin, 1997. vii–xxxii.

Freneau, Philip. *The Poems of Philip Freneau: Poet of the American Revolution*. 3 vols. Ed. Fred Lewis Pattee. Princeton, NJ: C.S. Robinson and Co. University Press, 1902.

Furet, François, *Interpreting the French Revolution*. Trans. Elborg Forster. New York: Cambridge University Press, 1990.

Gallagher, Catherine. *Nobody's Story: The Vanishing Acts of Women Writers in the Literary Marketplace*. Berkeley: University of California Press, 1994.

Galloway, Colin. *The American Revolution in Indian Country: Crisis and Diversity in Native American Communities*. New York: Cambridge University Press, 1995.

Gilmore, Michael T. "James Fenimore Cooper." In *The Cambridge History of American Literature*, vol. I. Ed. Sacvan Bercovitch. Cambridge: Cambridge University Press, 1994. 676–93.

Godwin, William. *An Enquiry Concerning Political Justice: and its Influence on Modern Morals and Happiness*. 1793. Reprint, New York: Penguin, 1985.

Gould, Philip. *Covenant and Republic: Historical Romance and the Politics of Puritanism*. Cambridge: Cambridge University Press, 1996.

Grabo, Norman S. "Crèvecoeur's American: Beginning the World Anew." *William and Mary Quarterly* 48.2 (April 1991): 159–72.

Greene, Jack P., ed. *Colonies to Nation, 1763–1789: A Documentary History of the American Revolution*. New York: Norton, 1975.

Gross, Robert A., ed. "The Confidence Man and the Preacher: The Cultural Politics of Shays' Rebellion." In *In Debt to Shays: The Bicentennial of an Agrarian Revolution*. Ed. Robert A. Gross. Charlottesville: University Press of Virginia, 1993. 297–320.

Gunderson, Joan. "Independence, Citizenship, and the American Revolution." *Signs: Journal of Women in Culture and Society* 13.1 (1987): 59–76.

Gura, Philip F. "Foreword." In Stephen Burroughs. *Memoirs of Stephen Burroughs*. Boston: Northeastern University Press, 1988. ix–xxiii.

Habermas, Jürgen. *The Structural Transformation of the Public Sphere*. 1962. Reprint, trans. Thomas Burger, Cambridge, MA: MIT Press, 1989.

Hagensick, Donna. "Irving: A Littérateur in Politics." In *Critical Essays on Washington Irving*. Ed. Ralph M. Aderman. Boston, MA: G.K. Hall and Co., 1990. 178–91.

Handlin, Oscar and Mary Handlin, eds. *The Popular Sources of Political Authority; Documents on the Massachusetts Constitution of 1780*. Cambridge, MA: Belknap Press of Harvard University Press, 1966.

Hart, Albert B. *American History Told by Contemporaries*, vol. III. New York: Macmillan, 1897.

Hazelton, John H. *The Declaration of Independence: Its History*. New York: Dodd, Mead and Co., 1906.

Hazlitt, William. *The Complete Works of William Hazlitt*. 21 vols. Ed. P.P. Howe. London: J.M. Dent and Sons, 1930–4.

Hedges, William. "The Theme of Americanism in Irving's Writings." In *Washington Irving: A Tribute*. Ed. Andrew B. Myers. Tarrytown, NY: Sleepy Hollow Restorations, 1972. 29–35.

Hill, Christopher. *The Century of Revolution, 1603–1714*. Edinburgh: Nelson, 1961.

Hofstadter, Richard. *The Paranoid Style in American Politics, and Other Essays*. New York: Knopf, 1965.

Hughes, Langston. *The Collected Poems*. Eds. Arnold Rampersad and David Roessel. New York: Alfred A. Knopf, 1994.

Hyneman, Charles S, and Donald S. Lutz, eds. *American Political Writing During the Founding Era, 1760–1805*. Indianapolis, IN: Liberty Press, 1983.

Irving, Washington. "Rip Van Winkle." In *History, Tales and Sketches*. New York: The Library of America, 1983. 767–85.

"*Salmagundi* No. VII (April 4, 1807)." In *History, Tales and Sketches*. New York: The Library of America, 1983. 143–50.

"A History of New York." In *History, Tales and Sketches*. New York: The Library of America, 1983. 363–729.

James, C.L.R. *The Black Jacobins: Toussaint L'Ouverture and the San Domingo Revolution*. New York: Vintage, 1989.

Jefferson, Thomas. *Collected Works of Thomas Jefferson*. 12 vols. Ed. Paul Leicester Ford. New York: Putnam, 1904–05.

"Notes of Proceedings." In *The Papers of Thomas Jefferson*. 25 vols. Eds. Julian Boyd *et al*. Princeton, NJ: Princeton University Press, 1959–. I, 315–19.

The Political Writings of Thomas Jefferson. Ed. Edward Dumbauld. New York: Macmillan, 1987.

Jehlen, Myra. "J. Hector St. John Crèvecoeur: A Monarcho-Anarchist in Revolutionary America." *American Quarterly* 31.2 (1979): 204–22.

Jehlen, Myra and Michael Warner, eds. *The English Literatures of America, 1500–1800*. New York: Routledge, 1997.

Jones, Christopher W. "Praying Upon Truth: The Memoirs of Stephen Burroughs and the Picaresque." *Early American Literature* 30.1 (1995): 32–50.

Kaminski, John P., ed. *A Necessary Evil?: Slavery and the Debate Over the Constitution*. Madison, WI: Madison House, 1995.

Kammen, Michael, ed. *The Origins of the American Constitution: A Documentary History*. New York: Penguin, 1986.

A Season of Youth: The American Revolution and the Historical Imagination. 1978. Reprint, Ithaca NY: Cornell University Press, 1988.

Kantorowicz, Ernst. *The King's Two Bodies*. Princeton, NJ: Princeton University Press, 1957.

Kaufman, Martin, ed. *Shays' Rebellion: Selected Essays*. Westfield, MA: Institute for Massachusetts Studies, 1987.

Kenyon, J.P., ed. *The Stuart Constitution, 1603–1688: Documents and Commentary*. Cambridge: Cambridge University Press, 1966.

Kerber, Linda. *Federalists in Dissent: Imagery and Ideology in Jeffersonian America*. Ithaca, NY: Cornell University Press, 1970.

Women of the Republic: Intellect and Ideology in Revolutionary America. Chapel Hill: University of North Carolina Press, 1980.

No Constitutional Right to be Ladies: Women and the Obligations of Citizenship. New York: Hill and Wang, 1998.

Ketcham, Ralph. *James Madison: A Biography*. New York: Macmillan, 1971.

Kettner, James H. *The Development of American Citizenship, 1608–1870*. (Published for the Institute of Early American History and Culture.) Chapel Hill: University of North Carolina Press, 1978.

Keyssar, Alexander. *The Right to Vote: The Contested History of Democracy in the United States*. New York: Basic Books, 2000.

King, Martin Luther. "I Have A Dream." In *Call and Response: The Riverside Anthology of the African American Tradition*. Eds. Patricia Liggins Hill *et al*. Boston: Houghton Mifflin Company, 1998. 1423–5.

Klinghoffer, Judith A. and Lois Elkin. "'The Petticoat Electors': Women's Suffrage in New Jersey." *Journal of the Early Republic* 12 (1992): 159–93.

Kramnick, Isaac. *Bolingbroke and His Circle*. Cambridge, MA: Harvard University Press, 1968.

"Introduction." In Thomas Paine. *Common Sense*. New York: Penguin, 1976. 7–59.

Laclau, Ernesto. *New Reflections on the Revolution of Our Time*. London: Verso, 1990.

"Power and Representation." In *Politics, Theory, and Contemporary Culture*. Ed. Mark Poster. New York: Columbia University Press, 1993. 277–96.

"Deconstruction, Pragmatism, Hegemony." In *Deconstruction and Pragmatism*. Ed. Chantal Mouffe. London: Routledge, 1996. 47–68.

Emancipation(s). London: Verso, 1996.

Laclau, Ernesto and Chantal Mouffe. *Hegemony and Socialist Strategy: Towards a Radical Democratic Politics*. New York: Verso, 1985.

Lauter, Paul, *et al.*, eds. *Heath Anthology of American Literature*, vol. 1. Boston: Houghton Mifflin Co., 1998.

Leary, Lewis. "Washington Irving and the Comic Imagination." In *Critical Essays on Washington Irving*. Ed. Ralph M. Aderman. Boston, MA: G.K. Hall and Co., 1990. 191–202.

Lefort, Claude. *The Political Forms of Modern Society*. Cambridge, MA: MIT Press, 1986.

Democracy and Political Theory. Minneapolis: University of Minnesota Press, 1988.

Lemay, J.A. Leo, ed. *Reappraising Benjamin Franklin: A Bicentennial Perspective*. Newark: University of Delaware Press, 1993.

Lincoln, Abraham. "Speech in Reply to Judge Douglas, Delivered in Representatives' Hall, Springfield, Illinois, June 26, 1857." In *Lives and Speeches of Abraham Lincoln and Hannibal Hamlin*. Eds. W. D. Howells *et al.*, Columbus, OH: Follett, Foster and Co. 1860. 170–87.

Looby, Christopher. *Voicing America: Language, Literary Form, and the Origins of the United States*. Chicago: University of Chicago Press, 1996.

Madison, James, Alexander Hamilton and John Jay. *The Federalist Papers*. Ed. Isaac Kramnick. New York: Penguin, 1987.

Madison, James. *The Papers of James Madison*. Ed. William T. Hutchinson and William M. E. Rachal. Chicago: University of Chicago Press, 1962–1977. Charlottesville: University Press of Virginia, 1977–1991.

Maier, Pauline. *From Resistance to Revolution: Colonial Radicals and the Development of American Opposition to Britain, 1765–1776*. 1972. Reprint, New York: Norton, 1991.

Main, Jackson Turner. "Government by the People: The American Revolution and the Democratization of the Legislatures." *William and Mary Quarterly* 23.3 (1966): 391–407.

Marin, Louis. *Portrait of the King*. Trans. Martha M. Houle. Minneapolis: University of Minnesota Press, 1988.

Martin, Terence. "Rip, Ichabod, and the American Imagination." In *Washington Irving: The Critical Reaction*. Ed. James W. Tuttleton. New York: AMS Press, 1993. 56–60.

Martineau, Harriet. *Society in America.* Garden City, New York: Anchor Books, 1962.

Marx, Karl. *Capital: A Critique of Political Economy.* 1867. Reprint, New York: Modern Library, 1906.

"The Eighteenth Brumaire of Louis Bonaparte." 1852. Reprint, in *The Marx–Engels Reader.* Ed. Robert C. Tucker. New York: Norton, 1978. 594–617.

Mayhew, Jonathan. "A Discourse Concerning Unlimited Submission and Non-Resistance to the Higher Powers." In *American Sermons: The Pilgrims to Martin Luther King Jr.* Ed. Michael Warner. New York: Library of America, 1999. 380–421.

McCormick, Richard P. *The History of Voting in New Jersey: A Study of the Development of Election Machinery, 1664–1911.* New Brunswick, NJ: Rutgers University Press, 1953.

McKeon, Michael. *The Origins of the English Novel, 1600–1740.* Baltimore, MD: Johns Hopkins University Press, 1991.

McWilliams, John P. Jr. *Political Justice in a Republic: James Fenimore Cooper's America.* Berkeley: University of California Press, 1972.

Miller, Joshua S. "The Ghostly Body Politic: The Federalist Papers and Popular Sovereignty." *Political Theory* 16:1 (1988): 99–119.

Milton, John. *The Defence of the English People by John Milton, Englishman, in Answer to the Defence of the King by Claudius Anonymous, alias Salmasius (Claude de Saumaise).* 1651. Reprint, trans. Paul Weldon Blackford. Dissertation, University of Chicago, 1950.

Minot, George. *The History of the Insurrections in Massachusetts in 1786.* Worcester, MA: Isaiah Thomas, 1788.

Montesquieu, Charles de Secondat, Baron de. *The Spirit of the Laws.* 1748. Reprint, trans. and ed. Anne M. Cohler, Basia Carolyn Miller and Harold Samuel Stone. Cambridge: Cambridge University Press, 1989.

Moore, Dennis, ed. *More Letters From the American Farmer: An Edition of the Essays in English Left Unpublished by Crèvecoeur.* Athens, GA: University of Georgia Press, 1995.

Morgan, Edmund S. *American Slavery, American Freedom: The Ordeal of Colonial Virginia.* 1975. Reprint, New York: Norton, 1995.

Murray, Judith Sargent. "Sketch of the Present Situation of America, 1794." In *Selected Writings of Judith Sargent Murray.* Ed. Sharon M. Harris. New York: Oxford University Press, 1995. 49–68.

Murray, Laura. "The Aesthetic of Dispossession: Washington Irving and Ideologies of (De)Colonization in the Early Republic." *American Literary History* 8.2 (1996): 205–31.

Myers, Andrew B., ed. *Washington Irving: A Tribute.* Tarrytown, NY: Sleepy Hollow Restorations, 1972.

Myers, Gustavus. *The History of Tammany Hall.* New York: Boni and Liveright, 1917.

Nancy, Jean-Luc. *The Sense of the World.* Trans. Jeffrey S. Librett. Minneapolis: University of Minnesota Press, 1997.

Nash, Gary B. *The Urban Crucible: The Northern Seaports and the Origins of the American Revolution.* Cambridge, MA: Harvard University Press, 1986.
    Race and Revolution. Madison, WI : Madison House, 1990.
Nelson, Dana D. *National Manhood: Capitalist Citizenship and the Imagined Fraternity of White Men.* Durham, NC: Duke University Press, 1998.
Nelson, William H. *The American Tory.* Boston: Beacon Press, 1971.
    "The Tory Rank and File." In *Major Problems in the Era of the American Revolution, 1760–1791.* Ed. Richard D. Brown. Lexington, MA: D.C. Heath and Co., 1992. 283–8.
Norwood, Joseph White. *The Tammany Legend.* Boston: Meador Publishing Company, 1938.
O' Toole, G. J. A. *Honorable Treachery: A History of US Intelligence, Espionage, and Covert Action from the American Revolution to the CIA.* New York: Atlantic Monthly Press, 1991.
Oberg, Barbara B. "'Plain, insinuating, persuasive': Benjamin Franklin's Final Speech to the Constitutional Convention of 1787." In *Reappraising Benjamin Franklin: A Bicentennial Perspective.* Ed. J.A. Leo Lemay. Newark: University of Delaware Press, 1993: 175–92.
Owen, William. "Reevaluating Scott: Washington Irving's 'Abbotsford.'" In *The Old and New World Romanticism of Washington Irving.* Ed. Stanley Brodwin. Westport, CT: Greenwood Press, 1986. 69–78.
Paine, Thomas. "The Forester's Letters." In *The Complete Writings of Thomas Paine.* 2 vols. Ed. Philip S. Foner. New York: Citadel Press, 1945. II, 60–87.
    "A Dialogue Between the Ghost of General Montgomery and An American Delegate." In *The Complete Writings of Thomas Paine.* 2 vols. Ed. Philip S. Foner. New York: Citadel Press, 1945. II, 88–93.
    Common Sense. New York: Penguin, 1976.
    "Dissertations on Government, the Affairs of the Bank, and Paper Money." In *The Thomas Paine Reader.* Eds. Isaac Kramnick and Michael Foot. New York: Penguin, 1987. 167–200.
    "An Essay For the Use of New Republicans in their Opposition to Monarchy." In *The Thomas Paine Reader.* Eds. Isaac Kramnick and Michael Foot. New York: Penguin, 1987. 387–93.
    The Rights of Man. In *The Thomas Paine Reader.* Eds. Isaac Kramnick and Michael Foot. New York: Penguin, 1987. 201–364.
Parmenter C.O. *History of Pelham, Mass. From 1738 to 1898.* Amherst, MA: Carpenter and Morehouse, 1898.
Pateman, Carole. *The Sexual Contract.* Stanford, CA: Stanford University Press, 1988.
Pearce, Roy Harvey. *Savagism and Civilization: A Study of the Indian and the American Mind.* 1953. Reprint, Berkeley: University of California Press, 1988.
Philbrick, Thomas. *Hector St. John de Crèvecoeur.* New York: Twayne, 1970.
Pitkin, Hannah. "Commentary: The Paradox of Representation." In *Representation.* Eds. J. Roland Pennock and John W. Chapman. New York: Atherton Press, 1968. 38–42.

Plumstead, A. W. "Hector St. John de Crèvecoeur." In *American Literature 1764–1789: The Revolutionary Years*. Ed. Everett Emerson. Madison: University of Wisconsin Press, 1977. 213–31.

Pocock, J.G.A. *The Machiavellian Moment: Florentine Political Thought and the Atlantic Republican Tradition*. Princeton, NJ: Princeton University Press, 1975.

  Virtue, Commerce, and History: Essays on Political Thought and History Chiefly in the Eighteenth Century. Cambridge: Cambridge University Press, 1985.

Pole, J.R. *Political Representation in England and the Origins of the American Republic*. New York: Macmillan, 1966.

Quarles, Benjamin. *The Negro in the American Revolution*. 1961. Reprint, Chapel Hill: University of North Carolina Press, 1996.

Rice, Howard C. *Le Cultivateur Américain: Etude sur l'oeuvre de Saint John de Crèvecoeur*. Paris: Champion, 1933.

Ringe, Donald A. "The American Revolution in American Romance." *American Literature* 49 (1977): 352–65.

Roth, Martin. *Comedy and America: The Lost World of Washington Irving*. Port Washington, NY: Kennikat Press, 1976.

Rousseau, Jean-Jacques. *Contrat social*. In *Oeuvres complètes*, 4 vols. Eds. B. Gagnebin and M. Raymond. Paris: Editions Gallimard, 1959. III, 351–470.

  The Social Contract. 1762. Reprint, trans. Christopher Betts. Oxford: Oxford University Press, 1999.

Rubin-Dorsky, Jeffrey. *Adrift in the Old World: The Psychological Pilgrimage of Washington Irving*. Chicago: University of Chicago Press, 1988.

Rush, Benjamin. *Selected Writings of Benjamin Rush*. Ed. Dagobert D. Runes. New York: New York Philosophical Library, 1947.

Ruttenburg, Nancy. *Democratic Personality: Popular Voice and the Trial of American Authorship*. Stanford, CA: Stanford University Press, 1998.

Saito, Miwa. "Tears of Blood: Charles I and the Execution Elegy." *Studies in English Literature* (2000): 1–15.

Sedgwick, Catharine Maria. *Hope Leslie*. 1827. Reprint, New Brunswick, NJ: Rutgers University Press, 1987.

Shaw, Peter. *American Patriots and the Rituals of Revolution*. Cambridge, MA: Harvard University Press, 1981.

Shell, Marc. *The End of Kinship: "Measure for Measure" and the Ideal of Universal Siblinghood*. Stanford, CA: Stanford University Press, 1988.

Shurr, William H. "Now, Gods, Stand Up for Bastards." *American Literature* 64.3 (1992): 435–52.

Silverman, Kenneth. *A Cultural History of the American Revolution: Painting, Music, Literature, and the Theatre in the Colonies and the United States from the Treaty of Paris to the Inauguration of George Washington, 1763–1789*. New York: T.Y. Crowell, 1976.

Simpson, Lewis P. "Federalism and the Crisis of Literary Order." *American Literature* 32.3 (1960): 253–66.

Smith, Adam. *Wealth of Nations*. 1776. Reprint, New York: Penguin, 1970.

Smith, Daniel Scott. "Population and Political Ethics: Thomas Jefferson's Demography of Generations." *William and Mary Quarterly* 56.3 (1999): 591–612.

Smith-Rosenberg, Carroll. "Dis-Covering the Subject of the 'Great National Discussion,' 1786–1789." *Journal of American History* 79 (1992): 841–73.

Soderlund, Jean R. "Women's Authority in Pennsylvania and New Jersey Quaker Meetings, 1680–1760." *William and Mary Quarterly* 44.4 (1987): 722–49.

St. George, Robert Blair. *Conversing by Signs: Poetics of Implication in Colonial New England Culture.* Chapel Hill: University of North Carolina Press, 1998.

Stauffer, Vernon. *New England and the Bavarian Illuminati.* New York, 1918.

Stern, Julia A. *The Plight of Feeling: Sympathy and Dissent in the Early American Novel.* Chicago: University of Chicago Press, 1997.

Szatmary, David P. *Shays' Rebellion: The Making of an Agrarian Insurrection.* Amherst: University of Massachusetts Press, 1980.

Thoreau, Henry David. *Journal.* vol. 1. Ed. Elizabeth Hall Witherell *et al.* Princeton, NJ: Princeton University Press. 1981.

"Civil Disobedience." In *The Essays of Henry David Thoreau.* Ed. Richard Dillman. Albany, NY: NCUP, Inc, 1990. 16–34.

Walden; Or Life in the Woods. New York: Dover, 1995.

Tocqueville, Alexis de. *Democracy in America.* Ed. Richard D. Heffner. New York: Signet, 1984.

De la démocratie en Amérique. Paris: Librairie Philosophique J. Vrin, 1990.

Tompkins, Jane. *Sensational Designs: The Cultural Work of American Fiction, 1790–1860.* New York: Oxford University Press, 1985.

Traister, Bryce. "Libertinism and Authorship in America's Early Republic." *American Literature* 72.1 (2000): 1–30.

Turner, Edward Raymond. "Women's Suffrage in New Jersey, 1790–1807." *Smith College Studies in History* 1.4 (1916): 165–87.

Tuttleton, James W., ed. *Washington Irving: The Critical Reaction.* New York: AMS Press, 1993.

Voices of the American Revolution. The People's Bicentennial Commission. New York: Bantam, 1975.

Voloshin, Beverly. "*Edgar Huntly* and the Coherence of the Self." *Early American Literature* 23.3 (1988): 262–80.

Waldstreicher, David. *In the Midst of Perpetual Fetes: The Making of American Nationalism, 1776–1820.* Chapel Hill: University of North Carolina Press, 1997.

Wallace, James D. "Cultivating An Audience: From *Precaution* to *The Spy.*" In *James Fenimore Cooper: New Critical Essays.* Ed. Robert Clark. London: Vision Books, 1985. 38–54.

Warner, Michael. *The Letters of the Republic: Publication and the Public Sphere in Eighteenth-Century America.* Cambridge, MA: Harvard University Press, 1990.

Warner, Michael, ed. *American Sermons: The Pilgrims to Martin Luther King Jr.* New York: Library of America, 1999.

Watts, Steven. *The Republic Reborn: War and the Making of Liberal America, 1790–1820*. Baltimore, MD: Johns Hopkins University Press, 1987.

The Romance of Real Life: Charles Brockden Brown and the Origins of American Culture. Baltimore, MD: Johns Hopkins University Press, 1994.

Webster, Noah. "On the Education of Youth in America." In *A Collection of Essays and Fugitiv Writings on Moral, Historical, Political and Literary Subjects*. Boston: I. Thomas and E.T. Andrews, 1790. 1–37.

Weston, Corinne C. and Janelle R. Greenberg. *Subjects and Sovereigns: The Grand Controversy Over Legal Sovereignty in Stuart England*. New York: Cambridge University Press, 1981.

Williams, Daniel E. "In Defense of Self: Author and Authority in *The Memoirs of Stephen Burroughs*." *Early American Literature* 25 (1990): 96–122.

Williamson, Chilton. *American Suffrage: From Property to Democracy, 1760–1860*. Princeton, NJ: Princeton University Press, 1960.

Wills, Garry. *Inventing America: Jefferson's Declaration of Independence*. New York: Vintage, 1979.

Explaining America: The Federalist. Garden City, NY: Doubleday, 1981.

Wood, Gordon S. *The Creation of the American Republic, 1776–1787*. New York: Norton, 1972.

"Conspiracy and the Paranoid Style: Causality and Deceit in the Eighteenth Century." *William and Mary Quarterly* 39.3 (1982): 401–41.

"Interests and Disinterestedness in the Making of the Constitution." In *Beyond Confederation: Origins of the Constitution and American National Identity*. Eds. Richard Beeman *et al.* Chapel Hill: University of North Carolina Press, 1987. 69–109.

"The Liberation of Print." *The New Republic* 203.20 (November 12, 1990), 41.

The Radicalism of the American Revolution. New York: Vintage, 1991.

Wright, Marion Thompson. "Negro Suffrage in New Jersey, 1776–1875." *Journal of Negro History* 33.2 (1948): 168–224.

X, Malcolm. "The Ballot or the Bullet." In *The Heath Anthology of American Literature*. vol. II. Ed. Paul Lauter *et al.* Boston: Houghton Mifflin Company, 1998. 2542–56.

Young, Philip. "Fallen From Time: The Mythic 'Rip Van Winkle.'" In *Washington Irving: The Critical Reaction*. Ed. James W. Tuttleton. New York: AMS Press, 1993. 67–84.

Ziff, Larzer. *Writing in the New Nation: Prose, Print, and Politics in the Early United States*. New Haven, CT: Yale University Press, 1991.

Žižek, Slavoj. *The Sublime Object of Ideology*. London: Verso, 1989.

Index